INTRODUCTION TO DBMS

CS-06

For

Bachelor of Computer Applications
[B.C.A.]

Dinesh Verma
MCA, BCA, 'A' & 'O' Level, SCJP(USA), JP
Dr. A.K. Saini
Ph.D, M.PHIL., MCA., MBA

Useful For

IGNOU, Vinayaka Mission University, IP University, Delhi University, CCS University, JMI University, B. M. V. Open University (KOTA), M. P. Bhoj Open University(M.P.), Tamilnadu Open University, YCM Open University (Maharashtra), Mahatma Gandhi University (Kottyam), M. D. University, and all other Indian Universities.

GULLYBABA PUBLISHING HOUSE (P) Ltd.
AN ISO 9001:2008 CERTIFIED CO.

GullyBaba Publishing House (P) Ltd.

2525/193, Ist Floor, Onkar Nagar-A,
Tri Nagar, Delhi-110035
Ph: 9350849407, 9312235086, 011-27387998
E-mail: info@gullybaba.com / info@degreewala.com
Website: www.gullybaba.com / www.ignouonline.com

First Edition : March, 2012

ISBN : 978-81-89086-33-6

Preface

This book is mainly targeted for BCA and MCA exam of Introduction to database management system. It has been introduced in market after seeing the huge demand of ready to grasp material for exams with high level of quality, and its un-availability in market. We the GullyBaba Publishing House took a step ahead to publish the quality material focusing on exams at the same time giving you indepth knowledge about the subject.

GPH Book is the poineer effort that provides a unique methodology so as to perform better in exams. If your goal is to attain higher grade use this powerful study tool independently or along with your text.

*On the Web : **www.gullybaba.com** is the vital resource for your exams acting as catalyst to boost up your preparation. Gullybaba.com has been Listed **no.1** in www.google.com and www.yahoo.com when you search "IGNOU MCA BCA MBA". Now you can access us on the net through **www.doctorignou.com, www.doeacconline.com, www.gphindia.com, and www.gullybabapublishinghouse.com.***

Feedback about the book can be sent at **cs06writers@gullybaba.com.**

Acknowledgments :

We appreciate the staff and facility support provided by GullyBaba Publishing House. In particular, we appreciate the encouragement and professional advises received from Mr. Ajay Saini, Mr. Tarun Sharma, B. K. Krishna and many more.

Also we would like to thank typesetting and designing team Mrs. Bhawna Verma, Mr. Shravan Vats, Mr. Parveen, and Mr. Mukesh.

We gratefully acknowledges the significant contributions of Mr. Mahesh Chand, Mrs. Bimla Devi, Mrs. Bhawna Verma and our experts in bringing out this publication.

New Delhi ***Publishers***

Feedback is the breakfast of Champions.

Ken Blanchard

You can Help other students.
"Inform any error or mistake in this book."

We and Universe
will reward you for Your Kind act.

Email at : feedback@gullybaba.com
or
WhatsApp on 9350849407

Contents

Question Papers

CHAPTER-1

DATABASE CONCEPTS

Collections of data

Data may be collected, manipulated and retrieved in various ways:

- plain text editor - simple editing and retrieval
- word processor - adds tables and simple calculations
- spreadsheet programme - adds more sophisticated calculations
- database management system (DBMS) - adds formats, structures, rules, ...

Reasons for a DBMS

A DBMS is a software package for defining and managing a *database*. OR a dbms is a system to manage database (a organised collection of data), here organised means data will be in the form of tables (collection of rows and column).
A 'real' database includes

- definitions of
- field names
- data formats (text? binary? integer? etc.)
- record structures (fixed-length? pointers? field order, etc.)
- file structures (sequential? indexed? etc.)
- rules for validating and manipulating data
- data

A DBMS provides **Data independence**.
One must be able to change storage mechanisms and formats without having to modify all application programmes. For example:

- method of representation of alphanumeric data (e.g., changing date format to avoid Y2000 problem)
- method of representation of numeric data (e.g., integer vs. long integer or floating-point)
- units (e.g., metric vs. furlongs)
- record structure
- file structure (sequential, sorted, indexed, etc.)

Database organization

Four main types of database organization are :

(i) Flat
(ii) Hierarchical
(iii) Relational
(iv) Object-oriented

(i) Flat databases

A single kind of record with a fixed number of fields.
Notice the repetition of data, and thus an increased chance of errors.

(ii) Hierarchical databases

Hierarchical relationships among different types of data :

- can be very easy to answer some questions, but very difficult to answer others
- if one-to-many relationship is violated (e.g., a patient can have more than one physician) then the hierarchy becomes a network.

A hierarchical schema for part of the company database.

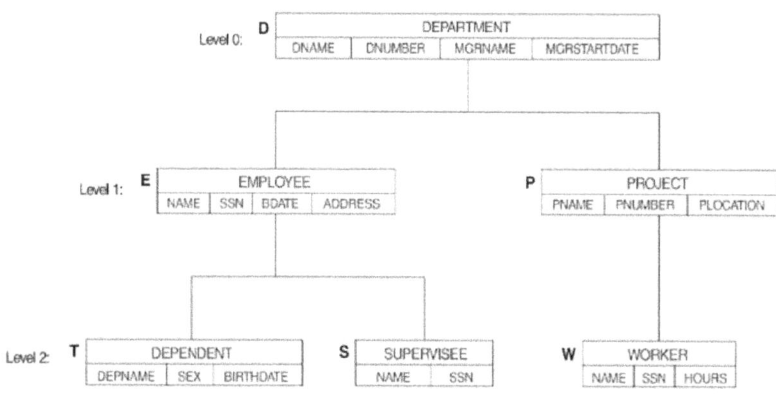

Advantages :

1. Hierarchical Model is simple to construct and operate on
2. Corresponds to a number of natural hierarchically organized domains - e.g., assemblies in manufacturing, personnel organization in companies

3. Language is simple; uses constructs like GET, GET UNIQUE, GET NEXT, GET NEXT WITHIN PARENT etc.

Disadvantages :

1. Navigational and procedural nature of processing
2. Database is visualized as a linear arrangement of records
3. Little scope for "query optimization"

(iii) Relational databases

Data are organized as logically independent tables. Features:

- 'Natural'
- Not so strongly biased towards specific questions
- Expresses relationships by means of shared data rather than explicit pointers
- Theoretical basis: relational algebra, calculus; closure
- Operations on tables (Join, Project, Select) to form new tables

Operations on tables

- `JOIN`: combine tables having common columns
- `PROJECT`: extract specified columns, remove duplicate rows
- `SELECT`: select rows satisfying a condition

(iv) Object-oriented databases

Object-oriented analysis is another way to model the world, involving *abstraction, encapsulation, modularity* and *hierarchy* (with *inheritance*).

An *object* consists of data and *methods.*

Classes are used to group objects which have the same types of data and the same methods.

Abstraction

Consider only features which are necessary for the problem at hand.
For example, a *person* may be defined by the ability to ask for the ID number, age, height and weight.

Encapsulation

The internal structure of an object is hidden.
For example, all we know is that we can ask for the age, not whether the age is
(1) periodically updated or
(2) calculated on demand from birth date and current date.

Modularity

Grouping classes and objects into 'cohesive and loosely coupled modules'. For example, the classes *person* and *cat* might be implemented within the same module because they share many things (like how to calculate age).

Hierarchy

Objects are *instances* of classes, e.g., *Vijay* is an *instance* of the class *patient* Classes and objects form two different hierarchies.

- Class hierarchy ('kind'): e.g., *patient* is a **kind of** *person*. A class inherits (and specializes) the characteristics of its parent class.
- Object hierarchy ('part'): e.g., the object *Vijay.height* is a **part of** the object *Vijay*.

Examples of class hierarchies

- Event
    - Ultrasound
    - Delivery
- Person
    - Physician
    - Patient
        - Mother
        - Baby
- Numeric_value
    - Height
    - Weight
        - Weight_m
        - Weight_b
    - Date
        - Date_of_birth
        - Date_of_event
    - ID_num
        - Phys_num
        - Pat_num
- String_value

- Name

Centralized databases

A centralized database (e.g., hospital information system) can be very big and complex, but offers the following advantages:

- shared data, reduced redundancy
- fewer inconsistencies in data

- enforcement of standards
- security restrictions
- balancing of conflicting requirements

A centralized DBMS will offer different *views* of the data.
Different applications will need to look at data in different ways. For example:

- Clinical lab doesn't need to see patient demographics
- Admission/discharge office doesn't need to see lab results
- Neither needs to see payroll data

Q1. Discuss why navigation is simpler in the Relational data model than in the Hierarchical data model. [4]

In the network model, it is possible that several identical occurrences of the same logical record type could exist. These multiple identical occurrences are distinguished by their membership in different occurrences of the sets. Similarly, in the hierarchical model, their associations with different ancestor record type occurrences distinguish identical occurrences of a record type.

The relational model allows for a fairly straightforward method of selecting certain entities or relationships. Selecting those tuples of the relation corresponding to the entity or relationship that meet certain selection conditions does this.

In the network model, the selection operation on a record type is similar to that in the relational model. However, the operation corresponding to the join operation of the relational model is handled differently.

Selection operations for the record type corresponding to the root of a hierarchical tree are similar to operations for its counterpart in the relational and network models. As in the case of the network model, we have to traverse pointers from parent to child since there is no method of traveling from descendant to parent.

The process of joining relations in the case of the relational model or following the pointers from owner to member, from member to owner, or from parent to child is known as navigating through the database. Navigating through relations that represent an M:N relationship is just as simple as through a 1::M relationship. This leads us to conclude that it is easier to specify how to manipulate a relational database that a network or hierarchical one. This in turn leads to a query language for the relational model that is correct, clear, and effective in specifying the required operations. Unfortunately, the join operation is inherently inefficient and demands a considerable amount of processing and retrieval of unnecessary data. The structure for the network and hierarchical models can be implemented efficiently. Such an implementation would mean that navigating though these databases, though awkward, requires the retrieval of relatively little unnecessary data.

Q2. Name the major advantages of a Database Management System (DBMS) over a File Management System. [4]

Major advantages of Database Management over a File Management System are as under :

1. Time required in maintaining record is reduced.
2. Computer does calculations, hence human error is over.
3. Generally data redundancy not occurs.
4. The data may be used in proportional to its sequence or physical presence.
5. Lack of duplication.
6. Assured backup system.
7. Data storage at single place.
8. Data manager enforces central and concurrent control and enforces integrity among the users.
9. Granting of authorization for data access.
10. The data in the database is stored in tables, each table contains number of records and each record in a table is a unique set of related fields.
11. A DBMS can create a file, add data to it, delete data from it or modify data in a file.
12. The stored data can be indexed at user's will.
13. A selective or collective retrieval of data is possible.
14. DBMS give selective view of data to its users.

DBMS provides a facility termed as DDL whereby one can define conceptual scheme and give details of how to implement conceptual scheme in physical device.

CHAPTER-2

INTRODUCTION TO DATABASE NORMALIZATION

Introduction

The normalization process, as first proposed by Codd (1972). Initially, Codd proposed three normal forms, which he called **first, second,** and **third normal form.** A stronger definition of 3NF was proposed later by Boyce and Codd and is known as **Boyce-Codd normal form (BCNF).** All these normal forms are based on the functional dependencies among the attributes of a relation. Later, a **fourth normal form (4NF)** and **a fifth normal form (5NF)** were proposed, based on the concepts or multivalued dependencies and join dependencies, respectively.

Normalization is the process of reducing data redundancy. **Normalization of data** can be looked on as a process during which unsatisfactory relation schemas are decomposed by breaking up their attributes into smaller relation schemas that possess desirable properties. Objective of the original normalization process is to ensure that the update / insert / delete anomalies do not occur.
Normal forms provide database designers with :

· A formal framework for analyzing relation schemas based on their keys and on the functional dependencies among their attributes.
· A series of tests that can be carried out on individual relation schema so that the relational database can be **normalized** to any degree. When a test fails, the relation violating that test must be decomposed into relations that individually meet the normalization tests.

Definitions

A relation is defined as a *set of tuples*. By definition, all elements of a set are distinct; hence, all tuples in a relation must also be distinct. This means that no two tuples can have the same combination of values for *all* their attributes.
Any set of attributes of a relation schema is called a **superkey**. Every relation has at least one superkey—the set of all its attributes. A **key** is a *minimal superkey*, i.e., a superkey from which we cannot remove any attribute and still have the uniqueness constraint hold.

In general, a relation schema may have more than one key. In this case, each of the keys is called a **candidate key.** It is common to designate one of the candidate keys as the **primary key** of the relation. A **foreign key** is a key in a relation R but it's not a key (just an attribute) in other relation R' of the same schema.

Integrity Constraints: the **entity integrity constraint** states that no primary key value can be null. This is because the primary key value is used to identify individual tuples in a relation; having null values for the primary key implies that we cannot identify some tuples. The **referential integrity constraint** is specified between two relations and is used to maintain the consistency among tuples of the two relations. Informally, the referential integrity constraint states that a tuple in one relation that refers to another relation must refer to an *existing tuple* in that relation.

An attribute of a relation schema R is called a **prime attribute** of the relation R if it is a member of *any key* of the relation R. An attribute is called **nonprime** if it is not a prime attribute—that is, if it is not a member of any candidate key.

A **functional dependency,** denoted by X->Y, between two sets of attributes X and Y that are subsets of R specifies a constraints on the possible tuples that can form a relation instance of R.

Normal Forms

The normalization procedure consists of a sequence of *projections* — that is, some attributes are extracted from one table to form a new one. In other words, tables are split up vertically. The decomposition is lossless, only if you can restore the original table by joining its projections.

Through such non-loss decompositions it is possible to transform an original schema into a resulting one that satisfies certain conditions, known as **Normal Forms**:

· The **First Normal Form (1NF)** addresses the structure of an isolated table.
· The **Second (2NF), Third (3NF),** and **Boyce-Codd (BCNF) Normal Forms** address one-to-one and one-to-many relationships.
· The **Fourth (4NF)** and **Fifth (5NF) Normal Forms** deal with many-to-many relationships.

These Normal Forms form a hierarchy in such a way that a schema in a higher normal form automatically fulfills all the criteria for all of the lower Normal Forms. The Fifth Normal Form is the ultimate normal form with respect to projections and joins — it is guaranteed to be free of anomalies that can be eliminated by taking projections.

In the following discussion we have taken utmost care to make the students clear the concept of normalization. Normalization is most important part in any software development and your exam also. Lets begin,

First Normal Form (1NF)

First normal form is now considered to be part of the formal definition of a relation; historically, it was defined to disallow *multivalued attributes, composite attributes, and their combinations.* It states that the domains of attributes must include only *atomic* (simple, indivisible) *values* and that the value of any attribute in a tuple must be a single *value* from the domain of that attribute.

Practical Rule : *"Eliminate Repeating Groups,"* i.e., make a separate table for each set of related attributes, and give each table a primary key.

Formal Definition[2]: A relation is in **first normal form** (1NF) if and only if all underlying simple domains contain atomic values only.

The following relation violates 1NF because the SupplierID forms a repeating group (here and in the following examples and text, primary key fields are in **bold**):

Part ID	Supplier 1 ID	Supplier 2 ID	Supplier 3 ID

Repeating groups indicate a one-to-many relationship — in other words, a relationship which in relational databases is treated using foreign keys. Note that the problem of repeating groups cannot be solved by adding any number of fields to a record; even if the number of elements of the vector-valued data was fixed, finite, and predetermined, searching for a value in all these parallel fields is prohibitively cumbersome.

To achieve 1NF, eliminate repeating groups by creating separate tables for each set of related data.

To demonstrate the typical anomalies that occur in tables that are only 1NF, consider the following example:

Customer ID	Order ID	Customer Address	Order Date

Note the following problems :

1. Insert : It is not possible to add a record for a customer who has never placed an order.
2. Update : To change the address for a customer, this change has to be repeated for all of the customer's existing orders.
3. Delete : Deleting the last order for a customer loses all information about the customer.

Functional dependency

The Second and Third Normal Forms address dependencies among attributes, specifically between key and non-key fields.

By definition, a key uniquely determines a record: Knowing the key determines the values of all the other attributes in the table row, so that given a key, the values of all the other attributes in the row are fixed.

This kind of relationship can be formalized as follows. Let *X* and *Y* be attributes (or sets of attributes) of a given relationship. Then *Y* is **functionally dependent** on *X* if, whenever two records agree on their *X*-values, they must also agree on their *Y*-values. In this case, *X* is called the **determinant** and *Y* is called the **dependent**. Since for any *X* there must be a *single Y*, this relationship represents a **single-valued functional dependency**. If the set of attributes in the determinant is the smallest possible (in the sense that after dropping one or more of the attributes from *X*, the remaining set of attributes does no longer uniquely determine *Y*), then the dependency is called **irreducible**.

Note that functional dependency is a semantic relationship: It is the business logic of the problem domain, represented by the relation, which determines whether a certain *X* determines *Y*.

Second Normal Form

A table is in Second Normal Form (2NF) if every non-key field is a fact about the *entire* key. In other words, a table is 2NF if it is 1NF and all non-key attributes are functionally dependent on the entire primary key (that is, the dependency is irreducible).
Clearly, 2NF is only relevant when the key is composite (that is, consisting of several fields). The following example describes a table which is not 2NF since the WarehouseAddress attribute depends only on WarehouseID but not on PartID :

Part ID	**Warehouse ID**	Quantity	WarehouseAddress

To achieve 2NF, create separate tables for sets of values that apply to multiple records and relate these tables through foreign keys. The determinants of the initial table become the primary keys of the resulting tables.

Third Normal Form

A relation is in Third Normal Form (3NF) if it is 2NF and none of its attributes is a fact about another non-key field. In other words, no non-key field functionally depends on any other non-key field. (Such indirect dependencies are known as **transitive dependencies**.)

The following example violates 3NF since the Location is functionally dependent on the Department ID:

Employee ID	Department ID	Location

To achieve 3NF, eliminate fields that do not depend on the key from the original table and add them to the table whose primary key is their determinant.

To summarize the normalization procedure up to and including Third Normal Form: Every field in a record must depend on The Key (1NF), the Whole Key (2NF), and Nothing But The Key (3NF).

Boyce-Codd Normal Form

Boyce-Codd Normal Form (BCNF) is an extension of 3NF in the case with two or more candidate keys which are composite and overlapping (that is, they have at least one field in common). If these conditions are not fulfilled, 3NF and BCNF are equivalent. A table is BCNF if, and only if its only determinants are candidate keys. In the following table, both {SupplierID, PartID}, as well as {SupplierName, PartID}, are candidate keys. The table is not BCNF since it contains two determinants (SupplierID and SupplierName) which are not candidate keys. (SupplierID and SupplierName are determinants, since they determine each other.)

Supplier ID	Part ID	Supplier Name	Quantity

However, either of the following decompositions is BCNF:

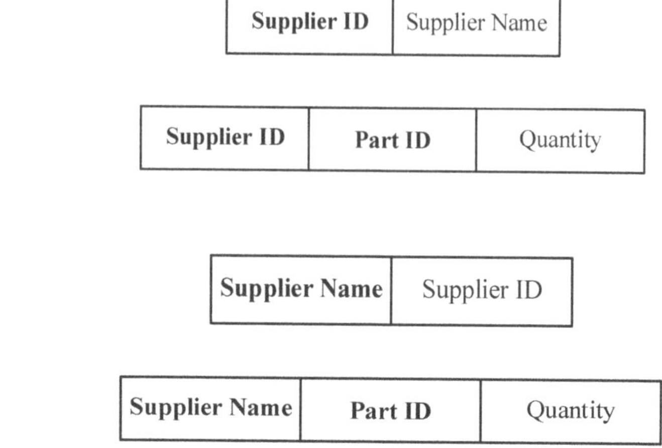

Supplier ID	Supplier Name

Supplier ID	**Part ID**	Quantity

or

Supplier Name	Supplier ID

Supplier Name	**Part ID**	Quantity

To achieve BCNF, remove the determinants which are not candidate keys.

Many-to-many relationships and higher Normal Forms

Fourth and Fifth Normal Forms apply to situations involving many-to-many relationships. In relational databases, many-to-many relationships are expressed through cross-reference tables.

As an example, consider a case of class enrollment. Each student can be enrolled in one or more classes and each class can contain one or more students. Clearly, there is a many-to-many relationship between classes and students. This relationship can be represented by a Student/Class cross-reference table:

Student ID	Class ID

The key for this table is the combination of StudentID and ClassID. To avoid violation of 2NF, all other information about each student and each class is stored in separate Student and Class tables, respectively.

Note that each StudentID determines not a unique ClassID, but a well-defined, finite *set* of values. This kind of behavior is referred to as **multi-valued dependency** of ClassID on StudentID.

Fourth Normal Form

A table is in Fourth Normal Form (4NF) if it is 3NF and it does not represent two or more independent many-to-many relationships.

Consider an example with two many-to-many relationships, between students and classes and between classes and teachers. Also, a many-to-many relationship between students and teachers is implied. However, the business rules do not constrain this relationship in any way—the combination of StudentID and TeacherID does not contain any additional information beyond the information implied by the student/class and class/teacher relationships. Consequentially, the student/class and class/teacher relationships are **independent** of each other—these relationships have no additional constraints. The following table is, then, in violation of 4NF:

Student ID	Class ID	Teacher ID

As an example of the anomalies that can occur, realize that it is not possible to add a new class taught by some teacher without adding at least one student who is enrolled in this class.

To achieve 4NF, represent each independent many-to-many relationship through its own cross-reference table.

Fifth Normal Form

A table is in Fifth Normal Form (5NF) if it is 4NF and its information content cannot be reconstructed from several tables containing fewer attributes.

Consider again the student/class/teacher example, but now assume that there is an additional relationship between students and teachers. The previous example table is now 4NF, since all the relationships it describes are interrelated. However, it is not 5NF, since it can be reconstructed from three cross-reference tables, each representing one of the three many-to-many relationships :

Student ID	Class ID

Class ID	Teacher ID

Teacher ID	Student ID

To achieve 5NF, isolate interrelated many-to-many relationships, introducing the required number of new tables to represent all business domain constraints.

Domain Key Normal Form (DKNF)

We can also always define stricter forms that take into account additional types of dependencies and constraints. The idea behind **domain-key normal form** is to specify, (theoretically, at least) the "ultimate normal form" that takes into account all possible dependencies and constraints. A relation is said to be in **DKNF** if all constraints and dependencies that should hold on the relation can be enforced simply by enforcing the domain constraints and the key constraints specified on the relation.

For a relation in DKNF, it becomes very straightforward to enforce the constraints by simply checking that each attribute value in a tuple is of the appropriate domain and that every key constraint on the relation is enforced. However, it seems unlikely that complex constraints can be included in a DKNF relation; hence, its practical utility is limited.

Q1. Why is 4 NF preferable to BCNF ? **[5]**

Normalization is a process to reduce the redundancy by removing functional dependencies. BCNF (Boyce Code Normal Form) has all functional dependencies A $\rightarrow$ B are trivial or discriminator should be superkey. To get relation in BCNF, splitting the relational schema not necessarily preserve all functional dependency. Loss less decomposition and dependency are main points for the normalization. Sometime, it is not possible to get a BCNF decomposition that is dependency preserving. While 4NF has very similar definition as BCNF. A relational schema is in 4NF, if all multivalued dependencies A $\rightarrow$ B are trivial and determinant A is superkey of schema. If a relational schema is in 4NF, it is already in BCNF. And 4NF decomposition preserve the all functional dependency. So, 4NF is preferable than to have BCNF.

Q2. Compare and contrast BCNF and 3NF. Show that if a relation scheme is BCNF, then it is also in 3NF **[9]**

Boyce-Codd Normal Form (BCNF)

Boyce-Codd normal form is stricter than 3NF, meaning that every relation in BCNF is also in 3NF; however, a relation in 3NF is *not necessarily* in BCNF. A relation schema is an **BCNF** if whenever a functional dependency X->A holds in the relation, then X is a superkey of the relation. The only difference between BCNF and 3NF is that condition

of 3NF (i.e. 3NF also require prime attribute), which allows A to be prime if X is not a superkey, is absent from BCNF.

Formal Definition: A relation is in **Boyce/Codd normal form** (BCNF) if and only if every determinant is a candidate key. [A determinant is any attribute on which some other attribute is (fully) functionally dependent.]

CHAPTER-3

MAKE PERFECT ER DIAGRAMS

Introduction - Modelling databases

There are many different ways of modelling databases :

- Hierarchical model
- Network model
- Relational model
- Entity-Relationship model
- Semantic-Object model
- Object-oriented model

and many different graphical techniques for representing the models. You could rigorously apply the modelling techniques to any given database but a wide-spread practice is to combine the techniques. We tend to use a graphical modelling technique which borrows bits from various models. We use symbols and notions from the ERM or ERD to model relations and their associations and the symbols and techniques are influenced by notions borrowed from the network model. We am going to start with the ERM (Entity-Relationship Model).

Entity - Relationship Model

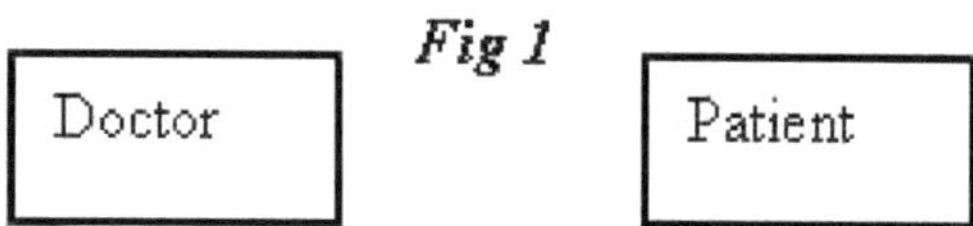

Fig 1

The ERM is based on entity sets and the relationships between the sets of entities. Figure 1 shows two entity sets, Doctor and patient. These could represent flat-files or tables or just the contents of a filing cabinet. Whatever the means of storage you know, from your own experience, that a doctor has many patients and that a patient has many doctors. There is some practical relationship between doctors and patients.

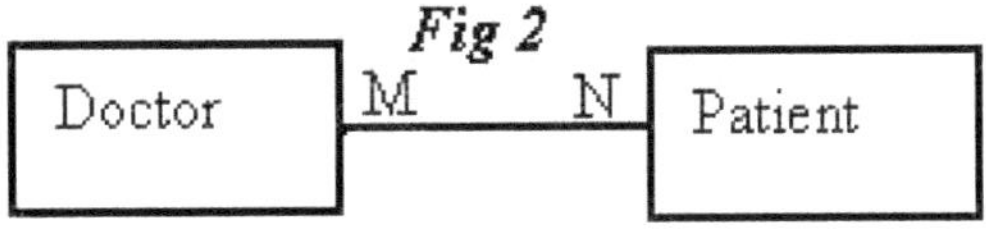

We can show the relationship between the entity sets: a doctor has many patients and a patient has many doctors. M and N are symbols which represent number.

In the ERM the relationship is shown as a diamond, and the entity sets are shown as rectangles. The entity sets are tables, the diamonds express some kind of relationship like: *has many, has one, has zero or one, may have.*

If figure 3 represents a medical practice then given a specific doctor, say Dr Verma we can safely assume that Dr Verma has many patients. Likewise a given patient, say Mrs Sharma might, over time, see many doctors in the practice.

You can see from this simple model that We are making some assumptions about the medical practice we are modelling. We are assuming that it has more than one doctor, that the doctors will see many patients and that the patients will not always be treated by the same doctor. It need not be this way. In the case of a specialist practice it may be that all patients have only one doctor.

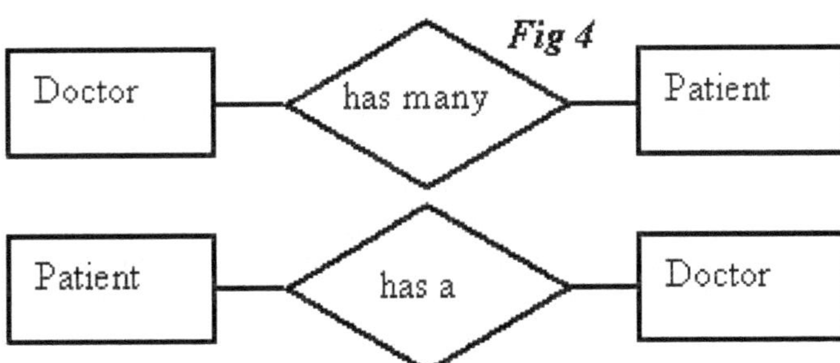

Figure 4 shows that one doctor has many patients and that one patient has one doctor. We can say that this model represents a practice with a single doctor and many patients.

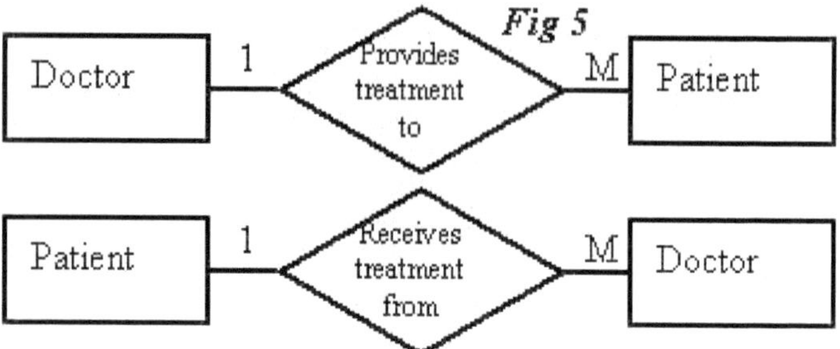

In the model we are developing we assume that the medical practice is the more usual general practice. You can see that we have changed the relationship to show something more practical - doctors treat patients. The practice has a number of doctors, the doctors treat many patients and the patients see are treated by many doctors.

If we look at the doctor and patient tables without the assistance of the treatment relationship we can't tell which doctor treated which patient on any given occasion. In complex entity-relationships like the many-to-many relationship between doctors and patients we need to resolve the confusions. How do we tell which doctor treated which patient when?

Relationships as relations

Obviously the treatment the doctor provides and the treatment the patient receives are the same thing. Like doctors and patients the the treatment is an entity itself. The difference is that the treatment entity expresses the relationship between the doctors and the patients. It is a record of a point at which a doctor and a patient interact at on specific occasion. Since it is a record we can use it resolve the confusions.

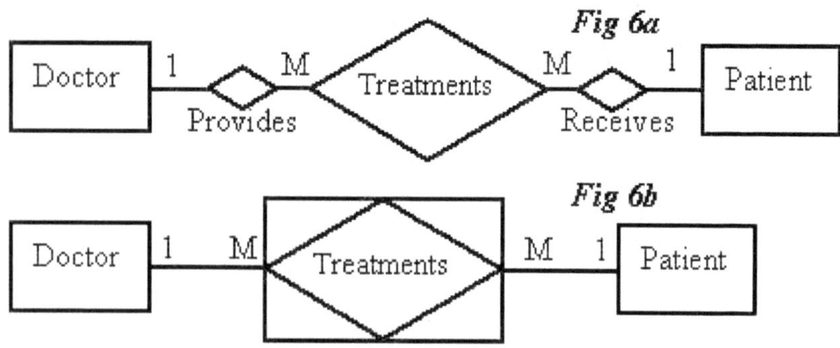

Figure 6a shows the model in all its detail. Figure 6b simplifies this by showing both the entity and the relationships in a single symbol. This is known as a composite entity or an intersection entity.

Figure 6b is a pure Entity-Relationship model or diagram (ERM or ERD). It depicts three relations: Doctors, Patients and Treatments. we use some simplifications, based on network database modelling, which are shown in Figures 7 and 8. These aren't really standard or recommended practice but do simplify the modelling process once you understand what the particular ERD represents. In brief, there is less drawing to do. For most of your work you should use the ERM.

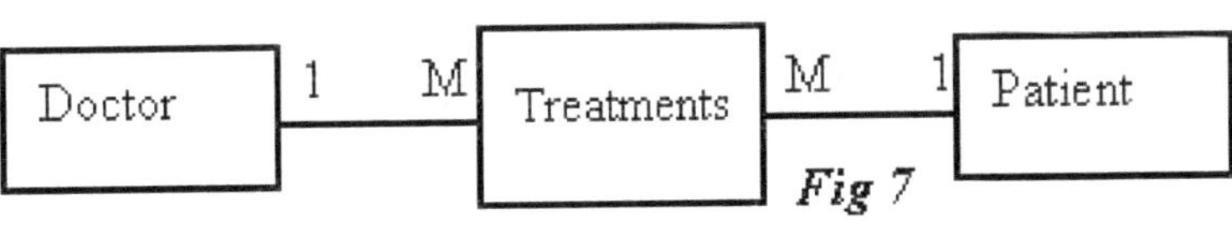

Fig 7

A simplified model using numbers and symbols.

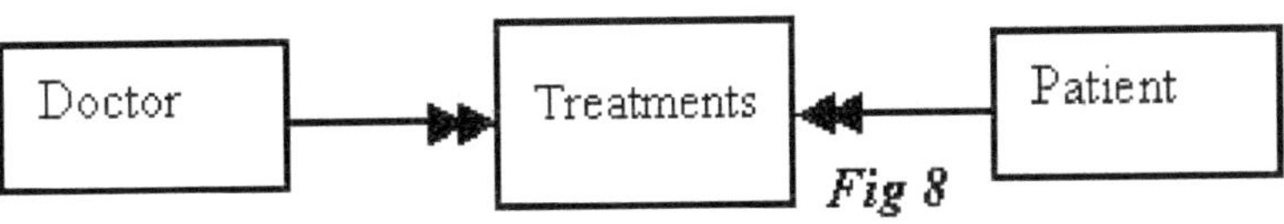

Fig 8

A simplified model using arrowheads.

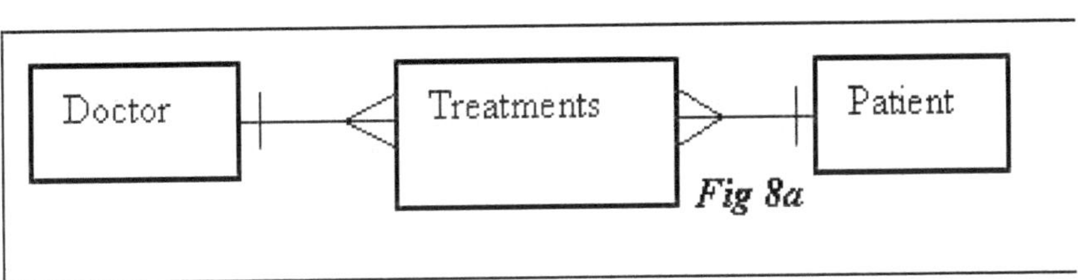

Fig 8a

A simplified model using crowsfeet.

The Entity-Relationship Model and the Relational Model.

In an earlier lesson we said of the relational model that:
a relational data base is a collection of relations, there need not be any explicit links between the files and that a relation was a two-dimensional table. You were also introduced to the intension (a way of stating a relation's structure) of a relation, for example :

Customer(Name, Address, Town, Balance)

The relational model (RM) depicts the database in a verbal form (the intension), the ERM depicts the database in a graphical form (the ERD). Both models are depicting the same thing, a database or a part of a database. We should know enough now to compare, in a very limited way, the RM and the ERM.

The ERM is particularly useful for modelling the relationships between entities but it doesn't tell us much about the structure of the entities. The RM is particularly good for detailing the structure of the entities but doesn't tell us much about the relationships between the entities.

If we combined both models then we would have a modelling technique that gave us the best of both worlds. A graphical model that showed the relationships between the entities and a verbal model that showed the internal structures of the entities.

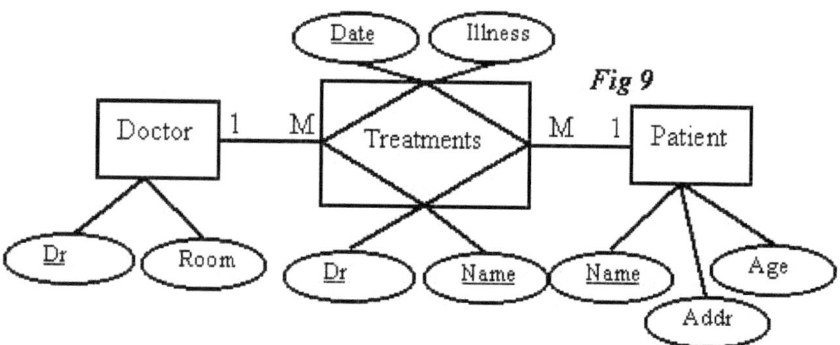

Fig 9

One way to do this would be to extend the ERD to include the attributes of each entity, as shown here in figure 9. A problem here is that the ERD would soon become very complex. In this example I have shown on a few of the likely attributes of each entity and already the ERD is starting to get unwieldy.

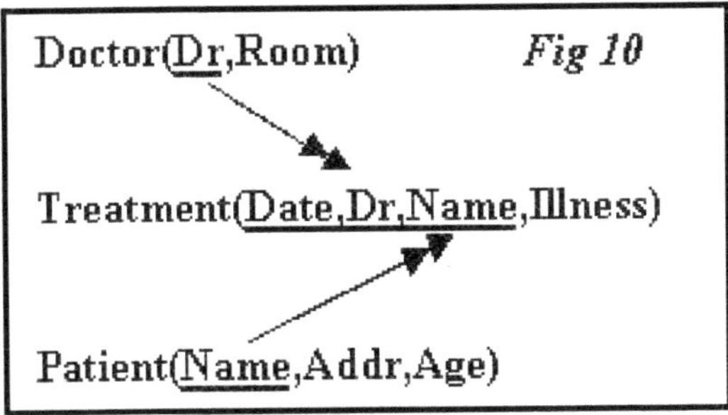

We could use the intension as the basis of a diagram and add directed lines which show the relationships. Figure 10 shows the three intensions and, a one-to-many relationship for doctor-treatment and patient-treatment relationships. This has a problem too since it loses the clarity of the ERD.

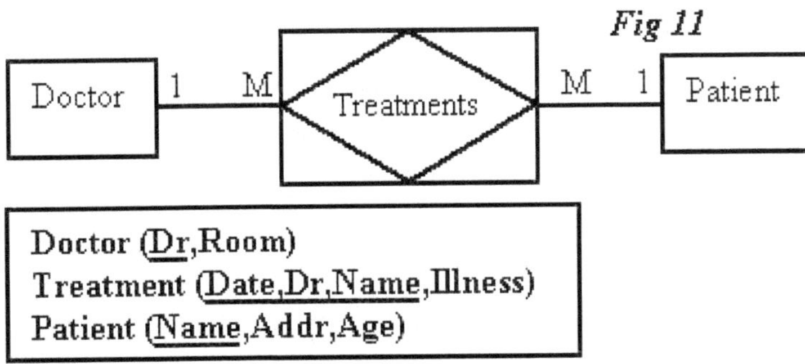

We find that the best way for me is to use both the ERD and the intension but to keep them separate as shown in figure 11.

Q1. Construct an E-R diagram for a car insurance company that has a set of customers, each of whom owns one or more cars. Each car has associated with it zero or any number of accidents. [10]

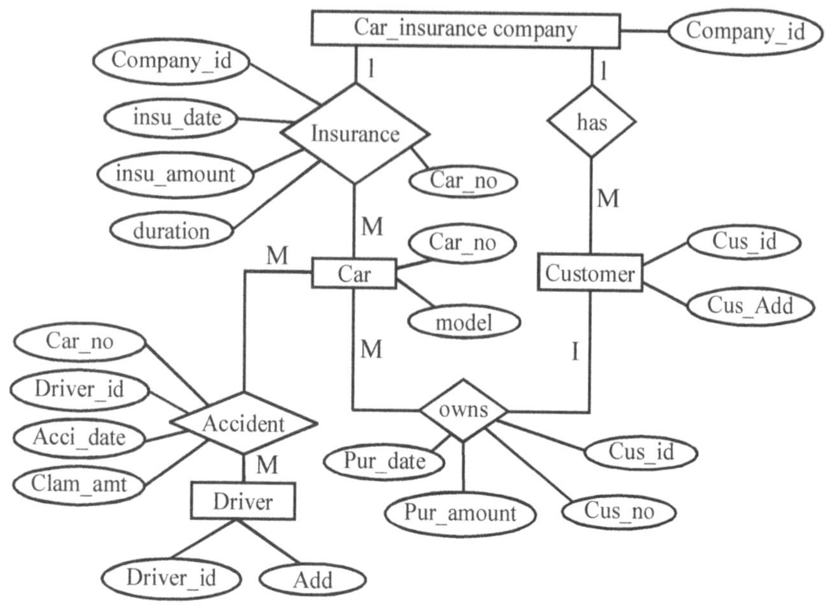

entity set CAR_INSURANCE COMPANY
company_id : string ; (**PK**)

entity set CAR
car_no : string ; (**PK**)
mode : string ;

entity set CUSTOMER
cus_id : string ; (*unique indentification)
cus_add : string ;
company_id : string ;

entity set DRIVER
driver_id : string ; (*unique identification)
Add : string ;

relationship set OWNS
cus_id : string ;
car_no : string ;
pur_date : date ;
pur_amount : integer ;

relationship set ACCIDENT

car_no : string ;
dri_id : string ;
acc_date : date ;
dam_amt ; integer ;

relationship set INSURANCE

car_no : string ;
company_id : string ;
insu_date : date ;
duration : date ;
insu_amount : integer ;

Date structure :

(1) Company

company_id : char(9)

PK(Primary Key) ⇒ company_id

(2) Customer

cus_id : char(9) cus_Add : varchar(100) company_id : char(9)

PK(Primary Key) ⇒ cus_id
FK(Foreign Key) ⇒ company_id reference (company)

(3) Car

car_no : char(9) model : char(9)

PK ⇒ car_no

(4) Driver

Driver_id : char(9) Add : varchar(100)

PK ⇒ Driver_id

(5) Owns

cus_id : char(9)
cus_no : char(9)
pur_date : date
pur_amount : integer

FK ⇒ company_id references (company)

FK ⇒ car_no references (car)

(6) Accident

car_no : char(9)
Driver_id : char(9)
Acci_date : date
dam_amt : integer

FK ⇒ car_no references (car)

FK ⇒ Driver_id references (Driver)

(7) Insurance

car_no : char(9)
company_id : char(9)
insu_date : date
insu_amount : integer
duration : date

FK ⇒ company_id references (company)

FK ⇒ car_no references (car)

Q2. Design a Relational Database corresponding to the E-R diagram given below: [8]

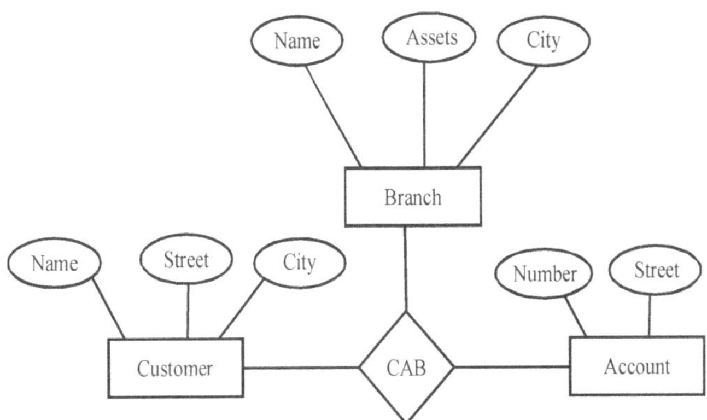

RDBMS of a Given ER Diagram

CUSTOMER TABLE
ACCOUNT_NUMBER *NAME* *STREET* *CITY*
BRANCH_NAME

BRANCH TABLE
NAME *ASSESTS* *BCITY*

ACCOUNT TABLE
NUMBER *BALANCE*

CAB TABLE
ACCOUNT_NUMBER *BRANCE_NAME* *CUSTOMER_NAME*

CHAPTER-4

INTRODUCTION TO STRUCTURED QUERY LANGUAGE

Structured Query Language (also known as **SQL**) allows users to access data in relational database management systems, such as Oracle, Sybase, Informix, Microsoft SQL Server, Access, and others, by allowing users to describe the data the user wishes to see. SQL also allows users to define the data in a database, and manipulate that data. This chapter will describe how to use SQL, and give examples.

Basics of the SELECT Statement

In a relational database, data is stored in tables. An example table would relate Social Security Number, Name, and Address:

EmployeeAddressTable

SSN	First Name	Last Name	Address	City	State
512687458	Nitin	Sharma	25/5,Tri Ng.	Jalandhar	Punjab
758420012	Naveen	Kumar	Sec.-5,Rohi.	Jaipur	Rajsthan
102254896	Ajay	Bhatt	B-88,Pu.Ba.	Luckhnow	U.P.

Now, let's say you want to see the address of each employee. Use the SELECT statement, like so:

SELECT FirstName, LastName, Address, City, State

FROM EmployeeAddressTable ;

The following is the results of your *query* of the database:

First Name	Last Name	Address	City	State
Nitin	Sharma	25/5,Tri Ng.	Jalandhar	Punjab
Naveen	Kumar	Sec.-5,Rohi.	Jaipur	Rajsthan
Ajay	Bhatt	B-88,Pu.Ba.	Luckhnow	U.P.

To explain what you just did, you asked for the all of data in the EmployeeAddressTable, and specifically, you asked for the *columns* called FirstName, LastName, Address, City, and State. Note that column names and table names do not have spaces...they must be typed as one word; and that the statement ends with a semicolon (;). The general form for a SELECT statement, retrieving all of the *rows* in the table is:

SELECT Column Name, Column Name, ...
FROM TableName;

To get all columns of a table without typing all column names, use:

SELECT * FROM TableName;

Conditional Selection

To further discuss the SELECT statement, let's look at a new example table :

EmployeeStatisticsTable

Employee IDNo	Salary	Benefits	Position
010	75000	15000	Manager
105	65000	15000	Manager
152	60000	15000	Manager
215	60000	12500	Manager
244	50000	12000	Staff
300	45000	10000	Staff
335	40000	10000	Staff
400	32000	7500	Entry-Level
441	28000	7500	Entry-Level

Relational Operators

There are six Relational Operators in SQL :

=	Equal
<> or ! = (see manaual)	Not Equal
<	Less than
>	Greater than
≤	Less than or Equal to
≥	Greater than or Equal to

The *WHERE* clause is used to specify that only certain rows of the table are displayed, based on the criteria described in that *WHERE clause.* It is most easily understood by looking at a couple of examples.

If you wanted to see the EMPLOYEEIDNO's of those making at or over Rs.50,000, use the following:

```
SELECT EMPLOYEEIDNO
FROM EMPLOYEESTATISTICSTABLE
WHERE SALARY>= 50000;
```

Notice that the >= (greater than or equal to) sign is used, as we wanted to see those who made greater than Rs.50,000, or equal to Rs.50,000, listed together. This displays:

```
EMPLOYEEIDNO
____________

0    1    0
1    0    5
1    5    2
2    1    5
244
```

The *WHERE* description, SALARY >= 50000, is known as a *condition* (an operation which evaluates to True or False). The same can be done for text columns:

```
SELECT EMPLOYEEIDNO
FROM EMPLOYEESTATISTICSTABLE
WHERE POSITION = 'Manager';
```

This displays the ID Numbers of all Managers. Generally, with text columns, stick to equal to or not equal to, and make sure that any text that appears in the statement is surrounded by single quotes (').

More Complex Conditions: Compound Conditions / Logical Operators
The *AND* operator joins two or more conditions, and displays a row only if that row's data satisfies **ALL** conditions listed (i.e. all conditions hold true). For example, to display all staff making over Rs.40,000, use:

```
SELECT EMPLOYEEIDNO
FROM EMPLOYEESTATISTICSTABLE
WHERE SALARY > 40000 AND POSITION = 'Staff';
```

The *OR* operator joins two or more conditions, but returns a row if **ANY** of the conditions listed hold true. To see all those who make less than Rs.40,000 or have less than Rs.10,000 in benefits, listed together, use the following query:

```
SELECT EMPLOYEEIDNO
FROM EMPLOYEESTATISTICSTABLE
WHERE SALARY < 40000 OR BENEFITS < 10000;
```

AND & OR can be combined, for example:

```
SELECT EMPLOYEEIDNO
FROM EMPLOYEESTATISTICSTABLE
WHERE POSITION = 'Manager' AND SALARY > 60000 OR BENEFITS > 12000;
```

First, SQL finds the rows where the salary is greater than Rs.60,000 and the position column is equal to Manager, then taking this new list of rows, SQL then sees if any of these rows satisfies the previous AND condition or the condition that the Benefits column is greater then Rs.12,000. Subsequently, SQL only displays this second new list of rows, keeping in mind that anyone with Benefits over Rs.12,000 will be included as the OR operator includes a row if either resulting condition is True. Also note that the AND operation is done first.

To generalize this process, SQL performs the AND operation(s) to determine the rows where the AND operation(s) hold true (remember: all of the conditions are true), then these results are used to compare with the OR conditions, and only display those remaining rows where any of the conditions joined by the OR operator hold true (where a condition or result from an AND is paired with another condition or AND result to use to evaluate the OR, which evaluates to true if either value is true). Mathematically, SQL evaluates all of the conditions, then evaluates the AND "pairs", and then evaluates the OR's (where both operators evaluate left to right).

To look at an example, for a given row for which the DBMS is evaluating the SQL statement Where clause to determine whether to include the row in the query result (the whole Where clause evaluates to True), the DBMS has evaluated all of the conditions, and is ready to do the logical comparisons on this result:

True AND False OR True AND True OR False AND False
First simplify the AND pairs:
False OR True OR False
Now do the OR's, left to right:
True OR False
True

The result is True, and the row passes the query conditions. Be sure to see the next section on NOT's, and the order of logical operations. I hope that this section has helped you understand AND's or OR's, as it's a difficult subject to explain briefly (especially when you write a version and the editor loses the changes—on multiple occasions no less!).

To perform OR's before AND's, like if you wanted to see a list of employees making a large salary (>Rs.50,000) or have a large benefit package (>Rs.10,000), and that happen to be a manager, use parentheses:

```
SELECT EMPLOYEEIDNO
FROMEMPLOYEESTATISTICSTABLE
WHERE POSITION = 'Manager' AND (SALARY > 50000 OR BENEFIT > 10000);
```

IN & BETWEEN

An easier method of using compound conditions uses *IN* or *BETWEEN*. For example, if you wanted to list all managers and staff:

```
SELECT EMPLOYEEIDNO
FROM EMPLOYEE STATISTICSTABLE
WHERE POSITION IN ('Manager', 'Staff');
```

or to list those making greater than or equal to Rs.30,000, but less than or equal to Rs.50,000, use:

```
SELECTEMPLOYEEIDNO
FROMEMPLOYEESTATISTICSTABLE
WHERE SALARY BETWEEN 30000 AND 50000;
```

To list everyone not in this range, try :

```
SELECT EMPLOYEEIDNO
FROM EMPLOYEE STATISTICSTABLE
WHERE SALARY NOT BETWEEN 30000 AND 50000;
```

Similarly, NOT IN lists all rows excluded from the *IN* list.
Additionally, NOT's can be thrown in with AND's & OR's, except that NOT is a unary operator (evaluates one condition, reversing its value, whereas, AND's & OR's evaluate two conditions), and that all NOT's are performed before any AND's or OR's.

SQL Order of Logical Operations (each operates from left to right)

NOT

AND

OR

Using *LIKE*

Look at the EmployeeStatisticsTable, and say you wanted to see all people whose last names started with "L"; try:

```
SELECT EMPLOYEEIDNO
FROM EMPLOYEE STATISTICSTABLE
WHERE LASTNAME LIKE 'L%';
```

The percent sign (%) is used to represent any possible character (number, letter, or punctuation) or set of characters that might appear after the "L". To find those people with LastName's ending in "L", use '%L', or if you wanted the "L" in the middle of the word, try '%L%'. The '%' can be used for any characters in the same position relative to the given characters. NOT LIKE displays rows not fitting the given description. Other possiblities of using LIKE, or any of these discussed conditionals, are available, though it depends on what DBMS you are using; as usual, consult a manual or your system manager or administrator for the available features on your system, or just to make sure that what you are trying to do is available and allowed. This disclaimer holds for the features of SQL that will be discussed below. This section is just to give you an idea of the possibilities of queries that can be written in SQL.

Joins

In this section, we will only discuss *inner* joins, and *equijoins*, as in general, they are the most useful. For more information, try the SQL links at the bottom of the page.

Good database design suggests that each table lists data only about a single *entity*, and detailed information can be obtained in a relational database, by using additional tables, and by using a *join*.

First, take a look at these example tables :

AntiqueOwners

OwnerID	OwnerLastName	OwnerFirstName
01	Sharma	Nitin
02	Kumar	Vijay
15	Bhatt	Ved
21	Gupta	Amit
50	Kant	Chandra

Orders

OwnerID	Item Desired
02	Table
02	Desk
21	Chair
15	Mirror

Antiques

SellerID	BuyerID	Item
01	50	Bed
02	15	Table
15	02	Chair
21	50	Mirror
50	01	Desk
01	21	Cabinet
02	21	Coffee Table
15	50	Chair
01	15	Jewellry Box
02	21	Pottery
21	02	Bookcase
50	01	Plant Stand

Keys

First, let's discuss the concept of *keys*. A *primary key* is a column or set of columns that uniquely identifies the rest of the data in any given row. For example, in the AntiqueOwners table, the OwnerID column uniquely identifies that row. This means two things: no two rows can have the same OwnerID, and, even if two owners have the same first and last names, the OwnerID column ensures that the two owners will not be confused with each other, because the unique OwnerID column will be used throughout the database to track the owners, rather than the names.

A *foreign key* is a column in a table where that column is a primary key of another table, which means that any data in a foreign key column must have corresponding data in the other table where that column is the primary key. In DBMS-speak, this correspondence is known as *referential integrity*. For example, in the Antiques table, both the BuyerID and SellerID are foreign keys to the primary key of the AntiqueOwners table (OwnerID; for purposes of argument, one has to be an Antique Owner before one can buy or sell any items), as, in both tables, the ID rows are used to identify the owners or buyers and sellers, and that the OwnerID is the primary key of the AntiqueOwners table. In other words, all of this "ID" data is used to refer to the owners, buyers, or sellers of antiques, themselves, without having to use the actual names.

Performing a Join

The purpose of these *keys* is so that data can be related across tables, without having to repeat data in every table—this is the power of relational databases. For example, you can find the names of those who bought a chair without having to list the full name of the buyer in the Antiques table...you can get the name by relating those who bought a chair with the names in the AntiqueOwners table through the use of the OwnerID, which *relates* the data in the two tables. To find the names of those who bought a chair, use the following query :

```
SELECT OWNER LAST NAME, OWNER FIRST NAME
FROM ANTIQUE OWNERS, ANTIQUES
WHERE BUYERID = OWNERID AND ITEM = 'Chair';
```

Note the following about this query...notice that both tables involved in the relation are listed in the FROM clause of the statement. In the WHERE clause, first notice that the ITEM = 'Chair' part restricts the listing to those who have bought (and in this example, thereby owns) a chair. Secondly, notice how the ID columns are related from one table to the next by use of the BUYERID = OWNERID clause. Only where ID's match across tables and the item purchased is a chair (because of the AND), will the names from the AntiqueOwners table be listed. Because the joining condition used an equal sign, this join is called an *equijoin*. The result of this query is two names: Sharma, Nitin & Kumar, Vijay.

Dot notation refers to prefixing the table names to column names, to avoid ambiguity, as such:

```
SELECT ANTIQUE OWNERS. OWNER LAST NAME,
ANTIQUE OWNERS. OWNER FIRST NAME
FROM ANTIQUE OWNERS, ANTIQUES
WHERE ANTIQUES.BUYERID = ANTIQUEOWNERS.OWNERID AND
ANTIQUES.ITEM = 'Chair';
```

DISTINCT and Eliminating Duplicates

Let's say that you want to list the ID and names of **only** those people who have sold an antique. Obviously, you want a list where each seller is only listed once—you don't want to know how many antiques a person sold, just the fact that this person sold one. This means that you will need to tell SQL to eliminate duplicate sales rows, and just list each person only once. To do this, use the *DISTINCT* keyword. First, we will need an equijoin to the AntiqueOwners table to get the detail data of the person's LastName and FirstName. However, keep in mind that since the SellerID column in the Antiques table is a foreign key to the AntiqueOwners table, a seller will only be listed if there is a row in the AntiqueOwners table listing the ID and names. We also want to eliminate multiple occurences of the SellerID in our listing, so we use *DISTINCT* **on the column where the repeats may occur.**

To throw in one more twist, we will also want the list alphabetized by LastName, then by FirstName (on a LastName tie). Thus, we will use the *ORDER BY* clause :

```
SELECT DISTINCT SELLERID, OWNERLAST NAME, OWNER FIRSTNAME
FROM ANTIQUES, ANTIQUEOWNERS
WHERESELLERID=OWNERID
ORDER BY OWNER LAST NAME, OWNER FIRST NAME;
```

In this example, since everyone has sold an item, we will get a listing of all of the owners, in alphabetical order by last name. For future reference (and in case anyone asks), this type of join is considered to be in the category of *inner joins.*

Aliases & *In*/Subqueries

In this section, we will talk about *Aliases*, *In* and the use of subqueries, and how these can be used in a 3-table example. First, look at this query which prints the last name of those owners who have placed an order and what the order is, only listing those orders which can be filled (that is, there is a buyer who owns that ordered item):

```
SELECT OWN.OWNERLASTNAME Last Name, ORD.ITEMDESIRED Item
Ordered
FROM ORDERS ORD, ANTIQUEOWNERS OWN
WHERE ORD.OWNERID = OWN.OWNERID
AND ORD.ITEMDESIRED IN

    (SELECT ITEM
    FROM ANTIQUES);
```

This gives:

Last Name Item Ordered

Kumar Table
Kumar Desk
Gupta Chair
Bhatt Mirror

There are several things to note about this query:
First, the "Last Name" and "Item Ordered" in the Select lines gives the headers on the report.

The OWN & ORD are aliases; these are new names for the two tables listed in the FROM clause that are used as prefixes for all dot notations of column names in the query (see above). This eliminates ambiguity, especially in the equijoin WHERE clause where both tables have the column named OwnerID, and the dot notation tells SQL that we are talking about two different OwnerID's from the two different tables.

Note that the Orders table is listed first in the FROM clause; this makes sure listing is done off of that table, and the AntiqueOwners table is only used for the detail information (Last Name).

Most importantly, the AND in the WHERE clause forces the In Subquery to be invoked ("= ANY" or "= SOME" are two equivalent uses of IN). What this does is, the subquery is performed, returning all of the Items owned from the Antiques table, as there is no WHERE clause. Then, for a row from the Orders table to be listed, the ItemDesired must be in that returned list of Items owned from the Antiques table, thus listing an item only if the order can be filled from another owner. You can think of it this way: the subquery returns a *set* of Items from which each ItemDesired in the Orders table is compared; the In condition is true only if the ItemDesired is in that returned set from the Antiques table.

Also notice, that in this case, that there happened to be an antique available for each one desired...obviously, that won't always be the case. In addition, notice that when the IN, "= ANY", or "= SOME" is used, that these keywords refer to any possible row matches, not column matches...that is, you cannot put multiple columns in the subquery Select clause, in an attempt to match the column in the outer Where clause to one of multiple possible column values in the subquery; only one column can be listed in the subquery, and the possible match comes from multiple *row* values in that *one* column, not vice-versa.

Q1. We are given the following record-types (relation types): **[4]**

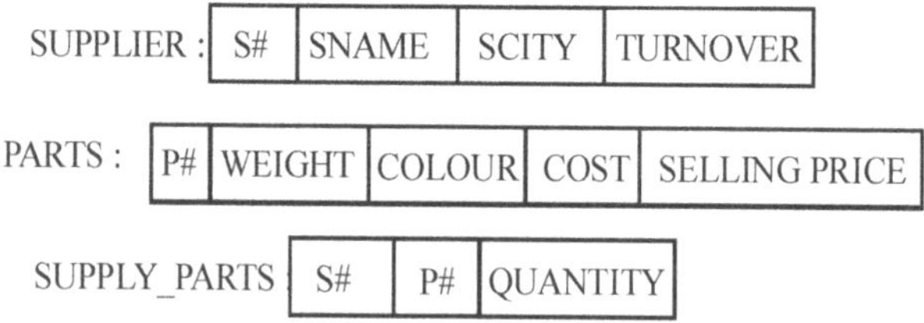

SUPPLIER :

S#	SNAME	SCITY	TURNOVER

PARTS :

P#	WEIGHT	COLOUR	COST	SELLING PRICE

SUPPLY_PARTS

S#	P#	QUANTITY

Express the following commands in SQL :

(i) Get P# for the parts for which weight of the part is 5 kg and colour is black.
SELECT P# FROM PARTS WHERE WEIGHT = 5 AND COLOUR = "BLACK"

(ii) Give the details of all suppliers from the city of Bombay and turnover of more than Rs. 50 lacs.

SELECT * FROM SUPPLIER WHERE SCITY = "BOMBAY" AND TURNOVER > 5000000

OTHER IMPORTANT SQL STATEMENTS

Aggregate Functions

We will discuss five important *aggregate functions*: AVG, MAX, MIN, SUM and COUNT. They are called aggregate functions because they summarize the results of a query, rather than listing all of the rows.

- SUM () gives the total of all the rows, satisfying any conditions, of the given column, where the given column is numeric.
- AVG () gives the average of the given column.
- MAX () gives the largest figure in the given column.
- MIN () gives the smallest figure in the given column.
- COUNT(*) gives the number of rows satisfying the conditions.

Looking at the tables at the begining of the chapter, let's look at three examples :

```
SELECTSUM(SALARY),AVG(SALARY)
FROM EMPLOYEESTATISTICSTABLE;
```

This query shows the total of all salaries in the table, and the average salary of all of the entries in the table.

```
SELECTMIN(BENEFITS)
FROMEMPLOYEESTATISTICSTABLE
WHERE POSITION = 'Manager';
```

This query gives the smallest figure of the Benefits column, of the employees who are Managers, which is 12500.

```
SELECTCOUNT(*)
FROMEMPLOYEESTATISTICSTABLE
WHERE POSITION = 'Staff';
```

This query tells you how many employees have Staff status (3).

Views

In SQL, you might (check your DBA) have access to create views for yourself. What a view does is to allow you to assign the results of a query to a new, personal table, that you can use in other queries, where this new table is given the view name in your FROM clause. When you access a view, the query that is defined in your view creation statement is performed (generally), and the results of that query look just like another table in the query that you wrote invoking the view. For example, to create a view:

```
CREATE VIEWANTVIEWAS SELECT ITEMDESIRED FROM ORDERS;
```

Now, write a query using this view as a table, where the table is just a listing of all Items Desired from the Orders table :

```
SELECTSELLERID
FROMANTIQUES,ANTVIEW
WHERE ITEMDESIRED=ITEM;
```

This query shows all SellerID's from the Antiques table where the Item in that table happens to appear in the Antview view, which is just all of the Items Desired in the Orders table. The listing is generated by going through the Antique Items one-by-one until there's a match with the Antview view. Views can be used to restrict database access, as well as, in this case, simplify a complex query.

Creating New Tables

All tables within a database must be created at some point in time...let's see how we would create the Orders table:

```
CREATE TABLE ORDERS
(OWNER ID INTEGER NOT NULL,
ITEMDESIRED CHAR(40) NOT NULL);
```

This statement gives the table name and tells the DBMS about each column in the table.

Altering Tables

Let's add a column to the Antiques table to allow the entry of the price of a given Item :

```
ALTER TABLE ANTIQUES ADD (PRICE DECIMAL(8,2) NULL);
```

The data for this new column can be updated or inserted as shown later.

Adding Data

To insert rows into a table, do the following:

INSERT INTO ANTIQUES VALUES (21, 01, 'Gullyman', 200.00);

This inserts the data into the table, as a new row, column-by-column, in the pre-defined order. Instead, let's change the order and leave Price blank:

INSERT INTO ANTIQUES (BUYERID, SELLERID, ITEM)

VALUES (01, 21, 'Gullyman');

Deleting Data

Let's delete this new row back out of the database:
DELETEFROMANTIQUES
WHERE ITEM = 'Gullyman';

But if there is another row that contains 'Gullyman', that row will be deleted also. Let's delete all rows (one, in this case) that contain the specific data we added before:
DELETE FROM ANTIQUES
WHERE ITEM = 'Gullyman' AND BUYERID = 01 AND SELLERID = 21;

Updating Data

Let's update a Price into a row that doesn't have a price listed yet :

UPDATE ANTIQUES SET PRICE = 500.00 WHERE ITEM = 'Chair';

This sets all Chair's Prices to 500.00. As shown above, more WHERE conditionals, using AND, must be used to limit the updating to more specific rows. Also, additional columns may be set by separating equal statements with commas.

GROUP BY & HAVING

One special use of GROUP BY is to associate an aggregate function (especially COUNT; counting the number of rows in each group) with groups of rows. First, assume that the Antiques table has the Price column, and each row has a value for that column. We want to see the price of the most expensive item bought by each owner. We have to tell SQL to *group* each owner's purchases, and tell us the maximum purchase price:

SELECT BUYERID, MAX(PRICE)
FROM ANTIQUES

```
GROUP BY BUYERID;
```

Now, say we only want to see the maximum purchase price if the purchase is over Rs.1000, so we use the HAVING clause:

```
SELECT BUYERID, MAX(PRICE)
FROM ANTIQUES
GROUP BY BUYERID
HAVING PRICE > 1000;
```

More Subqueries

Another common usage of subqueries involves the use of operators to allow a Where condition to include the Select output of a subquery. First, list the buyers who purchased an expensive item (the Price of the item is Rs.100 greater than the average price of all items purchased):

```
SELECT BUYERID
FROM ANTIQUES
WHERE PRICE >
(SELECT AVG(PRICE) + 100 FROM ANTIQUES);
```

The subquery calculates the average Price, plus Rs.100, and using that figure, an OwnerID is printed for every item costing over that figure. One could use DISTINCT BUYERID, to eliminate duplicates.

List the Last Names of those in the AntiqueOwners table, ONLY if they have bought an item :

```
SELECT OWNERLASTNAME
FROM ANTIQUEOWNERS
WHERE OWNERID IN
(SELECT DISTINCT BUYERID FROM ANTIQUES);
```

The subquery returns a list of buyers, and the Last Name is printed for an Antique Owner if and only if the Owner's ID appears in the subquery list (sometimes called a *candidate list*). *Note:* on some DBMS's, equals can be used instead of IN, but for clarity's sake, since a set is returned from the subquery, IN is the better choice.
For an Update example, we know that the gentleman who bought the bookcase has the wrong First Name in the database...it should be Gullybaba:

```
UPDATE ANTIQUEOWNERS
SET OWNERFIRSTNAME = 'Gullybaba'
WHERE OWNERID =
```

```
(SELECT BUYERID FROM ANTIQUES WHERE ITEM = 'Bookcase');
```

First, the subquery finds the BuyerID for the person(s) who bought the Bookcase, then the outer query updates his First Name.

Remember this rule about subqueries :

when you have a subquery as part of a WHERE condition, the Select clause in the subquery must have columns that match in number and type to those in the Where clause of the outer query. In other words, if you have "WHERE ColumnName = (SELECT...);", the Select must have only one column in it, to match the ColumnName in the outer Where clause, *and* they must match in type (both being integers, both being character strings, etc.).

Exists & All

EXISTS uses a subquery as a condition, where the condition is True if the subquery returns any rows, and False if the subquery does not return any rows; this is a nonintuitive feature with few unique uses. However, if a prospective customer wanted to see the list of Owners only if the shop dealt in Chairs, try:

```
SELECT OWNERFIRSTNAME, OWNERLASTNAME
FROM ANTIQUEOWNERS
WHERE EXISTS
(SELECT * FROM ANTIQUES WHERE ITEM = 'Chair');
```

If there are any Chairs in the Antiques column, the subquery would return a row or rows, making the EXISTS clause true, causing SQL to list the Antique Owners. If there had been no Chairs, no rows would have been returned by the outside query. ALL is another unusual feature, as ALL queries can usually be done with different, and possibly simpler methods; let's take a look at an example query:

```
SELECT BUYERID, ITEM
FROM ANTIQUES
WHERE PRICE >= ALL
(SELECT PRICE FROM ANTIQUES);
```

This will return the largest priced item (or more than one item if there is a tie), and its buyer. The subquery returns a list of all Prices in the Antiques table, and the outer query goes through each row of the Antiques table, and if its Price is greater than or equal to every (or ALL) Prices in the list, it is listed, giving the highest priced Item. The reason ">=" must be used is that the highest priced item will be equal to the highest price on the list, because this Item is in the Price list.

UNION & Outer Joins

There are occasions where you might want to see the results of multiple queries together, combining their output; use UNION. To merge the output of the following two queries, displaying the ID's of all Buyers, plus all those who have an Order placed:

```
SELECT BUYERID FROM ANTIQUES UNION
SELECT OWNERID FROM ORDERS;
```

Notice that SQL requires that the Select list (of columns) must match, column-by-column, in data type. In this case BuyerID and OwnerID are of the same data type (integer). Also notice that SQL does automatic duplicate elimination when using UNION (as if they were two "sets"); in single queries, you have to use DISTINCT. The *outer join* is used when a join query is "united" with the rows not included in the join, and are especially useful if constant text "flags" are included. First, look at the query :

```
SELECT OWNERID, 'is in both Orders & Antiques'
FROM ORDERS, ANTIQUES
WHERE OWNERID = BUYERID
UNION
SELECT BUYERID, 'is in Antiques only'
FROM ANTIQUES
WHERE BUYERID NOT IN
(SELECT OWNERID FROM ORDERS);
```

The first query does a join to list any owners who are in both tables, and putting a tag line after the ID repeating the quote. The UNION merges this list with the next list. The second list is generated by first listing those ID's not in the Orders table, thus generating a list of ID's excluded from the join query. Then, each row in the Antiques table is scanned, and if the BuyerID is not in this exclusion list, it is listed with its quoted tag. There might be an easier way to make this list, but it's difficult to generate the informational quoted strings of text.

This concept is useful in situations where a primary key is related to a foreign key, but the foreign key value for some primary keys is NULL. For example, in one table, the primary key is a salesperson, and in another table is customers, with their salesperson listed in the same row. However, if a salesperson has no customers, that person's name won't appear in the customer table. The outer join is used if the listing of **all** salespersons is to be printed, listed with their customers, whether the salesperson has a customer or not—that is, no customer is printed (a logical NULL value) if the salesperson has no customers, but is in the salespersons table. Otherwise, the salesperson will be listed with each customer.

Another important related point about Nulls having to do with joins: the order of tables listed in the From clause is very important. The rule states that SQL "adds" the second table to the first; the first table listed has any rows where there is a null on the join column displayed; if the second table has a row with a null on the join column, that row from the table listed second does not get joined, and thus included with the first table's row data. This is another occasion (should you wish that data included in the result) where an outer join is commonly used. The concept of nulls is important, and it may be worth your time to investigate them further. ENOUGH QUERIES!!! you say?...now on to something completely different...this is an Gullybaba way to make you comfortable with difficulties in your studies.

Q2. Consider the record-types given below:

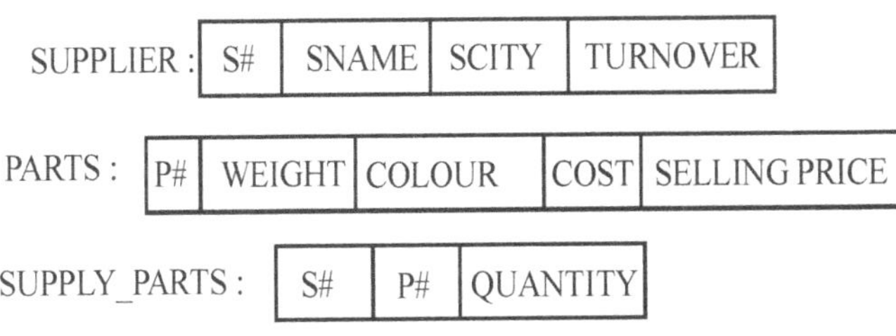

Where S# and P# are keys respectively for SUPPLIER and PARTS.
Express the following in SQL

(i) Get the part numbers weighting between 25 and 35
SELECT P# FROM PARTS WHERE WEIGHT BETWEEN 25 AND 35

(ii) Get the supplier names (S_NAME) who are located in the city of Hyderabad.
SELECT S_NAME FROM SUPPLIER WHERE CITY = "HYDRABAD"

(iii) Get the names of suppliers who supply at least one part of red colour
SELECT S_NAME FROM SUPPLIER WHERE S# = (SELECT SUPPLY_PARTS.S# FROM SUPPLY_PARTS WHERE P# = (SELECT P# FROM PARTS WHERE COLOUR = "RED")))

(iv) Delete all the suppliers involving red colored parts. **[8]**
DELETE FROM SUPPLIER WHERE S# = (SELECT S# FROM SUPPLY_PARTS WHERE P# = (SELECT P# FROM PARTS WHERE COLOUR = "RED")))

Chapter-5

Introduction To File Organisation

SEQUENTIAL FILES

Introduction

Access to records in a Sequential file is serial. To reach a particular record, all the preceding records must be read.

The organization of an **unordered** Sequential file means it is only practical to read records from the file and add records to the end of the file. It is not practical to delete or update records.

While it is possible to delete, update and insert records in an **ordered** Sequential file, these operations have some drawbacks.

Problems accessing ordered Sequential files

Records in an ordered Sequential file are arranged, in order, on some key field or fields. When we want to insert,delete or amend a record we must preserve the ordering. The only way to do this is to create a new file. In the case of an insertion or update, the new file will contain the inserted or updated record. In the case of a deletion, the deleted record will be missing from the new file.

The main drawback to inserting, deleting or amending records in an ordered Sequential file is that the entire file must be read and then the records written to a new file. Since disk access is one of the slowest things we can do in computing this is very wasteful of computer time when only a few records are involved.

For instance, if 10 records are to be inserted into a 20,000 record file, then 20,000 records will have to be read from the old file and 20,010 written to the new file. The average time to insert a new record will thus be very great.

Contrast with direct access files

While Sequential files have a number of advantages over other types of file organization the fact that a new file must be created when we delete, update or insert a records causes problems.

These problems are addressed by direct access files. Direct access files allow us to read, update, delete and insert individual records using a key.

Inserting records in an ordered Sequential file
To insert a record in an ordered Sequential file :

1. All the records with a key value less than the record to be inserted must be read and then written to the new file.
2. Then the record to be inserted must be written to the new file.
3. Finally, the remaining records must be written to the new file.

Deleting records from an ordered Sequential file
To delete a record in an ordered Sequential file :

1. All the records with a key value less than the record to be deleted must be written to the new file.
2. When the record to be deleted is encountered it is not written to the new file.
3. Finally, all the remaining records must be written to the new file.

Amending records in an ordered Sequential file
To amend a record in an ordered Sequential file :

1. All the records with a key value less than the record to be amended must be read and then written to the new file.
2. The amended record must then be written to the new file.
3. Finally, all the remaining records must be written to the new file.

Summary

The problem with Sequential files is that unless the file is ordered very few (only read and add) operations can be applied to it.
Even when a Sequential file is ordered; delete, insert and amend operations are prohibitively expensive (in processing terms) when only a few records in the file are affected (i.e. when the "hit rate" is low).

RELATIVE FILES

Introduction

As we have already noted, the problem with Sequential files is that access to the records is serial. To reach a particular record, all the proceeding records must be read.

Direct access files allow direct access to a particular record in the file using a key and this greatly facilitates the operations of reading, deleting, updating and inserting records.

Organization of Relative files

Records in relative files are organized on ascending Relative Record Number. A Relative file may be visualized as a one dimension table stored on disk, where the Relative Record Number is the index into the table. Relative files support sequential access by allowing the active records to be read one after another.

Relative files support only one key. The key must be numeric and must take a value between 1 and the current highest Relative Record Number. Enough room is allocated to the file to contain records with Relative Record Numbers between 1 and the highest record number.

For instance, if the highest relative record number used is 20,000 then room for 20,000 records is allocated to the file.

Accessing records in a Relative file

To access a records in a Relative file a Relative Record Number must be provided. Supplying this number allows the record to be accessed directly because the system can use

1. the start position of the file on disk,
2. the size of the record,
3. and the Relative Record Number

to calculate the position of the record.

Because the file management system only has to make a few calculations to find the record position the Relative file organization is the fastest of the two direct access file organizations. It is also the most storage efficient.

Organization and use of Relative files

To read, insert, delete or update a record directly, the Relative Record Number of the record must be placed in the key area and then the operation must be applied to the file.

Summary or definition of relative file

A Relative file is organized like a one dimension table on disk where each record is an element of the table. The Relative Record Number acts like a table index to allow access to the records.

INDEXED FILES

Introduction

While the usefulness of a Relative file is constrained by its restrictive key, Indexed files suffer from no such limitation.

Indexed files may have up to 255 keys, the keys can be alphanumeric and only the primary key must be unique.
In addition, it is possible to read an Indexed file sequentially on any of its keys.

Organization of Indexed files

An Indexed file may have multiple keys. The key upon which the data records are ordered is called the **primary key**. The other keys are called **alternate keys**.

Records in the Indexed file are sequenced on ascending primary key. Over the actual data records, the file system builds an index. When direct access is required, the file system uses this index to find, read, insert, update or delete, the required record.

For each of the alternate keys specified in an Indexed file, an alternate index is built. However, the lowest level of an alternate index does not contain actual data records. Instead, this level made up of base records which contain only the alternate key value and a pointer to where the actual record is. These base records are organized in ascending alternate key order.

As well as allowing direct access to records on the primary key or any of the 254 alternate keys, indexed files may also be processed sequentially. When processed sequentially, the records may be read in ascending order on the primary key or on any of the alternate keys.

Since the data records are in held in ascending primary key sequence it is easy to see how the file may be accessed sequentially on the primary key. It is not quite so obvious how sequential on the alternate keys is achieved.

The **algorithm** used for traversing the index is -

```
IF Record Key Value > Required Key Value
   take this branch
ELSE
  go to next index record
END-IF
```

Summary

An Indexed file may have multiple, alphanumeric, keys.
Only the primary key must be unique.
For each key specified for an Indexed file, an index will be built.

COMPARISON OF VARIOUS FILE ORGANIZATIONS

Introduction

In this section we examine the advantages and disadvantages of the three file organizations.

SEQUENTIAL FILES

Disadvantages :

1. Slow
The "hit rate" refers to the number of records in the file that are affected when updating a file. For instance, if only 100 records are to affected by an insert, delete or amend operation in a file of 10,000 records then the hit rate is low. But if 9,000 records are affected then the hit rate is high.

Sequential files are very slow to update when the hit rate is low because the entire file must be read and then written to a new file, just to update a few records.

2. Complicated
Sequential files are also complicated to change. Changes to Sequential files are batched together into a transaction file to minimize the low hit rate problem but this makes updating the Sequential file much more complicated than updating a direct access file.

The complications come from having to match the records in the transaction file with those in the master file (i.e. the file to be updated).

Advantages :

1. Fast

When the hit rate is high this is the fastest method of updating a file because the record position does not have to be calculated and no indexes have to be traversed.

2. Most storage efficient

This is the most storage efficient of all the file organizations. No indexes are required. Space from deleted records is recovered. Only room actually required to hold the records is allocated to the file.

3. Simple organization

This is the simplest file organization. Records are held serially.

4. Files may be stored on serial media

Sequential files may be stored on serial media such as magnetic tape.
These media are cheap, removable and voluminous.

RELATIVE FILES

Disadvantages :

1. Wastes storage if the file is only partially populated

If the file is only partially populated with records then this is a very wasteful file organization. The file will be allocated enough room to hold records from 1 to the highest Relative Record Number used, even if only a few records have actually been written to the file.

For instance, if the first record written to the file has a Relative Record Number of 10,000 then room for that many records is allocated to the file.
The fact that there is only one key and that it must be numeric and must take a value between 1 and the highest record number is limiting.

2. Cannot recover space from deleted records

Relative files cannot recover the space from deleted records.
When a record is deleted in a Relative file, it is simply marked as deleted but the actual space that used to be occupied by the record is still allocated to the file.

So if a Relative file is 560K in size when full, it will still be 560K when you have deleted half the records.

3. Only a single key allowed

The usefulness of Relative files is severely constrained by the fact that;

1. they can only have one key,
2. the key must be numeric
3. the key must have a value in the range - 1 to the highest key value.

The single key is limiting because it is often the case that we need to access the file on more than one key. For instance, in a file of student records we might want to access the records on Student Id, Student Name, CourseCode.

4. The key must be numeric

The mention of using StudentName, CourseCode or ModuleCode as a key, highlights another drawback with Relative files.
We frequently need to access the file using a key that is not numeric.

5. The key is inflexible

The fact that the key must be in the range 1 to the highest key value and that the file system allocates space for all the records between 1 and the highest Relative Record Number used, imposes severe constraints on the key.

For instance even though the StudentId is numeric we couldn't use it as a key because the file system would allocate space for records from 1 to the highest StudentId written to the file.

Suppose the highest StudentId written to the file was 987654. The file system would allocate space for 9,876,54 records.
Sometimes we can get around the limitations of the key by using a transformation function to map the actual key on to the range of Relative Record Numbers.

There are a number of possible transformation, or "hashing", functions, including truncation (only using some of the digits in the key as the Relative Record Number), folding (breaking the key into two or more parts and summing the parts), digit manipulation (manipulating some of the digits in the key to produce a Relative Record Number) and modulus division (using the remainder of a division operation as the Relative Record Number).

Some transformation functions might even allow keys that are not numeric.
Some transformation functions require special code to deal with duplication that occurs when the transformation of two different keys produces the same Relative Record Number.

6. Must be stored on direct access media

Because Relative files are direct access files they must be stored on direct access media such as a hard or floppy disks. They can not be stored on magnetic tape.

Advantages :

1. Fastest direct access organization

This is the fastest direct access organization. To reach a particular record, only a few simple calculations have to be done.

2. Can be read sequentially

As well as allowing direct access, Relative files allow sequential access to the records in the file.

3. Very little storage overhead

Unlike Indexed files, which must store the indexes as well as the data, Relative files have only a small storage overhead.

INDEXED FILES

Disadvantages :

1. Slowest direct access organization

Because Indexed file achieve direct access by traversing a number of levels of index this is the slowest direct access organization.

Indexed files must have a primary key index and an index for each alternate key.
Each level of index implies an I/O operation on the hard disk.
For instance, in the Indexed file animation three I/O operations were required to read the record (two for the index records and one for data record).

Because of this, Indexed files are substantially slower than Relative files. They are especially slow when writing or deleting records because the primary key index and the alternate key indexes may need to be rebuilt.

2. Not very storage efficient

Indexed files require more storage than other file organizations because file must store;

- **(i)** the primary key Index records
- **(ii)** the index records for each alternate key
- **(iii)** the actual data records
- **(iv)** the base records for each alternate key

In addition, the space from deleted records is only partially recovered.

3. Must be stored on direct access media

Because Indexed files are direct access files they must be stored on direct access media such as a hard or floppy disks. They cannot be stored on magnetic tape.

Advantages :

1. Versatile keys

Indexed files can have multiple alphanumeric keys and only the primary key has to be unique.

An indexed file may be read sequentially on any of its keys.
When we compare the number of disadvantages of Indexed files with the advantages we might be forgiven for thinking "Why would we ever use Indexed files?". But the versatility of its keys overrides all its disadvantages with the result that Indexed files are the most widely used direct access file organization.

Summary

There is no one best file organization. Choosing an appropriate file organization is a case of "horses for courses".

If the hit rate is high and we have no need for direct access to the records, a Sequential file might be best.

If the hit rate is low or if we require direct access to the records but one numeric key is sufficient, a Relative file might be the best choice.

If we need direct access on a number of keys or if the key must be alphanumeric, then we must choose an Indexed file.

Q1. Compare and contrast index sequential file with B^+ tree file. [6]

In a sequential file, records are maintained in the logical sequence of their primary key values. The processing of a sequential file is conceptually simple but inefficient for random file access. However, if access to the file is strictly sequential, a sequential file is suitable. A sequential file could be stored on a storage device such as magnetic tape.

Adding a record necessitates the shifting of all records from the appropriate point to the end of file to create space for the new record.

In the Tree based data organization scheme (B Tree and B+ Tree) are used both for primary and secondary key retrieval. B tree indices are similar to B+ tree indices. A B tree allows search key values to appear only once. In B tree, the leaf nodes do not contain information. During lookup, if the leaf node is reached without a match, the key does not exist.

Difference :

* The deletion in a B+ tree is always made in the leaf nodes.
* A lookup on a B+ tree enquires traversal of a path from the root of the tree to some leaf node. While in sequential file it is based on index.

Q2. Discuss the differences between the following file organization. [15]

(a) Serial
(b) Index-Sequential
(c) Hashed
(d) Inverted

Compare their storage and access efficiencies. To what type of application is each of the organisations suited?

(a) Serial File Organization : Serial organization offers the easy access to next record and the absence of auxiliary data structure. Records are maintained in a logical sequence of their primary key value. The search for a given record requires, an average, access to all the records, till you reach the desired one. Appending a record requires the creation of a new file, updation procedure allows only sequential updation and resulted updated file generates a new master file from the existing one. It uses magnetic tape for storage media.

(b) Index-Sequential file organization : Provides random access to records and the sequential nature of the file provides easy access to next record. Updation do not require generation of a new file. It uses magnetic disks for direct access. In indexed sequential file overflow is a real problem in volatile tables. ISAM is good for static tables because there are usually fewer index levels.

(c) Hashed : In direct file organization the key value is mapped directly to storage location. The usual method of direct mapping is by performing arithmetic manipulation of the key value. This procedure is called hashing.

(d) Inverted : The inverted file approach tends to exhibit better inquiry performance. Many types of queries can be answered by accessing inversion indexes without necessitating access to records, thereby reducing I/O access requirements.

Indexed sequential file organization is commonly used in business data processing. There are no indexes to traverse well designed hashing functions where collision are few, this is a great advantage, exact key matches are extremely quick. No disk space is used by this indexing method. But it has some drawbacks. It become difficult to predict overflow because the working of the hashing algorithm will not be visible to the DBA. No sorting of data occurs either physically or logically, so sequential access is poor. The organization usually takes a lot of disk space to ensure that no overflow occurs. There is a plus side to this though no space is wasted on index structure because they simply do not exist. The primary disadvantage of the index sequential file organization is that performance degrades as the file grows. To overcome this deficiency, we can use a B+-tree index.
Sequential file organizations require an index structure to locate data. File organization based on hashing by contrast, allow us to find the address of a data item directly by computing a function on the search key value of the desired record. Since we do not know at design time precisely which search key values will be stored in the file, a good hash function to choose is one that assigns search key values to buckets such that the distribution is both uniform and random. The inverted file approach tends to exhibit better inquiry performance. Many types of queries can be answered by accessing inversion indexes without necessitating access to data records, thereby reducing I/O access requirements. Inversion of a file can be transparent to a programmer who access that file, but does not use the inversion indexes.

Linked file organization considered as indexed file organization, inverted file organization considered as direct file organization.

1. Sequential file organization find its use in application areas where batch processing is more common. Whereas direct files are used extensively in application areas where interactive processing is used when accessing record is done sequentially by some key value and also to access record directly by the same key value. The collection of records may be organized in an effective manner called indexed sequential organization.

2. Sequential files are simple to use and can be stored on inexpensive media whereas a direct file must be stored on a direct access device, whereas an indexed sequential file stored on a direct access storage device.

Q3. What does VSAM stand for? Briefly describe the VSAM indexing and also, mention the advantages and disadvantages. [7]

VSAM stands for virtual storage access method.

The major disadvantage of the index-sequential organisation is that as the file grow, performance deteriorates rapidly because of overflows and consequently there arises the need for periodic reorganisation. Reorganisation is an expensive process and the file becomes unavailable during reorganistion. Through VSAM IBM's advanced version of the indexed-sequential organisation that avoids these disadvantages. The system is immune to the characteristics of the storage medium, which could be considered as a pool of blocks. The VSAM files are made up of two components : the offset and data. However, unlike index-sequential organisation, overflows are handled in a different manner. The VSAM index and data are assigned to distinct blocks of virtual storage called a control interval. To allow for growth, each time a data block overflows it is divided into two blocks and appropriate changes are made to the indexes to reflect this division.

Feedback is the breakfast of Champions.

Ken Blanchard

You can Help other students.
"Inform any error or mistake in this book."

We and Universe
will reward you for Your Kind act.

Email at : feedback@gullybaba.com
or
WhatsApp on 9350849407

SOLVED PAPERS CS-06

CS-06: DATABASE MANAGEMENT SYSTEM
TEE-DEC-1999

Note: *Question 1 is **compulsory**. Answer any **three** from the rest.*

1(a). Construct an E-R diagram for a car insurance company that has a set of customers, each of whom owns one or more cars. Each car has associated with it zero or any number of accidents. [10]

Refer to Study material,Q2, Page No. -21

(b)Consider the Relational database

Employee (emp_name, street, city)
Works (emp_name, company_name, salary)
Company (company_name, city)
Manages (emp_name, manager_name)
Give expressions in SQL for the following:

(i) Find the names of all employees who work for First Bank Corporation

SELECT EMP_NAME FROM WORKS WHERE COMPANY_NAME="First Bank Corporation"

(ii) Find all employees in the database who live in the same cities as the companies for which they work.

SELECT EMP_NAME, CITY FROM EMPLOYEE, WORKS, COMPANY WHERE (EMPLOYEE.EMP_NAME=WORKS.EMP_NAME AND WORKS.COMPANY_NAME=COMPANY.COMPANY_NAME)

(iii) Find all employees in the database who earn more than every employee of small Bank Corporation.

SELECT EMP_NAME FROM WORKS WHERE SALARY > (SELECT MAX(SALARY) FROM WORKS WHERE COMPANY_NAME = "SMALL BANK CORPORATION"

(iv) Find the names, street address and cities of residence of all employees who work for First Bank Corporation and earn more $10000.

SELECT EMP_NAME, STREET, CITY FROM EMPLOYEE, WORKS WHERE ((EMPLOYEE.EMP_NAME=WORKS.EMP_NAME AND COMPANY_NAME="FIRST BANK CORPORATION") AND WORKS.SALARY > 10000))

(v) Find all employees in the databases who live in the same cities and on the same street as do their managers. [10]

SELECT EMP_NAME EMPLOYEE WHERE EMP_NAME, MANAGES WHERE EMPLOYEE.EMP_NAME=MANAGES.EMP_NAME

(c) Define 2NF and 3NF. Produce 3NF table structures from the table below: [10]

Enrol No.	Sname	Dept.	Year	Block Name
1024	Mathews	Physics	1	G
1126	John	Chemistry	1	G
1016	Bill	Mathematics	2	K
1420	James	Botany	2	K
1503	Charles	Geology	3	L
1001	Dickens	Zoology	4	M

Second Normal Form (2NF)

Second normal form is based on the concept of *fully functional dependency.* A functional X->Y is a **fully functional dependency** is removal of any attribute A from X means that the dependency does not hold any more. A relation schema is in **2NF** if every nonprime attribute in relation is *fully functionally dependent* on the primary key of the relation. It also can be restated as: a relation schema is in **2NF** if every nonprime attribute in relation is not partially dependent on *any key* of the relation.

Practical Rule: *"Eliminate Redundant Data,"* i.e., if an attribute depends on only part of a multivalued key, remove it to a separate table.

Formal Definition: A relation is in **second normal form** (2NF) if and only if it is in 1NF and every nonkey attribute is fully dependent on the primary key.

Third Normal Form (3NF)

Third normal form is based on the concept of *transitive dependency.* A functional dependency X->Y in a relation is a **transitive dependency** if there is a set of attributes Z that is *not a subset* of any key of the relation, and both X->Z and Z->Y hold. In other words, a relation is in **3NF** if, whenever a functional dependency X->A holds in the relation, either (a) X is a superkey of the relation, or (b) A is a prime attribute of the relation.

Practical Rule : *"Eliminate Columns not Dependent on Key,"* i.e., if attributes do not contribute to a description of a key, remove them to a separate table.
Formal Definition: A relation is in **third normal form** (3NF) if and only if it is in 2NF and every nonkey attribute is nontransitively dependent on the primary key.

The following is the 3NF structure

ENROLL_No SNAME DEPT Year

The table further divided into another table for YEAR & Block NAME

YEAR BLOCK NAME

2(a). Is it possible in general to have two primary indices on the same relation for different search keys? Explain your answer.

Yes, It is possible in general to have two primary indices on he same keys because if the file containing the records is sequentially ordered, the index whose search key specifies the sequential order of the file is the primary index. Primary index are also called Clustering Index. The search key of a primary is usually the primary key. Index whose search key specifies an order different from the sequential order of the file is called Secondary Index.

(b)Explain the distinction between open and closed hashing. Discuss the relative merits of each technique in database applications. [9]

In closed hashing, the hash function is used on the search key to identify a bucket *b.* We must examine all the records in bucket b to see whether they match the search key. If bucket, b has overflow buckets, the records in all the overflow buckets of b must also be examined. This form of hashing is sometimes referred to as closed hashing. It is used for database systems because deletion under open hashing is troublesome.

In open hashing, the set of buckets is fixed, there are no overflow chains. Instead if bucket is full, records are inserted in some other bucket in the initial set of buckets B. It is used in construction of symbol tables for compilers and assemblers. Compilers and assemblers perform only lookup and insertion operations on their symbol tables. Open hashing is of only minor importance in database implementation.

In open hashing, the hash function must be chosen when we implement the system and it cannot be changed easily thereafter if the file being indexed grows or shrinks. Since the function h maps search-key values to a fixed set B of bucket addresses. is made large, then we waste space and if B is too small then the buckets contain records of many different search-key values and bucket overflows can occur.

In the index-sequential file organisation the mapping from the search-key value to the storage location is via index entries. In direct file organisation, the key value is mapped directly to the storage location. The usual method of direct mapping is by performing some arithmetic manipulation of the key value.

Key value Address

This process is called *hashing.* Let us consider a hash function h that maps the key value k to the value h(k). The value h(k) is used as an address and for our application we require that this value be in some range. If our address area for the records lies between S1 and S2, the requirement for the hash function h(k) is that for all values of k it should generate values between S1 and S2.

Open Hashing :

* Open hashing is used in construction of symbol tables for compilers and assemblers.
* Deletion in Open hashing is trouble some.
* Open Hashing is of minor importance in database implementation.

Closed Hashing :

* Closed hashing is used for database system.
* Deletion and Insertion is easily handled in closed hashing.
* Closed hashing is of minor importance in database implementation.

Q3(a). Compare and contrast BCNF and 3NF. Show that if a relation scheme is BCNF, then it is also in 3NF [9]

Refer to Study material,Q2, Page No. -14

(b) List the three design goals of relational databases and explain why each desired [6]

Refer to DEC01,Q5(c), Page no. 15

4(a). Discuss the design issues related to distributed database through an example. [9]

Following are the three design issues related to distributed database : -

(i) & (ii) Repeated in June 2002, 3 (a) Page No. 137

(iii) Replication and Fragmentation : This is a combination of the above two notions. The relation is partitioned into several fragments. The system maintains several identical replicas of each such fragment.

(b) Explain the trade offs in distributing the database [6]

The disadvantages of the distributed approach are its cost and complexity. A distributed system, which hides its distributed nature from the end user, is more complex than the centralized DBMS. Increased complexity means that the acquisition and maintenance costs of the system are higher than those for a centralized DBMS. The parallel nature of the system means that errors are harder to avoid and those in the applications are difficult to pinpoint. In addition, the distributed system, by its very nature entails a large communication overhead in coordinating messages between sites. These messages not only clutter up the network, but degrade the system's performance as well. Out-of-sequence delivery or nondelivery of messages creates problems such as phantom deadlocks and blocked transactions.

5(a). What are the techniques available for the knowledge representation? Explain them briefly through an example. [10]

Following are the various techniques available for the knowledge representation :

(i) Rule Based System (Production System)
Refer to JUNE02,Q6(a), Page no. -148

(ii) Frames
Refer to JUNE02,Q6(a), Page no. -148

(iii) Semantic Networks
Refer to DEC01,Q6(a), Page no. -160

(iv) First-order Logic (Predicate Logic)
Refer to JAN01,Q5(c)(iii), Page no. -187

(b) What is the difference between declarative and procedural knowledge? [5]

Knowledge may be declarative or procedural.

Declarative : Declarative knowledge express as statements of facts about the world.

Personnel data in a database is typical of declarative knowledge. Such data are explicit pieces of independent knowledge.

Procedural : Procedural knowledge is complied knowledge related to the performance of some tasks. For example the steps used to solve an algebraic equation can be expressed as procedural knowledge.

Declarative Knownledge : Declarative Knowledge on the other hand is passive knowledge expresses as statements of facts about the world.

Procedural Knowledge : Procedural Knowledge is complied knowledge related to the performance of some taks.

Declarative Knowledge : Personnel data in database is typical example of declarative knowledge. Such data are explicit pieces of independent knowledge.

Procedural Knowledge : e.g. The steps used to solve an algebraic equation are expressed as procedural knowledge.

6(a). Describe various Relational operators that are used in Relational Algebra. Perform Union, Difference, Intersection and Cartesian Product for the following relations. [10]

P

id	Name
101	Ram
103	Krishna
104	Kishore
107	Ravi
110	Varun
112	Rahul

Q

id	Name
103	Krishna
104	Kishore
106	Kishan
110	Varun

Union

The *union* operation of two relational tables is formed by appending rows from one table with those of a second table to produce a third. Duplicate rows are eliminated. The notation for the union of Tables A and B is A UNION B.

The relational tables used in the union operation must be union compatible. Tables that are union compatible must have the same number of columns and corresponding columns must come from the same domain. Below is the figure shows the union of P and Q.

Note that the duplicate rows has been removed.

Figure1: P UNION Q

id	Name
101	Ram
103	Krishna
104	Kishore
106	Kishan
107	Ravi
110	Varun
112	Rahul

Difference

The *difference* of two relational tables is a third that contains those rows that occur in the first table but not in the second. The Difference operation requires that the tables be union compatible. As with arithmetic, the order of subtraction matters. That is, P - Q is not the same as Q - P. Figure below shows the different results.

Figure : The Difference Operator

id	Name
106	Kishan

id	Name
101	Ram
107	Ravi
112	Rahul

Intersection

The intersection of two relational tables is a third table that contains common rows. Both tables must be union compatible. The notation for the intersection of P and Q is P [intersection] Q = R or P INTERSECT Q. Figure below shows the single rows in P and Q.

Figure : Intersection

id	Name
103	Krishna
104	Kishore
110	Varun

Product

The product of two relational tables, also called the Cartesian Product, is the concatenation of every row in one table with every row in the second. The product of table P (having m rows) and table Q (having n rows) is the table R (having m x n rows). The product is denoted as P X Q or P TIMES Q.

Figure : Product

P id	P name	Q id	Q name
101	Ram	103	Krishna
101	Ram	104	Kisore
101	Ram	106	Kishan
101	Ram	110	Varun
103	Krishna	103	Krishna
103	Krishna	104	Kisore
103	Krishna	106	Kishan
103	Krishna	110	Varun
104	Kisore	103	Krishna
104	Kisore	104	Kisore
104	Kisore	106	Kishan
104	Kisore	110	Varun
107	Ravi	103	Krishna
107	Ravi	104	Kisore
107	Ravi	106	Kishan
107	Ravi	110	Varun
110	Varun	103	Krishna
110	Varun	104	Kisore
110	Varun	106	Kishan
110	Varun	110	Varun
112	Rahul	103	Krishna
112	Rahul	104	Kisore
112	Rahul	106	Kishan
112	Rahul	110	Varun

(b) Write short notes on Client-Server approach. **[5]**

Earlier system normally preferred the concept of centralized system. Centralized system are those that run on a single computer system and do not interact with other systems. Now as the personal computer used are having a very great speed therefore there is a shift from centralized system to client/server approach. Terminals connected to centralized system are now being supplanted by personal computers. Therefore user-interface functionality now can be handled directly by the personal computers. The main system which renders its services to resolve various queries is called the server. The systems through which the users send the request is called the client machine.

The general structure of the client-server system is as shown in the following diagram.

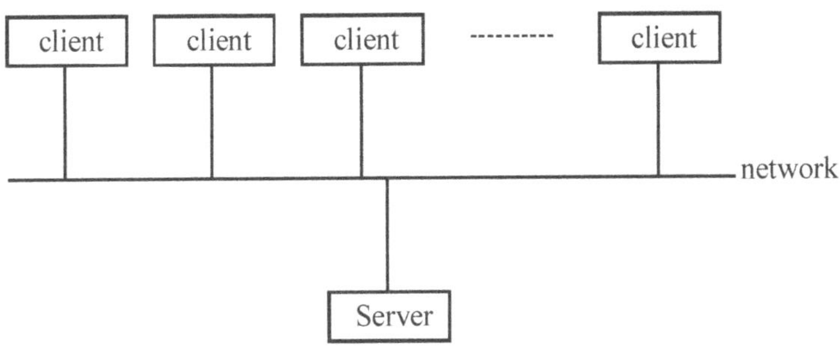

Database functionality is divided into two parts. The first is called front-end and the second as back-end. The back-end manages access structure, query evaluation and optimization, concurrency control and recovery. The front-end of a database system consists of tools such as forms, report writers and graphical user interface facilities. The interface between front-end and back-end is performed by the languages like SQL(Structured Query Language) or some application programs :

The functionality between Front-end and back-end can be graphically shows as below :

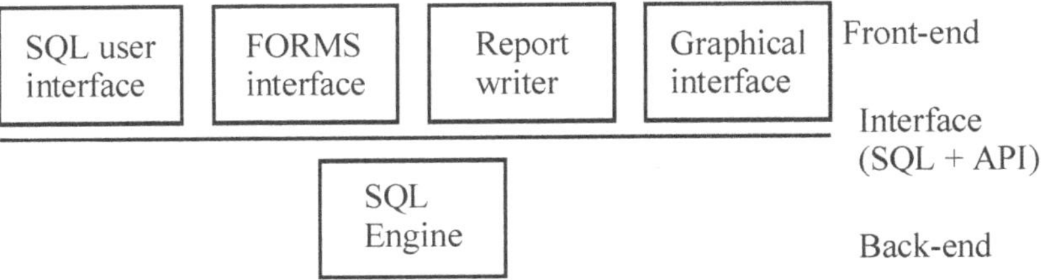

CS-06: DATABASE MANAGEMENT SYSTEM
TEE-JUNE-2000

Note: *Question 1 is* ***compulsory****. Answer any* ***three*** *from the rest.*

1(a). List all functional dependencies and multi-valued dependencies satisfied by the relation of the figure below: [10]

A	B	C	D
a_1	b_1	c_1	d_1
a_1	b_2	c_1	d_1
a_2	b_2	c_2	d_2
a_2	b_3	c_2	d_3
a_3	b_3	c_2	d4

Refer to JUNE02,Q3(b), Page No-140

(b) When designing an E-R diagram for a particular enterprise, there exist several alternative designs. [10]

(i) What criteria should you consider in deciding on the appropriate choice?

The E-R diagram is based on the perception of the real world as a collection of basic objects called entities and the relationships among these objects.

There is no fixed E-R diagram for a particular situation as it depends on the analysis of database and designing from person to person. It may be possible that E-R diagram or Database designed by three persons are different from one another.

As there exists weak and strong entities in the E-R diagram so based upon these entities a criteria for a appropriate E-R diagram can be set. An entity set is called a weak entity set if its existence depends on other entities (called strong entities). Thus a weak entity set does not have sufficient attributes to form a primary key. A entity set which has a primary key, is termed a strong entity set.

Thus based on the obove discussion one can say that a E-R diagram consisting of highest or all strong entities will be appropriate.

(ii) Come up with several alternative E-R diagrams to represent an enterprise. List the merits of each alternative and argue in favour of one of the alternatives. [15]

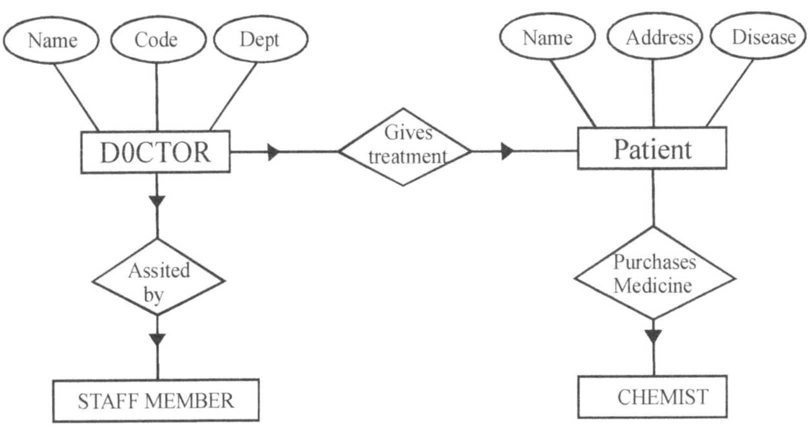

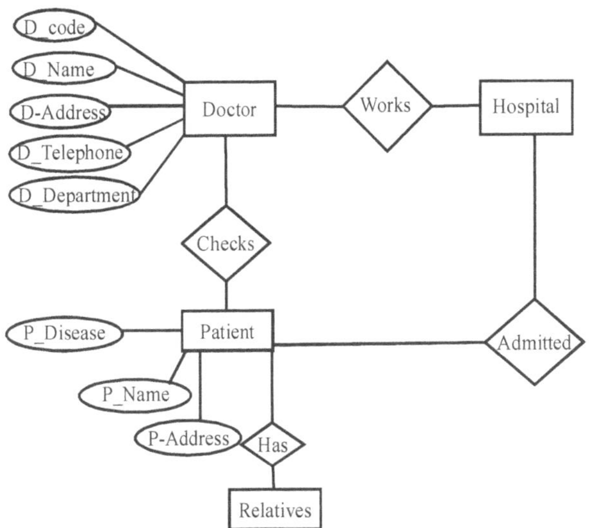

As shown above E-R Diagram (i) is favourable for the Hospital System. In the (i) diagram there exists strong entities while in (ii) ERD there is Patient Entity which is weak entity as no primary key is given. Also relationships are represented without attributes in (ii) while (i) ERD shows all of the eligible attributes with relation to make ERD more clear and understandable, the system. Also (i) ERD represents Relatives Entity which is of no use for this system.

All this make us to select (i) ERD as appropriate for the Hospital Management System.

(c)Given the EMPLOYEE and SALARY relations.
Find the natural Join(EMPLOYEE ⋈ SALARY)

EMPLOYEE :

ENO	ENAME
600	ALEXANDER
607	BRITES
610	CHARLES
612	DAVID

SALARY :

ENO	ESALARY
600	1400
607	1600
610	1300
612	1800

A *join* operation combines the product, selection, and, possibly, projection. The join operator horizontally combines (concatenates) data from one row of a table with rows from another or the same table when certain criteria are met. The criteria involve a relationship among the columns in the join relational table. If the join criterion is based on equality of column value, the result is called an *equijoin*. A *natural join*, is an equijoin with redundant columns removed.
Below is the Natural Join of Employee and Salary Tables given in the question :

E NO	E NAME	E SALARY
600	ALEXANDER	1400
607	BRIJES	1600
610	CHARLES	1300
612	DAVID	1800

2(a)(i). Explain how each view is defined by a schema. Discuss the different views.
Views by Schema :
Each view is defined by a schema, there exists several schema in the database and these schema are partitioned in following three levels of data abstraction or views.

External level or Subschema :

The external level is at the highest level of database abstraction where only those portions of the database of concern to a user or application program are included. Any number of user views may exist for a given global or conceptual view.

Internal level or Physical schema :

We find this view at the lowest level of abstraction, closest to the physical storage method used. It indicates how the data will be stored and describes the data structures and access methods to be used by the database.

(ii) Discuss levels of architecture for a DBMS. **[7]**

Refer to JUNE02,Q2(iii), Page No.-134

(b)Design a Relational Database corresponding to the E-R diagram given below: **[8]**

Refer to Study material,Q2, Page No. -24

3(a). Compare and contrast Sequential and Indexed Sequential file organisations **[3]**

In a sequential file, records are maintained in the logical sequence of their primary key values. The processing of a sequential file is conceptually simple but inefficient for random file access. However, if access to the file is strictly sequential, a sequential file is suitable. A sequential file could be stored on a storage device such as magnetic tape. Adding a record necessitates the shifting of all records from the appropriate point to the end of file to create space for the new record.

A sequential (or sorted on primary keys) file that is indexed is called an index-sequential file. The index provides for random access to records, while the sequential nature of the file provides easy access to the subsequent records as well as sequential processing. In an index-sequential file the physical location of a record in the sequential file is maintained in a set of indexes. These indexes provides fast and random access to the records in the file. An additional feature of this file system is the overflow area. This feature provides additional space for record addition without necessitating the creation of a new file.

(b)Why is a B^+ tree a better structure than a B-tree for implementation of an indexed sequential file? Discuss **[7]**

B Trees :

B Trees are multi-way trees. That is each node contains a set of keys and pointers. A B Tree with four keys and five pointers represents the minimum size of a B Tree node. A B Tree contains only data pages. B Trees are dynamic. That is, the height of the tree grows and contracts as records are added and deleted.

B+ Trees A B+ Tree combines features of ISAM and B Trees. It contains index pages and data pages. The data pages always appear as leaf nodes in the tree. The root node and intermediate nodes are always index pages. These features are similar to ISAM. Unlike ISAM, overflow pages are not used in B+ trees.

The index pages in a B+ tree are constructed through the process of inserting and deleting records. Thus, B+ trees grow and contract like their B Tree counterparts. The contents and the number of index pages reflects this growth and shrinkage

B+ Trees and B Trees use a "fill factor" to control the growth and the shrinkage. A 50% fill factor would be the minimum for any B+ or B tree. As our example we use the smallest page structure. This means that our B+ tree conforms to the following guidelines.

Number of Keys/page	4
Number of Pointers/page	5
Fill Factor	50%
Minimum Keys in each page	2

As this table indicates each page must have a minimum of two keys. The root page may violate this rule.

4. Consider the following tables A, B and AB in which S# is supplier code. P# is product code and QTY is quantity and others carry their respective meaning.

A

S#	SNAME	SCITY	TURNOVER
110	XXX	BHOPAL	50
111	YYY	MUMBAI	100
112	ZZZ	DEHRADUN	70
113	SSS	HYDERABAD	20

B

P#	WEIGHT	COLOUR	COST	SELLING PRICE
1	25	VIOLET	10	30
2	30	BROWN	15	55
3	35	VIOLET	17	55

AB

S#	P#	QTY
100	1	100
111	1	5
110	2	50
111	2	30
110	3	10
112	3	100
113	1	20

Write appropriate SQL statements for the following :

(i) Get the part numbers for the parts being supplied with no duplicates.
SELECT DISTINCT B# FROM SP

(ii) Get the supplier number and part number in ascending order of supplier number and descending order for the part supplied for each supplier.
SELECT A#, B#, QTY FROM SP ORDER BY A#, B# DESC

(iii) Get the details of suppliers who operate from MUMBAI with turnover > 50.
SELECT A.* FROM A WHERE CITY='BOMBAY' AND TURNOVER > 50

(iv) Get the part numbers weighing between 25 and 35.
SELECT B#, WEIGHT FROM B WHERE WEIGHT BETWEEN 25 AND 35

(v) Get the names and cities of suppliers whose names begin with XXX. [15]
SELECT SNAME, SCITY FROM A WHERE SNAME LIKE 'XXX%'

5(a). Describe HISAM as the internal access methods for a hierarchical data base illustrating their features and implications thereof in database performance. [9]

Hierarchical Sequential Access Method (HSAM) is one of DL/I's sequential-access methods. In a sequential-access database, segments are stored in a hierarchical sequence, one segment after another. HSAM provides sequential access to root segments and dependent segments. One can access data in HSAM databases, but you cannot update any of the data.

Hierarchical Indexed Sequential Access Method (HISAM) processes data sequentially, but has an index that enables , to directly access records in the database.

The simplest IMS data structure is the hierarchical sequential access method (HSAM). With this organization, the segments that make up a physical database record are stored in physical sequence within one or more stored records. The root segment is stored first, followed by its dependent segments. The segments are stored in **hierarchical sequence**, which is a top-to-bottom, left-to-right ordering within the PDBR. Thus, the hierarchical sequence is represented by physical adjacency in HSAM.

The hierarchical indexed sequential access method (HISAM) provides an indexed sequential organization for segments. As a result, the segments of a physical database record can be retrieved either sequentially or by direct access. HISAM uses either ISAM or VSAM as its underlying access method. ISAM is used with a special IMS access method called OSAM (overflow sequential access method).

In HISAM example, two data sets (or physical storage files) are used, an ISAM data set and an OSAM data set. Each of these data sets is divided into fixed-length stored records. When an IMS database is first loaded, each root segment that is stored causes a new ISAM stored record to be created.

(b) Discuss the 3 most important Code's commandments through examples. [6]
Following are the 3 most important Code's commandments :

* All information must be held in tables e.g. In simple terms this means that if an item of data doesn't reside somewhere in a table in the database then it doesn't exist and this should be extended to the point where even such information as table, view and column names to mention just a few, should be contained somewhere in table form.
* Retrieval of data must be possible using the following types of operations: SELECT , JOIN and PROJECTe.g. ORACLE
* All relationship between data must be represented explicitly in that data itself e.g. ORACLE

6(a). Compare and contrast knowledge database and DBMS. Give any two examples of knowledge database applications and explain. [7]
One difference between the DBMS and KBMS that has been proposed is that the knowledge base system handles a rather small amount of knowledge, whereas a

DBMS efficiently (as measured by response performance) handles large amounts of shared data. However, this distinction is fallacious since the amount of knowledge has no known boundaries and what this says is that existing knowledge base systems handle a very small amount of knowledge. This does not mean that at some future date we couldn't develop knowledge base systems to efficiently handle much larger amounts of shared knowledge.

In a knowledge base system, the emphasis is placed on a robust knowledge representation scheme and extensive reasoning. Robust signifies that the scheme is rich in expressive power and at the same time it is efficient. In a DBMS, emphasis is on efficient access and management of the data that model a portion of the real world. A knowledge base system is concerned with the meaning of information, whereas a DBMS is interested in the information contained in the data. However, these distinctions are not absolute.

Definition :

A knowledge base management system is a computer system that manages the knowledge in a given domain or field of interest and exhibits reasoning power to the level of a human in this domain.

Database technology has already addressed the problems of improving system performance, concurrent access, distribution and friendly interface; these features are equally pertinent in a KBMS. There will be a continuing need for current DBMSs and their functionalities coexisting with an integrated KBMS. However, the reasoning power of a KBMS can improve the ease of retrieval of pertinent information from a DBMS.

(b) Compare and contrast production rule system and frame base representation with appropriate examples. [8]

Refer to JUNE02,Q6(a), Page no.-148

CS-06: DATABASE MANAGEMENT SYSTEM
TEE-JAN-2001

Note: *Question 1 is* ***compulsory****. Answer any* ***three*** *from the rest.*

1(a). Name six major components of a DataBase Management System. [4]

Database Management System is a system to manage database (a organised collection of data), here organised means data will be in the form of tables(collection of rows and columns). Following are the major Six components of Database Management System.

(i) Data :

Data stored in a database include numerical data which may be integers (whole numbers only) or floating point numbers (decimal), and non-numerical data such as characters (alphabetic and numeric characters), date or logical (true or false). More advanced systems may include more complicated data entities such as pictures and images as data types.

(ii) Standard operations :

Standard operations are provided by most DBMS. These operations provide the user basic capabilities for data manipulation. Examples of these standard operations are sorting, deleting and selecting records.

(iii) Data definition language (DDL) **:**

DDL is the language used to describe the contents of the database. It is used to describe, for example, attribute names (field names), data types, location in the database, etc.

(iv) Data manipulation and query language :

Normally a query language is supported by a DBMS to form commands for input, edit, analysis, output, reformatting, etc. Same degree of standardisation has been achieved with SQL (Structured Query Language).

(v) Programming tools :

Besides commands and queries, the database should be accessible directly from application programs through function calls (subroutine calls) in conventional programming languages.

(vi) File structures :

Every DBMS has its own internal structures used to organise the data although some common data models are used by most DBMS

(b)Define the following concepts in context of DBMS.

(i) Inverted List

An inverted list contains the list of all records, satisfying the particular <attribute, value> pair in the index. The list contains a pointer to every record with a given value for the attribute.

Let us consider a list containing some records with certain field whose values are taken from the set of values D which is domain of Field F maybe a part of a set of fields. It is possible that the value of field F uniquely determines a record. A secondary index for field F is relationship between domain D and the set of records of the file. A list with secondary index on a field F is said to be inverted list. Hence using the fields normally other than the key field we reach in a position to retrieve the specific entity.

For example in case of a supplier (SNAME, STATUS, CITY) we can have a secondary key. Through this key we can reach to the requisite entity. Hence retrieving entity through secondary key is called Inverted List.

(ii) Foreign Key

A foreign key is a primary key of one table that is embedded in another table. (Referential Integrity) is concerned with foreign key i.e. with attributes of relation having domains that are those of the primary key of another relation.

(iii) Referential Integrity **[4]**

Refer to DEC01,Q1(b, ii) Page No. -152

(c)What does ISAM stand for? Briefly describe the advantages of ISAM indexes/Indices. **[4]**

An Index Sequential Organization can be used to fit a specific file hardware configuration. To do so save both access time and storage space. ISAM stands for Index Sequential Access Method. The records are sorted by their key values. The file is organized in blocks. The blocks are searched with the help of the key values and the requisite record is searched into that block sequentially. Therefore, this method is called Indexed Sequential Access Method.

The advantages of ISAM are as follows :

1. Records may be accessed sequentially or directly by some key value.

2. Index part and data part reside on a separate file.

3. Main data file changes due to insertions and deletions, the static index contents may change but the structure does not change.
4. This is most feasible in the application areas where the interactive processing is required.
5. It supports both index and sequential access by the key values and direct access to a particular record giving its key value.
6. Because the whole structure is ordered to a large extent, partial and range based retrievals can often benefit from the use of this type of index.
7. ISAM is good for static tables because there are usually fewer index levels.
8. No locking contention problems occurs in case of ISAM.

A fewer disk I/O is required to access the data.

(d) For the set of following two relations:

P:

B
b_1
b_2

And Q:

A	B
a_1	b_1
a_2	b_1
a_3	b_1
a_1	b_2
a_4	b_2
a_5	b_2

Find out which of the following operation(s) are defined on this set of record types :

(i) Union
Not Union Compatible, as number of columns are not same.

(ii) Difference
For Difference also, tables must be Union Compatible.

(iii) Projection
The *project* operator retrieves a *subset of columns* from a table, removing duplicate rows from the result.

(iv) Division
It is possible here.

Apply one of the definable operation (s) **[4]**
Q Division P
Output will be :

a1
a2
a3
a4
a5

(e) Briefly describe the properties of a normalized relation. **[4]**

Ideal relations after normalization should have the following properties :

1. No data value should be duplicated in different rows unnecessarily.
2. A value must be specified (and required) for every attribute in a row.
3. Each relation should be self-contained. In other words, if a row from a relation is deleted, important information should not be accidentally lost.
4. When a row is added to a relation, other relations in the database should not be affected.
5. A value of an attribute in a tuple may be changed independent of other tuples in the relation.

The idea of normalizing relations to higher and higher normal forms is to attain the goals of having a set of ideal relations meeting the above criteria.

(f) Write briefly about the advantages of Data distribution. **[4]**

Data Sharing and Distributed Control

The primary advantage to accomplish data sharing by means of data distribution is that each site is able to retain a degree of control over data stored locally. There is a global database administrator responsible for the entire system.

Reliability and Availability

If one site fails in distributed system, the remaining sites may be able to continue operating. In particular, if data are replicated in several sites, transaction needing a particular data item may find it in several sites. Thus, the failure of a site does not necessarily imply the shutdown of the system.

The failure of one site must be detected by the system, and appropriate action may be needed to recover from the failure. The system must no longer use the service of the failed site. Finally, when the failed site recovers or is repaired, mechanisms must be available to integrate it smoothly back into the system.

The ability of the system to continue to operate despite the failure of one site results in increased availability.

Speedup Query Processing

If a query involves data at several sites, it may be possible to split the query into subqueries that can be executed in parallel by several sites. Such parallel computation allows for faster processing of user's query. In those cases in which data is replicated, queries may be directed by the system to the least heavily loaded sites.

(g) Name the fundamental ideas underlying Object Oriented Technology (OOT) [3]

1. The fundamental ideas under OOT are :

✔ **Abstraction :** It is the act of removing certain distinctions between objects, so that we can see commonalties. The result of an abstraction process is a concept or object type. One of the form of abstraction is data abstraction.

✔ **Object :** An object is anything, real or abstract, about which we store data and those methods that manipulate the data. In an encapsulated abstraction that includes state information and a clearly defined set of protocol (messages to which object responds). It is a software package which contains related data and procedures. The basic concept is to define software objects that can intersect with each other just as their real-world counterparts do.

✔ **Encapsulation :** Encapsulation is the combination of packaging data and methods. It has following advantages :
(i) Avoid unnecessary details.
(ii) Avoid unintentional data modification
(iii) Presents interference with the internals and also hides the complexity of the compounds.

✔ **Classes and Instance :** A class is an implementation of an object type and is defined by a class description that defines both the attributes and message for an object.

It specifies a data structure and the permissible operational methods that apply to each of its objects.

An object is an instance of a class. The properties of any instance (object) are given by the class description of its class. Thus,
(i) Class is template that helps us to create objects.
(ii) Classes have names (class identifier) that indicates the kind of objects they represent.
(iii) Classes may be arranged in hierarchy with subclass representing more specific kinds of objects than their super class.

✔ **Inheritance :** Inheritance allows developer to create a new class for object from an existing one by inheriting the behavior and then modifying or adding to it. It provides an ability to create classes that will automatically model themselves on other classes. Sometimes a class inherits properties of more than one super class, then it is called MULTIPLE INHERITANCE. It leads to a "Class hierarchy". Thus the power of an OOT is defined by the class hierarchy and its capabilities. It has the following advantages :

(i) Reusability of code

(ii) Avoid duplication of code

(iii) Reduce cost of maintenance

✔ **Message :** A message is defined as :

(i) A specific symbol, identifier and keyword(s) with or without parameters that represents an action to be taken by an object.

(ii) A message is not restricted to one recipient object but to multiple object.

✔ **Methods :** These are also called selectors that enable the system to select code to be executed. Some of the characteristics of method are :

(i) These are descriptions of operations.

(ii) It appears as component of object.

(iii) There is a one-to-one correspondence between message and methods that are executed.

(iv) The same message might result to different method.

(h) Briefly explain what do you understand by a Knowledge Base System. [3]

Refer to DEC02,Q5(a), Page No. -123

Q2(a). Explain briefly the levels of an architecture of a DBMS. Viz., Internal level. Conceptual level and External level. [6]

Refer to JUNE02,Q2(iii), Page No.-134

(b) Draw E-R diagram for any one of the following two organization viz., (i) Public Library, (ii) Hospital, after determining the entities of interest and the relationship that exist between these entities. [6]

Refer to JUNE01,Q2(b), Page No. -167

(c) Define the following terms:

(i) Aggregation

Aggregation is the process of compiling information on an object, thereby abstracting a higher-level object. In this manner, the entity person is derived by aggregating the characteristics a relationship between object and viewing the relationship as an object. As such, the ENROLLMENT relationship between entities student and course could be viewed as entity REGISTRATION. Examples of aggregation are shown in figure : -

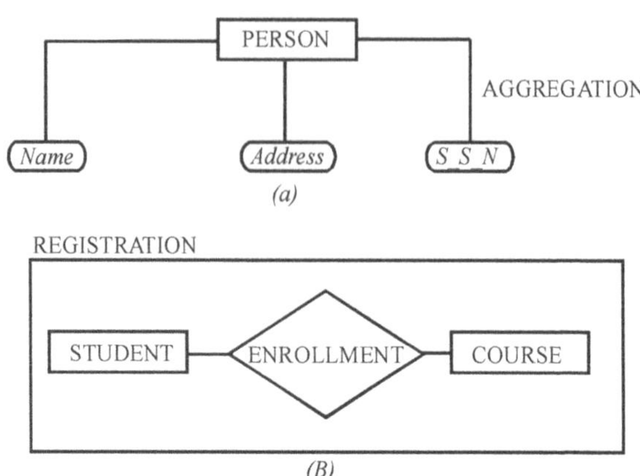

(ii) Specialization

Refer to DEC01,Q2(d, ii), Page No. -154

(iii) Generalization **[3]**

Refer to DEC01,Q2(d, iii), Page No. -154

Below is the Diagrammatic Representation of Specialization and Generalization : -

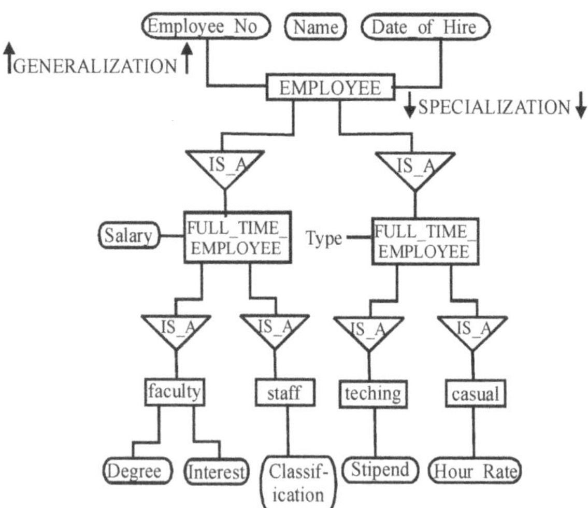

3(a). Draw diagrammatic representation of a university, which runs a number of program say P_i …….. P_m ; The program P_i has n_i course C_{ij} of P_i for each i is pursued by a set S_{ij} of students. The diagrammatic representation is to reflect the hierarchical structure of the university system. [5]

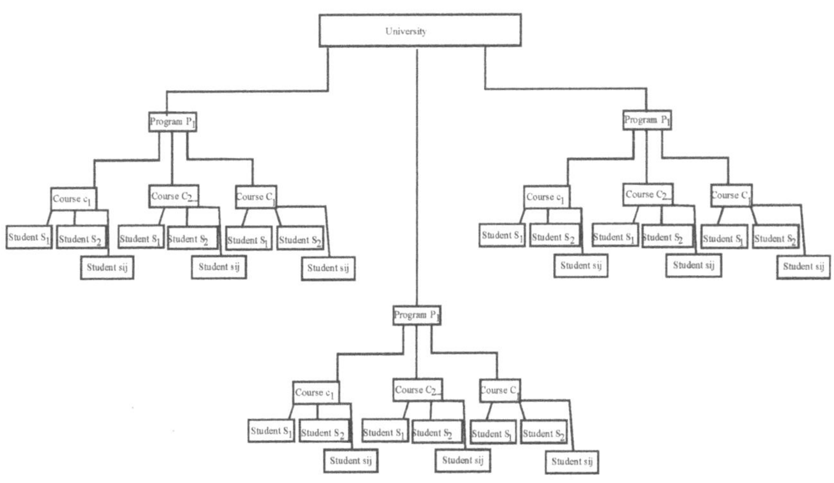

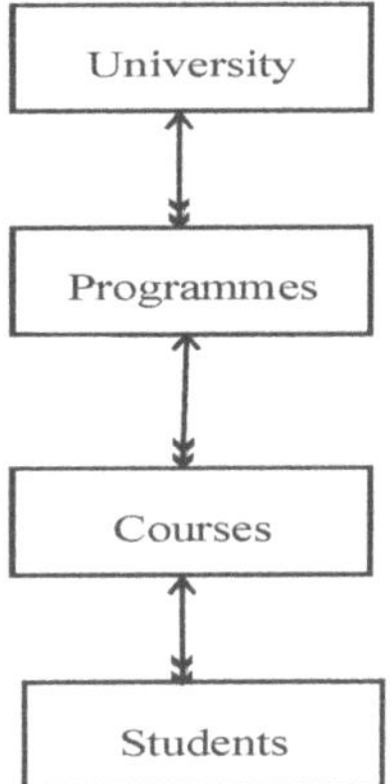

A simple hierarchy

(b) Given the relational schemes:

ENROLL (S#, C#, Section)
TEACH (Prof, C#, Section)
ADVISE (Prof, S#)
PRE_REQ (C# , Pre_C#)

GRADES (S#, C#, Grade, Year)
STUDENT (S#, Sname)

Where S#, C# represent respectively ‘student number’ and ‘course number’: Sname is student name. Prof is thesis advisor of S# in ADVISE, Pre_C# is prerequisite course.
Express the following queries in relational algebra :

(i) List all student taking courses with Mr. Ram and Mr. Abdul.
Sname$^{(student[x])}$ (‘Prof=”Mr. Ram”$^{(Advisor)}$) &
Sname (‘Prof=”Mr. Abdul”$^{(Advisor)}$)

(ii) List all those professors who teach more than one section of the same course.
Name$^{(student[x])}$ (‘C’<=1$^{(teach)}$)

(c) What are the essential components of a DBMS? **[4]**
Refer to Study material,Q2, Page No.-6

4(a). For the following record type, tell whether it is Third Normal From or Not: EMPLOYEE (Employee – Code, Employee-name, department, salary, project–no., Termination–date-of-project)
Where each project-no has unique Termination-Date-of-Project. Justify your answer, if it is in third normal form. It is not in third normal form, being it into third normal form through normalization. **[5]**
A table is said to be in the Third Normal Form, if all the non-key fields of the table are independent of all other non-key fields of the same table. So 3NF removes fields that depend on other non-key fields can be calculated or derived from logic.

So in this question this table is not in 3NF, because Termination-Date-Of-Project is dependent on Project-No. To achieve 3NF , we made another table to remove this dependency the new table contains only two fields Termination-Date-Of-Project & Project-No. The following structure shows 3NF

EMPLOYEE_CODE *EMPLOYEE_NAME* *DEPARTMENT* *SALARY* *Project-No*

New TABLE

Project-No *Termination-Date-Of-Project*

(b) Consider the record-types given below:

SUPPLIER :

S#	SNAME	SCITY	TURNOVER

PARTS :

P#	WEIGHT	COLOUR	COST	SELLING PRICE

SUPPLY_PARTS :

S#	P#	QUANTITY

Where S# and P# are keys respectively for SUPPLIER and PARTS.
Express the following in SQL

(i) Get the part numbers weighting between 25 and 35
(ii) Get the supplier names (S_NAME) who are located in the city of Hyderabad.
(iii) Get the names of suppliers who supply at least one part of red colour
(iv) Delete all the suppliers involving red colored parts. [8]

Refer to Study material,Q2, Page No.- 43

5(a). Briefly discuss the alternative Object-Oriented Database strategies. [5]

Following are the alternative Object-Oriented Database strategies :
* *Novel Database data language/data model approach* --> pursued in research work, most aggresstive approach to develop entirely new database language and database management system with object orientation capabilities.
* *Extending an existing database language with object oriented capabilities* --> used by most vendors of relational system. SQL is a standard and the most popular database language, the most reasonable solution is to extend this language with object-oriented constructs, reflecting the object orientation capabilitities of the underlying database management system.
* *Extending an existing object-oriented programming language with database.*
* *Embedding object-oriented database language constructs in a host (conventional) language* --> Database language can be embedded in host of programming languages. e.g., SQL statements can be embedded in PL/I, C, FORTRAN and Ada.

(b) Briefly explain, the main features of client/server computing. [5]

Following are the alternative Object-Oriented Database strategies :

(i) Client / Server computing caters to low cost & user friendly environment.
(ii) It can be used to develop highly complex multiuser database application being handled by any mainframe computers until about 5 years back.

(iii) It offers expandability.
(iv) It ensures that the performance degradation is not much with increased load.
(v) It allows connectivity with the hetrogeneous machines & also with real time date feeders like ATMs, Numerical machines.
(vi) It allows database management inlcuding security, performance, backup etc.

(c) Explain briefly, with atleast one suitable example any one of the following knowledge representation schemes. [5]

(i) Semantic Nets

Refer to JUNE03,Q6(iii), Page No.-109

(ii) Frame Based

Refer to JUNE03,Q6(ii), Page No.-108

(iii) Logic

Used to describe and understand the world around us. This schema is based upon logic. Logic may be "Propositional" or "Predicate". Here, proposition is declarative sentence e.g. "Today is raining", "Raju is a boy". Propositional logic establishes the validity of a proposition in a given set of propositions. It determines whether the proposition is true or false relative to a given set. Simple propositions can be combined using connectives. For example a combined proposition, which is always true, is given as: - "If today is raining then today is not sunny". A predicate is statement about an object or a relationship between one or more objects i.e. in the propositions. "Today is raining". "is raining" is a predicate. More than one predicates can be combined by the operators ^ (and), v (or), -/ (negation), a (implication). For example let P and Q are the two predicates then P ^ Q is true when both are true. P v Q is true when at least one is true. -/ is true when P is false.

6(a). Discuss main difference between Relational database Management system and Object oriented database management system. [5]

The following points show the difference between RDBMS and OODBMS :

1. RDBMS does not provide the nested structure, instead it allows the hierarchical structure.
2. In the RDBMS the data structure used is in the form of tuple, table and records rather than an object which model the real world in OODBMS.
3. Relational database drive a virtual structure at runtime based on values from sets of data records in tables. OODBMS traverse the data from object to object.
4. Relational database have a limited number of in-built data types such as integer, float etc. whereas we can create very complex data types by using the concepts of class inheritance, polymorphism etc..

5. The object model supports browsing of object class libraries, which allows reuse, rather than reinvention of commonly used data elements.
6. In relational database, complex objects must be broken up and stored in separate tables.
7. The relational database does not understand a global request and thus cannot optimize multiple requests, OODBs can issue a single message (request) that contains multiple transactions.
8. In a relational database, it is difficult to express semantics of complex objects with only a table for data storage.

(b) Discuss the following with reference to distributed computing environment.
(i) Remote Procedure Call **[5]**
Refer to DEC01,Q6(c), Page No.-163

(ii) Object Linking and Embedding.
Abbreviation of ***O****bject* ***L****inking and* ***E****mbedding,* pronounced as separate letters or as *oh-leh.* OLE is a compound document standard developed by Microsoft Corporation. It enables you to create objects with one application and then link(To paste a copy of an object into a document in such a way that it retains its connection with the original object. Updates to the original object can be reflected in the duplicate by updating the link.) or embed them in a second application. Embedded objects retain their original format and links to the application that created them.

Support for OLE is built into the Windows and Macintosh operating systems. A competing compound document standard developed jointly by IBM, Apple Computer, and other computer firms is called OpenDoc.

(c) Explain the steps required for client server application development. **[5]**
Client/Server (C/S) application development divides the application development into two categories. The first category is called **Server Coding** and the second is called **Client Coding**. Various tasks involved are as follows :

1. Creation of Database :
The database is first designed and then created. The design includes planning file limits, size and location of initial data file etc. Then by using SQL command we can create the database.

2. Creation of Tables :
Once database is created then various tables to be kept under this database are created. The table comprises of columns called fields.

3. Creation of database triggers :

Triggers ensure that when a specific action is performed actions are performed.

4. Creation of Stored Procedures :

A stored procedure is a schema object that logically groups a set of SQL and PL/ SQL programming language. These are normally used in case of Oracle (One of the most powerful RDBMS).

5. Creation of server forced validation checks :

This is done through some database integrity rules. It ensures that the data in a database adheres to a pre-defined set of constraints.

6. Creation of Indexes :

Indexes are used to provide quick access to rows in a table. It provides a faster access to data for operations that returns a small portion of rows of a table. Indexes should be created after loading data table. One should Index those columns which re-used for joins to improve performance of joins of multiple tables.

7. Creation of views :

Views are created to see the same data that is in database tables, but with a different perspective. A view is a virtual table, deriving its data from base tables. Views are used to limit access to specific table columns and create value based security by defining a view for a specific rows. Views can also be used to derive other columns not present in any table. For example calculated fields.

CS-06: DATABASE MANAGEMENT SYSTEM
TEE-JUNE-2001

Note: *Question 1 is* ***compulsory****. Answer any* ***three*** *from the rest.*

1(a). Name the major advantages of a Database Management System (DBMS) over a File Management System. [4]

Refer to Study material,Q2, Page No.-6

(b) Define the following concepts in the context of DBMS: [4]

(i) Bit Map

A bit-map is a matrix created for each relationship. Each row corresponds to the relative record number of a source record and each column corresponds to the relative record number of a target record of the relationship. A 1 bit in a cell for row x and column y means that the records corresponding to row x and column y are associated in this relationship; a zero means no association.

(ii) Candidate Key

In general, a relation schema may have more than one key. In this case, each of the keys is called a **candidate key.**

In some instances, an entity will have more than one attribute that can serve as a primary key. Any key or minimum set of keys that could be a primary key is called a *candidate key*. Once candidate keys are identified, choose one, and only one, primary key for each entity.

(iii) Referential integrity

Refer to DEC01,Q1(b, iii), Page No. 152

(c) What does VSAM stand for ? Briefly describe VSAM. [4]

VSAM stands for Virtual Storage Access Method.

The major disadvantage of the index-sequential organisation is that as the file grows, performance deteriorates rapidly because of overlows and consequently there arises the need for periodic reorganisation. Reorganisation is an expensive process and the file becomes unavailable during reorganistion. Through VSAM IBM's advanced version of the indexd-sequential organisation that avoids these disadvantages. The system is immune to the characteristics of the storage medium, which could be considered as a pool of blocks. The VSAM files are made up of two components : the offset and data. However, unlike index-sequential organisation, overflows are handled in a different manner. The VSAM index and data are assigned to distinct blocks of virtual storage called a control interval. To allow for growth, each time a data block overflows it is divided into two blocks and appropriate changes are made to the indexes to reflect this division.

(d) Discuss briefly the possible problem with an unnormalized database. [4]

PROBLEM WITH AN UNNORMALZIED DATABASE

An Un-Normalized database contains redundant and disorganized data, which needs to be organized, by dividing the data over several tables to avoid redundancy. That of

REDUNDANCIES

In non database system each application has its own private files. This fact can often lead to considerable redundancy in stored data, with resultant waste in storage space. Other than this following are the problems caused by redundancy

- Inconsistency occur
- Extra space
- add/deletion/modify will not easy.

In RDBMS all redundancy can or necessarily should be eliminated. Normalization process is used to remove redundancy.

The Network model solves the problem of data redundancy by representing relationships in terms of sets rather than hierarchy. Redundancy that is properly controlled at the physical level is invisible at the logical level, so it has no effect on the correctness of that logical level there are two broad kind of such redundancy :

- The first involves maintaining exact copies or replicas of the base data.
- The second involves maintaining derived data in addition to the base data, most often in the form of summary tables and/or calculated – or computed or derived - columns.

(e)We are given the following record-types (relation types): [4]

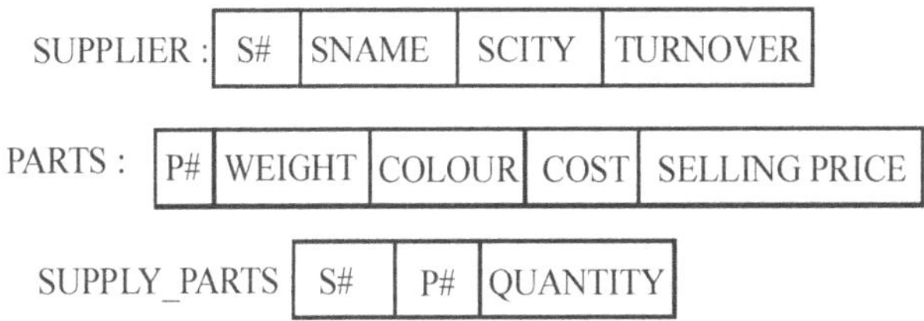

SUPPLIER :

S#	SNAME	SCITY	TURNOVER

PARTS :

P#	WEIGHT	COLOUR	COST	SELLING PRICE

SUPPLY_PARTS

S#	P#	QUANTITY

Express the following commands in SQL :

(i) Get P# for the parts for which weight of the part is 5 kg and colour is black.
(ii) Give the details of all suppliers from the city of Bombay and turnover of more than Rs. 50 lacs.
Refer to Study material,Q2, Page No.-36

(f) Compare object oriented and Relational approaches to Database design. [4]
The comparison between Object-oriented and Relation approaches to Database design is :

1. Object-oriented Database designs are used for facilities of multimedia-CAD, whereas this type of facility is not available in Relation approach.
2. Object-oriented database provides a unique system generated Object Identifier (OID) for each object, whereas in relation approaches each relation must have a primary key attribute whose value identifies each tuple uniquely.
3. Relational databases derived a virtual structure at run-time based on values from sets of data stored in tables, whereas OODBS traverse the data from object to object.
4. Relational databases have a limited number of simple, built-in data types as integer and string and limited number of built-in operations that can handle these data types. We can create complex data types in relation database, but we must do it on a linear basis, whereas OODBS allows arbitrary data types or sub-classing with inheritance.
5. The integrity of data in relational database sometimes creates inconsistent versions, whereas it does not happen in OODBS.
6. Object-oriented databases are favoured for applications, where the relationship among elements in the database carry the key information. Relational databases are favoured when the values of the database elements carry the key information.
7. Object-oriented models capture the structure of the data, relational models organize the data itself. If a record can be understood in isolation, then the relational database is probably suitable. If a record makes sense only in the context of other records, then OODBS is more appropriate.

(g) Explain briefly what do you understand by Distributed computing environment. [4]

Distributed computing environment integrates computers in geographically distant locations and underlying applications. These computers could be of different types with different operating systems, even the RDBMSs. It can also utilize heterogeneous client environment like VB.

This also includes the following :

1. Global Dictionary

The data dictionary of these geographically separate database is stored centrally to take action on distributed transactions. This caters to location transparency e.g. if the salary of all the people in a corporation belonging to grade G2 is higher by 25 %, the transaction statement need not specify the location name where G2's data has to be changed. A statement similar to increase salary of G2 by 25 % globally will do.

2. Two Phase Commit (2PC)

In 2PC, the commit server in phase one, checks out the availability of participating servers in all the locations. In phase two, after sending the transactions to the individual participating servers and receiving OK from them on updation, the commit server sends END COMMIT status to all the participating servers.

3. Replicated Server/Table

In this method, the tables required for distributed transaction are copied/replicated to all participating servers sites. The replication server ensures that when there is a change in the replicated table, the change transmitted to all the locations. This enables reduced network traffic and always prone to application storage owing to network failure.

2(a). Describe the problems that are caused by data redundancies. Can data redundancies be completely eliminated, when database approach is used? Give reasons in support of your answer. [5]

Refer to JUNE02,Q1(b), Page No. - 131

(b) Draw E-R diagram for any one of the following two organisations: (i) University, (ii) Hospital, after determining the entities of interest and the relationships that exist between these entities. [7]

(i) University

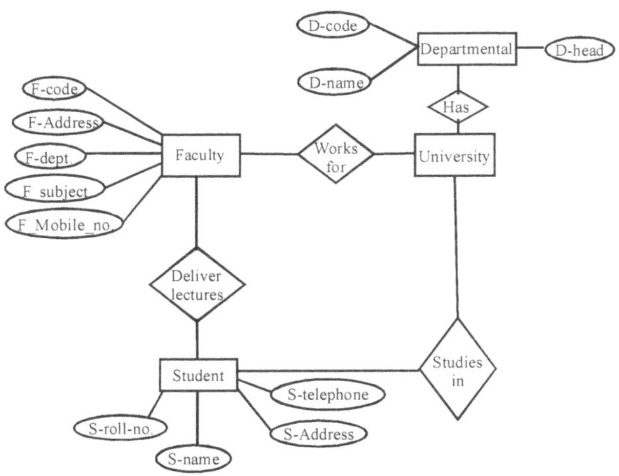

(ii) Hospital

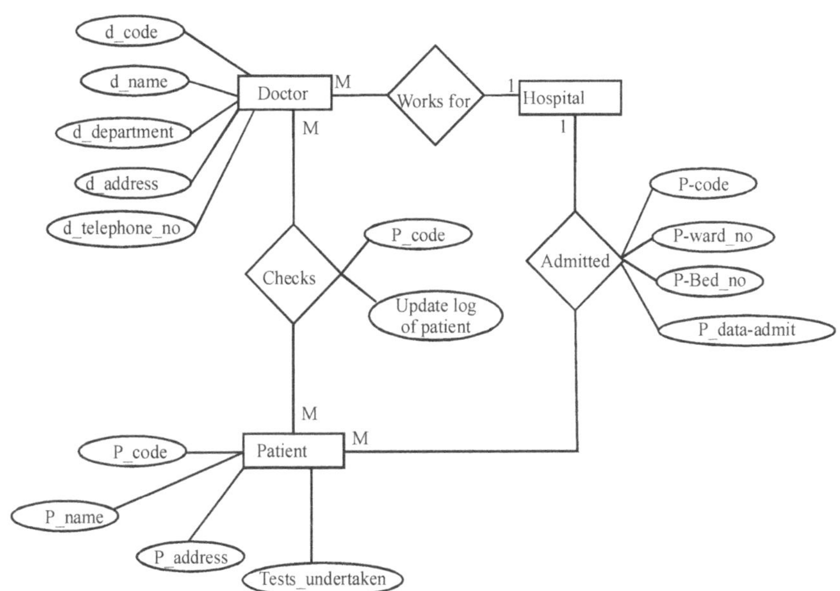

(c) Define the following terms: **[3]**

(i) Association

(ii) Relationship

(iii) Aggregation

ASSOCIATION

An association between two attributes indicates that the values of the associated attributes are interdependent.

Association tells that how the entities are related with each other either through 1:1, 1:M, M:1or M:N relationship.

RELATIONSHIPS

A Relationship represents an association between two or more entities. An example of a relationship would be:

* employees are assigned to projects
* projects have subtasks, departments manage one or more projects.
* Relationships are classified in terms of degree, connectivity, cardinality, and existence

AGGREGATION

Aggregation is the process of compiling information on an object, thereby abstracting a higher-level object. In this manner, the entity person is derived by aggregating the characteristics a relationship between object and viewing the relationship as an object. As such, the ENROLLMENT relationship between entities student and course could be viewed as entity REGISTRATION. Examples of aggregation are shown in figure : -

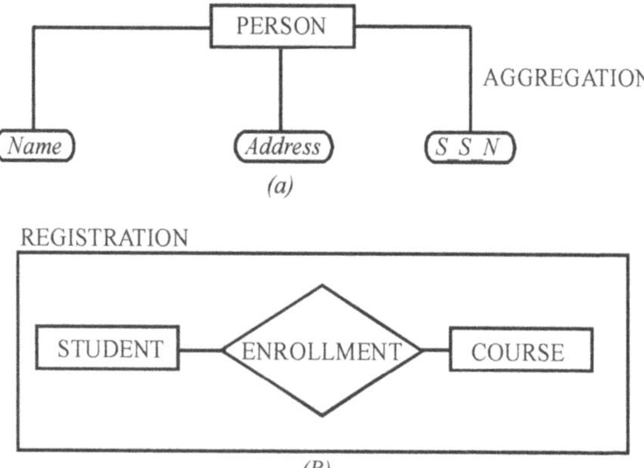

(a)

(B)

3(a). The People's Bank others five types of accounts: loan, checking, premium savings, daily interest saving and money market. It operates a number of branches, and a client of the bank can have any number of accounts. Accounts can be joint; i.e. more than one client may be able to operate a given account. Draw a diagrammatic representation of the Network model of the bank, after identifying the relevant concepts. [6]

Network data model :

There are two basic data structures in network model : records & sets.

Records :

Data is stored in record; each record consists of a group of related data values. Records are classified into record types, where each record type describes the structure of the group of records that store the same type of information. We give each record type a name, and we also give a name and format (data type) for each data item (or attributes) in the record type.

Set :

A set type is a description of a 1: N relationship between two record types. In set we represent a set type diagramatically as an arrow. This type of diagrammatic representation is called a *Bachman diagram.* Each set type definition consists of three basic elements.

- ✔ A name for the set type
- ✔ An owner record type
- ✔ A member record type

Diagrammatic representation of the network model :

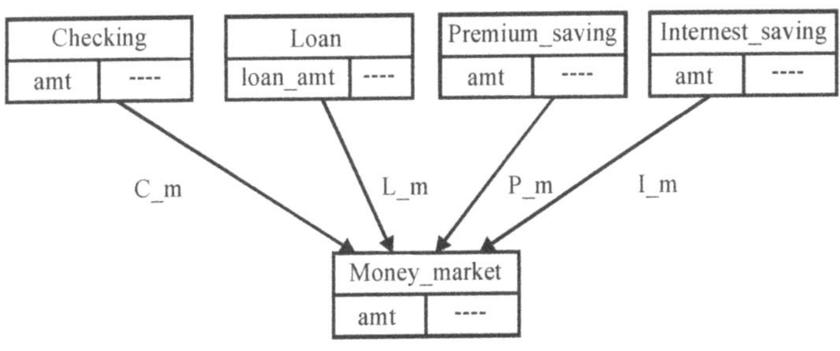

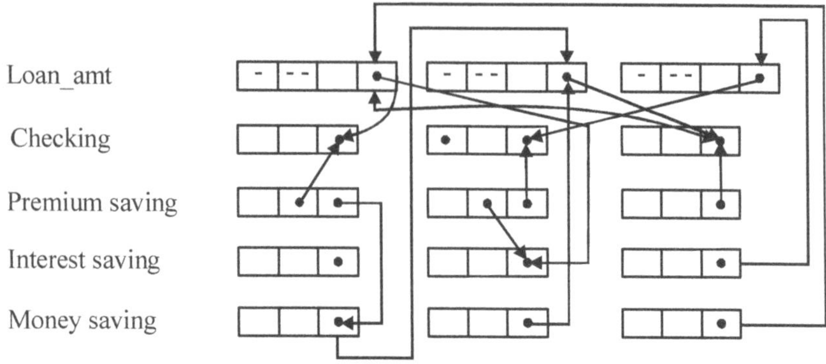

(b) In respect of project we are given the following record-types for the relational model of the database: **[6]**

EMPLOYEE : with fields as 'Emp#' and 'Name'

ASSIGNED_TO : with fields as 'Project#' and 'Emp#'

PROJECT : with fields and 'Project#', 'Project_Name', 'Chief_Architect'.

Where 'Chief_Architect' is a three-digit code and all other fields have obvious meanings. Then express the following queries in relational algebra:

(i) 'Get Emp# of employees working on project COMP353'

PEmp# (s project # = "COMP353" (ASSIGNED_TO))

(ii) 'Get details of employees (both number and name 3) working on project COMP353'

PEmp# , Name(s project # = 'COMP353" (EMPLOYEE ASSIGNED_TO))

(iii) 'Gather details of employees working on both COMP353 and COMP354'

PEmp# , Name(s project # = 'COMP353" A project # "COMP354" (EMPLOYEE ASSIGNED_TO))

(c) Briefly describe the various possible problems with a (not normalised) database. **[3]**

Refer to JUNE01,Q1(d), Page No.-165

Q4(a). Is the following relation in Third Normal Form? **[5]**

Roll No.	Name	Department	Year	Hostel Name
2101	Raman	Physics	I	Ganga

2102	**Krishna**	**Chemistry**	**I**	**Ganga**
2103	**Abdul**	**Mathematics**	**II**	**Kaveri**
2104	**John**	**Botany**	**II**	**Kaveri**

Justify your answer, if it is in Third Normal Form. If it is not, then bring it in Third Normal Form.

A table is said to be in the Third Normal Form, if all the non-key fields of the table are independent of all other non-key fields of the same table. So 3NF removes fields that

1. Depend on other non-key fields
2. Can be calculated or derived from logic

So in this question This table is not in 3NF, because YEAR and HOSTAL NAME are dependent on each other, to achieve 3NF, we made another table to remove this dependence, the new table contains only two fields YEAR & HOSTAL NAME. The following structure shows 3NF

ROLLNO	*NAME*	*DEPATMENT*	*YEAR*

New TABLE

YEAR	*HOSTALNAME*

(b) Again consider the record-types given in Question No. 1(e):
Where S# and P# are keys respectively for SUPPLIER and PARTS.
Express the following in SQL: [6]

(i) Get the part numbers that cost 20, 30 or 40 rupees.
SELECT P# FROM PARTS WHERE COST IN (20, 30, 40)

(ii) Get the supplier names who do not supply part.
SELECT S_NAME FROM SUPPLIER WHERE S# =
(SELECT S# FROM SUPPLY_PARTS WHERE P# <> 2)

(iii) Get the part numbers whose cost is greater than average cost
SELECT P# FROM PARTS WHERE COST > (SELECT AVG(COST) FROM PARTS)

(c) Discuss the issue of Data Replication or the issue of Data Fragmentation in respect of distributed database. [4]
Refer to JUNE02,Q3(a, i&ii) Page No. -137

5(a). Explain briefly any four approaches for incorporating object orientation in databases [5]
There are at least four approaches for incorporating object orientation capabilities in databases:

1. Novel database data model/data language approach :

The most aggressive approach is to develop entirely new database language and database management system with object orientation capabilities. Most of the research project in object-oriented databases has pursued this approach. In the industry introduces novel DML (Data Manipulation Language) and DDL (Data Definition Language) constructs for a data model based on semantic and functional data models.

2. Extending an existing database language with object orientation capabilities :

A number of programming languages have been extended with object-oriented constructs. C++ flavors (an extension of LISP), and Object Pascal are examples of this approach in programming languages. It is conceivable to follow a similar strategy with database languages. Since SQL is a standard and the most popular database language, the most reasonable solution is to extend this language with object-oriented constructs, reflecting the object orientation capabilities of the underlying database management system. This approach being pursued by most vendors of relational systems, as they evolve the next generation products. There have been many such attempts incorporating inheritance, function composition for nested entities, and even some support of encapsulation in an SQL framework.

3. Extending an existing object :

Object oriented programming language with database capabilities: Another approach is to introduce database capabilities to an existing object-oriented language. The object orientation features abstract data typing, inheritance, object identity—will already be supported by the object-oriented language. The extensions will incorporate database features (querying, transaction support, persistence, and so on).

4. Embedding object :

oriented database language constructs in a host (conventional) language: Database languages can be embedded in host programming languages. For examples, SWL statements can be embedded in PL/I C, Fortran and Ada. The types of SQL (that is relations and rows) are quite different from the type systems of these host languages.

(b) Explain:
(i) Advantages of client-server computing &
(ii) Major components of client-server computing. **[5]**

Refer to JUNE03,Q4(a), Page No. -100

(c) Discuss briefly any one of the following knowledge representation schemes:
(i) Rule based representation & (ii) Frame based representation **[5]**

Refer to JUNE02,Q6(a), Page No. -148

6. Discuss the following with reference to File organization for conventional DBMS:

(i) List the key features of B-tree and how it is different from B^+ - tree

The key features of B-tree are as follows :

1. There is no redundant storage of search key values. The search key values are stored only once in a node. The same node may contain some other search key values.
2. The B-tree is inherently balanced and is ordered by one type of search key.
3. The insertion and deletion operations are complex with the time complexity $O(\log_2 n)$.
4. The number of keys in the nodes is not always the same. The storage management is only complicated.
5. The B-tree grows at the node as opposed to the binary tree, BST and AVL trees.
6. For a B-tree of order N with n nodes the height is log n. The height of B-tree increases only because of a split at the root node.

The **advantages** of B-tree are as follows :

1. The B-tree is good for dynamic tables as there is no overflows.
2. It is good for 24-hours operation due to which it performs self management up to a large extent.
3. As data is retrieved via the index it is always presented in order.
4. 'Get Next' queries are efficient because of the inherent ordering of rows within the index blocks.
5. These are good for large tables as minimal reorganization is required.
6. The access time for retrieval of a key value is predictable.

One of the popular version of B-tree is B^+-tree and B*-tree. The main differences are as follows :

1. In a B^+-tree, the search keys are stored twice; each of the search key is found in some nodes.
2. In B-tree, there is no redundancy in storing search key values: the search key is found only one in the tree. Since search key values that are found in non leaf nodes are not found anywhere else in the B-tree, the insertion and deletion operations are complex and $O(\log_2 n)$, but the search operation is simple, efficient and $O(\log_2 n)$.

(ii) Why do we need multilist file organisation?

In Multi list file there is only one stored list for every pair. Therefore, the index of a multilist file contains only the single address. The records in the stored list are linked together in the form of a list. Thus, the record list of multilist file is implemented as a list of records.

We need This File organization because of following points :

1. IF data value in a number of fields are changed , this may require the travels land update of many lists. The process is simpler if records are double chained with pointers to both successor and predecessor records.

2. The performance of multi list file is satisfactory where the individual lists are short.
3. In a multilist file organization a pointer to the first member of every list is maintained in an index.

(iii) Explain comparison and trade-off in the design of a multikey file. [4]

Both inverted files and multi-list files have

* An index for each secondary key.

* An index entry for each distinct value of the secondary key.

* In either file organisation
The index may be tabular or tree-structured.
The entries in an index may or may not be sorted.
The pointers to data records may be direct or indirect.

* The indexes differ in that

An entry in an inversion index has a pointer to each data record with that value. An entry in a multi-list index has a pointer to the first data record with that value. Thus, an inversion index may have variable-length entries whereas a multi-list index has fixed-length entries. In either organization

* The data record pointers for a key value may or may not appear in some sorted order.

* Keeping entries in sorted order introduces overhead.

* The data record file
Is not affected by having an inversion index built on top of it.

* Must contain the linked lists of records with identical secondary key values in the multi-list structure.

*Some of the implications of these differences are the following :

Index management is easier in the multi-list approach because entries are fixed in length.
The inverted file approach tends to exhibit better inquiry performance. Many types of queries can be answered by accessing inversion indexes without necessitating access to data records, thereby reducing I/O-access requirements.

Inversion of a file can be transparent to a programmer who accesses that file but does not sue the inversion indexes, while a multi-list structure affects the file's record layout. The multi-list pointers can be made transparent to a programmer if the data manager does not make them available for programmer user and stores them at the end of each record.

Additionally, the multi-list structure has proven useful in linking together occurrences of different record types, thereby providing access paths based upon logical relationships. It is also possible to provide multiple sort orders through a single data collection, by linking the records together in order by various keys.

CS-06: DATABASE MANAGEMENT SYSTEM
TEE-DEC-2001

Note: *Question 1 is* ***compulsory****. Answer any* ***three*** *from the rest.*

1(a). Design a Relational database to the E- R diagram given below: **[7]**

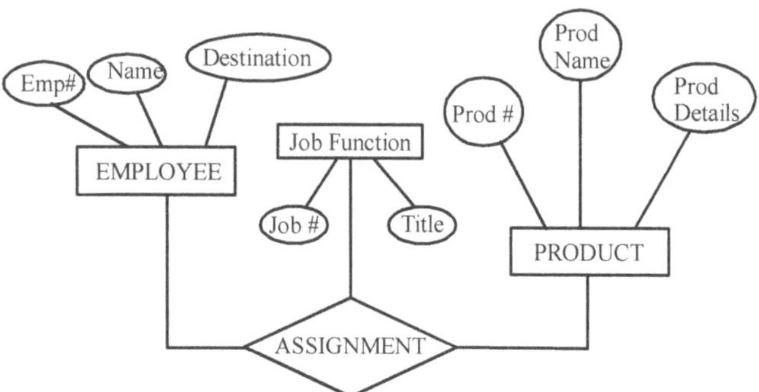

Tabular representation of the Relational Database for the above E-R Diagram :

Entities and its Attributes :

* Employee (Emp#, Name, Designation) -- This is Table 1
* Product (Prod#, Prod_Name, Prod_Details) -- This is Table 2

Relationships and its Attributes :

* Assignment is the Relationship between Employee and Product.
Job Function (Job#, Title) -- This is Table 3
Assignment (Emp#, Job#, Prod#) -- This is Table 4

Below are the attributes (or collections of attributes) in each entity set that would uniquely identify an instance of the entity set :

In Employee Entity - *Emp_Id* is the Primary Key
In Product Entity - *Prod_Code* is the Primary Key
In Job Function - *Job#* is the Key.

(b) Explain the following general integrity rules of Relational Mode: **[8]**

(i) Entity Integrity

The **entity integrity constraint** states that no primary key value can be null. This is because the primary key value is used to identify individual tuples in a relation; having null values for the primary key implies that we cannot identify some tuples.

(ii) Referential Integrity

The **'Referential Integrity Constraint** is specified between two relations and is used to maintain the consistency among tuples of the two relations. Informally, the referential integrity constraint states that a tuple in one relation that refers to another relation must refer to an *existing tuple* in that relation.

A feature provided by RDBMSs that prevents users or applications from entering inconsistent data. Most RDBMSs have various referential integrity rules that you can apply when you create a relationship between two tables. These rules help in preserving the integrity of the data. In simple terms referential integrity constraints make sure that there are no orphan records.

Let us say you have an 'employee' table that has a foreign key that points to 'department_id', which is a key in the 'department' table. Referential integrity will prevent you from deleting a department that has employees assigned to it. This is known as a restriction. If you are dealing with 'order' table and multiple items contained in an order, it is possible for you to set it up in such a way that all items in an order get deleted when you delete an order. This is known as a cascading delete.

(c) For the relations P and Q, perform the following operation: **[8]**

P

A	B	C	D
a_1	b_2	c_2	d_2
a_2	b_1	c_1	d_2
a_1	b_1	c_2	d_1
a_2	b_1	c_2	d_2
a_1	b_2	c_1	d_2
a_3	b_1	c_2	d_1
a_1	b_2	c_2	d_2
a_2	b_1	c_1	d_2
a_1	b_3	c_2	d_2

Q

B	C	D
b_1	c_1	d_2
b_3	c_1	d_2
b_2	c_2	d_1
b_1	c_1	d_2
b_3	c_2	d_2

(i) Find the projection of Q on the attributes (B,C)

Projection of attributes (B,C)

B	C
b_1	c_1
b_3	c_1
b_2	c_2
b_3	c_2

(ii) Find the natural join of P and Q on the common attributes.

B	C	D
b_1	c_1	d_2
b_1	c_1	d_2
b_2	c_2	d_2

(d) Write short notes on: **[7]**

(i) Object oriented databases

Object-Oriented Database Management Systems (OODBMSs) have been developed to support new kinds of applications for which semantic and content are represented more efficiently with the object model. Therefore, the OODBMSs present the two main problems :

Impedance mismatch is basically due to two reasons. Firstly, the no suitable abstractions of the operating systems, so when a client object has to invoke a method that is offered by a server object, and both objects are not into the same address space, it is necessary to use the mechanisms that are offered by the operating system, and these mechanisms do not became proper to the object-oriented paradigm since they are oriented to communicate processes. In order to solve this problem an intermediate software is included (e.g. COM or CORBA or Enterprise Java Beans).

In the second place, an impedance mismatch is also caused every time the object-oriented applications need to use the operating system services. The interface services are close to the procedural paradigm, generally in the shape of system calls. A solution can be the use of adaptation layers which encapsulate the operating system interface by means of a class library (e.g. MFC library).

Interoperability problem between object models. Although different system elements use the object-oriented paradigm, an interoperability problem can exist between them. So, an application implemented using the C++ language, with the C++ object model, can easily interact with its objects, but when it wants to use objects that have been created with another programming language or another object-oriented database an interoperability problem appears. It is due to the fact that an object model for an element is not necessarily compatible with the object model of other elements. This problem can be solved adding software layers, again. So, CORBA defines a proper object model with basic data types, and a mapping is specified between the object model of each language and its interface into the CORBA.

(ii) Specialization

Specialization is the abstracting process of introducing new characteristics to an existing class of object to create one or more new classes of objects. This involves taking a higher-level entity and, using additional characteristics, generating lower-level entities. The lower-level entities also inherit the characteristics of the higher-level entities. In applying the characteristic size to car we can create a full-size, mid-size, compact, or subcompact car. Specialization may be seen as the reverse process of generalization: additional specific properties are introduced at a lower level in a hierarchy of objects.

(iii) Generalization

Generalization is the abstracting process of viewing sets of objects as a single general class by concentrating on the general characteristics of the constituent sets while suppressing or ignoring their differences. It is the union of a number of lower-level entity types for the purpose of producing a higher-level entity type. For instance, student is a generalization of graduate or undergraduate, full-time or part-time students. Similarly, employee is a generalization of the classes of objects cook, waiter, cashier. Generalization is an IS_An relationship; therefore, manager IS_An employee, cook IS_An employee, waiter IS_An employee, and so forth.

(iv) Data independence

Rerer to JUNE02,Q2(iv), Page No.-136

(v) Query processor

Rerer to DEC02,Q1(c,iv), Page No.-115

3(a). Explain the distinction between the representation of association and relationship in the network and hierarchical models. [7]

Hierarchical Model

* Hierarchical data model uses tree structures to represent relationship among records. Tree structures occur naturally in many data organisations because some entities have an intrinsic hierarchical order. Example : an institute has a number of programmes to offer. Each program has a number of courses. Each course has a number of students registered in it.
* A hierarchical model consists of a collection of records which are connected with each other through links.
* A link is an association between precisely two records.
* Relationships and Association is represented by Tree Structure Diagram.
* Each child record type can have only one parent record type; thus a M:N Relationship cannot be directly expressed between two record types.

Network Model

* A *set type* is used to represent a directed relationship between two record types, the so-called owner record type, and the member record type. The set type, like the record type, is named and specifies that there is a one-to-many relationship (1:M) between the owner and member record type.
* To represent Logical Relationship implied by the set a graphical means called a data structure diagram is introduced by Bachman.
* The relationship through the database are predefined at database creation time.
* 1:1, 1:M, and M:1 relationship can all be represented.

(b) Explain why navigation is simpler in the relational model than in the hierarchical data model. [8]

The hierarchical data model uses the tree concept to represent data and the relationship among data. The nodes of the tree are the record types representing the entity sets and are connected by pointer or links, which can be viewed as pointers. The records in the database are organized as tree. Furthermore, the hierarchical data model restricts each record type to only one parent record type.

An example showing the part of company database is as under :

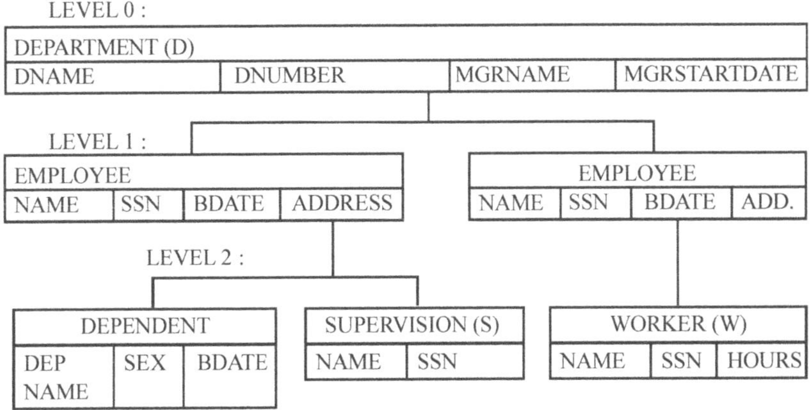

Fig. A Hierarchical Schema

It consists of a number of record types and PCR (Parent Child Relationship) types. Record type names are displayed in rectangular boxes and PCR types are displayed as lines connecting parent record type to the child record type. The hierarchical occurrence tree consist of all parent and child occurrences shown in the following figure :

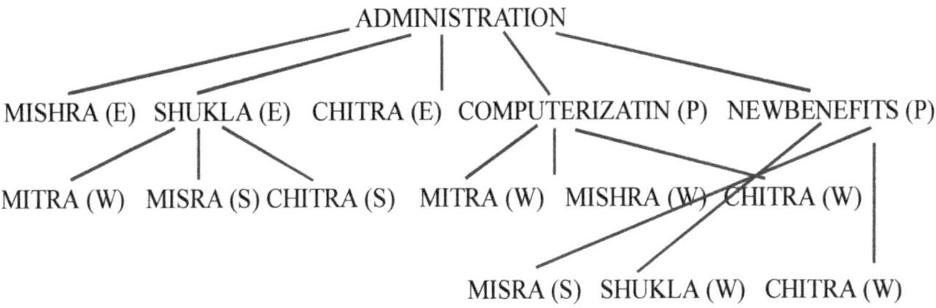

Fig. Hierarchical Occurrence (Occurrence Tree) of the Hierarchical Schema

The hierarchical sequence is also important because some hierarchical data manipulation language use it as basis for defining hierarchical database operation. It will traverse the data in Pre-order. For example the hierarchical sequence for the above schema is :

D Administration
E Mishra
E Shukla
T Ramita
S Mishra
S Chitra
E Chitra
P Computerization
W Mitra
W Misra
W Chitra
P Newbenefits
W Mishra
W Shukla
W Chitra

Fig. Hierarchical sequence for the occurrence tree

Navigation with the database includes the insertion, deletion or modification of data records in the database. When any of such operations are performed with the network or hierarchical model, a number of constraints exist in the hierarchical model like :

1. No record occurrences except root records can exist without being related to a parent record occurrence which mean :

(a) A child record cannot be inserted unless it is linked to a parent record.
(b) A child record may be deleted independently, but deletion of a parent record results in deletion of all its child records. Data regarding child record may be lost.

2. If a child record has more than two parent records from the same record type, the child record must be duplicated once under each parent record.
3. If a child record has more than two parent records of the different record types, the child can do so only by having at most one real parent, with all the other as virtual parents.

While, in Relational data model, each relation or relationship is displayed in forms of table and stored in separate file. The relational model differs from the network and hierarchical models in that it does not use pointers or links. Instead the relational model relates records by the values that they contain. The freedom from pointers allows defining mathematical foundation. Thus navigation becomes easy in relational data model.

4. Discuss the differences between the following file organization. [15]

(a) Serial

(b) Index-Sequential

(c) Hashed

(d) Inverted

Compare their storage and access efficiencies. To what type of application is each of the organisations suited?

(a) Serial File Organization : Serial organization offers the easy access to next record and the absence of auxiliary data structure. Records are maintained in a logical sequence of their primary key value. The search for a given record requires, an average, access to all the records, till you reach the desired one. Appending a record requires the creation of a new file, updation procedure allows only sequential updation and resulted updated file generates a new master file from the existing one. It uses magnetic tape for storage media.

(b) Index-Sequential file organization : Provides random access to records and the sequential nature of the file provides easy access to next record. Updation do not require generation of a new file. It uses magnetic disks for direct access. In indexed sequential file overflow is a real problem in volatile tables. ISAM is good for static tables because there are usually fewer index levels.

(c) Hashed : In direct file organization the key value is mapped directly to storage location. The usual method of direct mapping is by performing arithmetic manipulation of the key value. This procedure is called hashing.

(d) Inverted : The inverted file approach tends to exhibit better inquiry performance. Many types of queries can be answered by accessing inversion indexes without necessitating access to records, thereby reducing I/O access requirements.

Indexed sequential file organization is commonly used in business data processing. There are no indexes to traverse well designed hashing functions where collision are few, this is a great advantage, exact key matches are extremely quick. No disk space is used by this indexing method. But it has some drawbacks. It become difficult to predict overflow because the working of the hashing algorithm will not be visible to the DBA. No sorting of data occurs either physically or logically, so sequential access is poor. The organization usually takes a lot of disk space to ensure that no overflow occurs. There is a plus side to this though no space is wasted on index structure because they simply do not exist. The primary disadvantage of the index sequential file organization is that performance degrades as the file grows. To overcome this deficiency, we can use a B+-tree index.

Sequential file organizations require an index structure to locate data. File organization based on hashing by contrast, allow us to find the address of a data item directly by computing a function on the search key value of the desired record. Since we do not know at design time precisely which search key values will be stored in the file, a good hash function to choose is one that assigns search key values to buckets such that the distribution is both uniform and random. The inverted file approach tends to exhibit better inquiry performance. Many types of queries can be answered by accessing inversion indexes without necessitating access to data records, thereby reducing I/O access requirements. Inversion of a file can be transparent to a programmer who access that file, but does not use the inversion indexes.

Linked file organization considered as indexed file organization, inverted file organization considered as direct file organization.

1. Sequential file organization find its use in application areas where batch processing is more common. Whereas direct files are used extensively in application areas where interactive processing is used when accessing record is done sequentially by some key value and also to access record directly by the same key value. The collection of records may be organized in an effective manner called indexed sequential organization.
2. Sequential files are simple to use and can be stored on inexpensive media whereas a direct file must be stored on a direct access device, whereas an indexed sequential file stored on a direct access storage device.

5(a). What are the advantages of normalised relations over unnormalised relations? **[5]**

The normalized relational model is based on a fairly elegant mathematical theory. Relational databases derive a virtual structure at run time based on values from sets of data stored in tables.

An Un-normalized relations can contain redundant and disorganized data, which needs to be organized, by dividing the data over several tables to avoid redundancy and anomalies. This is achieved by going through the process of NORMALIZATION. Un-normalized data also increase any undesirable consequences, resulting from database activities like inserting, updating and deleting anamolies in a table. Storage space may also be conserved, thus resulting in a more efficient database.

1. Insertion of fields

If a new field is introduced into the system, it cannot be added to the database, until it becomes related to another existing field.

2. Deletion of fields

In information related to a specific column is to be deleted, the entire row has to be deleted, which result in loss of required information.

(b) Why is 4 NF preferable to BCNF ? **[5]**

Refer to Study material,Q2, Page No.-14

(c) Explain the design goals of a good relational database design. **[5]**

Following are the design goals suggested by Beeri and his co-workers should be satisfied.

1. Representation : The final structure must correctly represent the original specifications

2. Separation : The original specifications are separated into relations that satisfy certain conditions.

3. Redundancy : The final structure must not contain any redundant information.

6(a). Explain how the knowledge representation is done through Semantic Network. **[5]**

A lot of knowledge is default knowledge such as birds can fly. You don't want to have to list every attribute of every object, you'd end up with a large amount of data, it would surely be more sensible to create a hierarchy of information. If an entity is a bird you want to make certain assumptions automatically and this results in an inheritance hierarchy.

For example : Tweetie is a canary, canary is a bird, bird is an animal, etc. We would plug in the attributes at the highest possible level e.g..

Animal : Has skin, blood. Can move.
Bird : Is a type of animal. Has feathers. Can fly.
Canary : Is a type of bird. Is Yellow and Small.
Tweetie : Is a canary. Has a toe missing.

Using this technique is obviously efficient as it stores the important attributes only once and only exceptions and extra knowledge are included in each sub-level or sub-class. A structure like this has been shown to be a plausible explanation for the way people remember things.

Semantic nets work along these lines and all semantic nets are constructed from two basic components :

Nodes : These represent the objects, concepts, the things of the domain. Nodes are usually represented by a circle or oval diagrammatically.

Arcs : These represent the relationships between nodes. These can be actions between objects, abstract interactions between concepts, or any number of things in between! Arcs are drawn as arrows connecting the nodes.

(Semantic nets were initially created to demonstrate a theory of long term memory structure in humans by Ross Quillian. His initial aim was to build a program that could understand language but, surprisingly enough, this turned out to be a too ambitious so he dropped his specification down to comparing two word concepts. The results were to be expressed in a pseudo-English language.)

(b) Discuss the basics of Client\Server computing paradigm. **[5]**

A client is an application that initiates peer to peer communication and user usually involve client software when they use a network service. Most client software consists of conventional application programs. Each time a client application executes, it contacts a server, sends a request and awaits a response. When the response arrives, the client continues processing. Clients are often easier to build than servers and usually require special system privileges to operate. By comparison, a server is any program that provides services to requesting processing by client. It waits for incoming communication requests from a client. As soon as it receives a client's request it starts processing the request and sends the results to the client. The client may initiate a transaction with the server, while normally the server does not initiate a transaction with the client.

The client is therefore the more active partner in this association requesting specific functions, accepting corresponding results from the server, and acknowledging the completion of services and associated communication. Because servers need to access data, server software usually requires special system privileges. Because a server executes with special systems privilege, care must be taken to ensure that it does not inadvertently pass privileges on to the clients that use it.

Servers must contain code that handle the issue of

Authentication - Verifying the identify of a client.

Authorizations - Determining whether a given client is permitted to access the service by the server.

Data Security - Generating that data is not unintentionally revealed or compromised.

Privacy - Keeping information about an individual from unauthorised access.

Protection - Guaranteeing that network application cannot abuse system resources.

The general case client/server implementation shown in following figure.

client client client ---------- client

network

Server

Database functionality is divided into two parts. The first is called front-end and the second as back-end. The back-end manages access structure, query evaluation and optimization, concurrency control and recovery. The front-end of a database system consists of tools such as forms, report writers and graphical user interface facilities. The interface between front-end and back-end is performed by the languages like SQL(Structured Query Language) or some application programs :

The functionality between Front-end and back-end can be graphically shows as below :

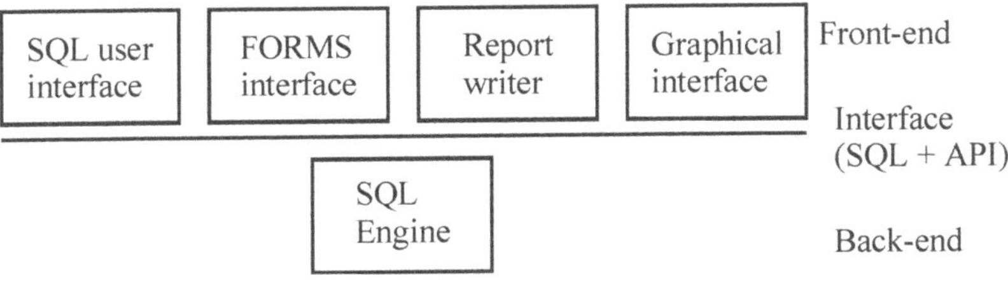

(c) Explain Dynamic Data Exchange and Remote Procedure Call. [5]

Dynamic Data Exchange

Through a set of APIs, windows provide calls that support to the DDE protocol for message-based exchange of data among applications. DDE can be used to construct HOT-LINKS between applications where data can be fed from window to window without operation intervention. DDE support WARM-LINKS that we can create so the server application notifies the client that the data have changed and client can issue an explicit request to receive it. We create REQUEST-LINKS to allow direct copy and paste operation between a server and client without the need for an immediate clipboard. No notification of change in data by the server application is provided. EXECUTIVE LINKS cause the execution of one application to be controlled by the another. This provides an easy to use batch processing capability. Thus, using DDE, applications can share data, execute commands remotely and check error conditions.

Remote Procedure Call

With RPC one component communicate with a remote component using simple procedure calls. This involves peer to peer messaging. If an application issues a functional request and this request is embedded in an RPC, the requested function can be located anywhere in the enterprise, the caller is authorized to access. The advantage of this process to process communication is evident when processors are involved in any simultaneous processes. New client applications that use object-level relationships between processes provide need for this type of communication e.g. a client requests information for a server by connecting to the server, making the request by calling low-level procedure native to the database server, and then disconnecting. To respond to a request, the server connects to the application and calls a low-level procedure in the application.

RPC is typically transparent to a user, making it very easy to use. The RPC provides facility for the invocation and execution of requests from processors running different operating systems and using different hardware platforms from the callers.

CS-06: DATABASE MANAGEMENT SYSTEM
TEE-JUNE-2002

Note: *Question 1 is **compulsory**. Answer any **three** from the rest.*

1(a). Draw E-R diagram for a departmental store, after determining the entities of interest and the relationship that exist between these entities. Also construct a tabular representation of the entities and relationships. Are there any attributes (or collections of attributes) in each entity set that would uniquely identify an instance of the entity set? [12]

Below is the Entity-Relationship diagram for a departmental store :-

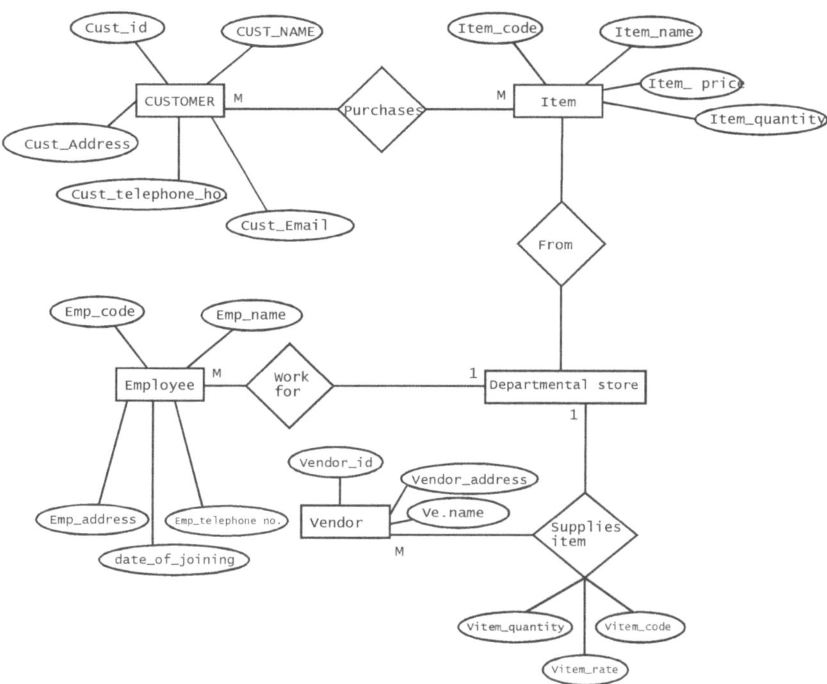

***Tabular representation of the entities and relationships* :**

Entities and its Attributes :

* Customer (Cust_Id, Cust_Name, Cust_Address, Cust_Telephone_No, Cust_Email)

* Item(Item_Code, Item_Name, Item_Price, Item_Quantity)

* Employee(Emp_Code, Emp_Name, Emp_Date_of_Joining, Emp_Addres, Emp_Telephone_No)

* Vendor (Vendor_Id, Vendor_Name, Vendor_Address, Vendor_Telephone_No)

Relationships and its Attributes :

* Purchases is the Relationship between Customer and Item

* Works_For is the Relationship between Employee and Departmental Store

* Supply_Items is the Relationship between Vendor and Departmental Store

*Supply_Items (Order_Id, vItem_Code, vItem_Rate, vItem_Quantity)

Below are the attributes (or collections of attributes) in each entity set that would uniquely identify an instance of the entity set :

In Customer Entity - *Cust_Id* is the Primary Key
In Item Entity - *Item_Code* is the Primary Key
In Employee Entity - *Employee_Code* is the Primary Key
In Vendor Entity - *Vendor_Id* is the Primary Key
In Supply_Items Relationship - Order_Id is the Primary Key

(b)What problems are caused by data redundancies? Can data redundancies be completely eliminated when the database approach is used? Explain. [7]

Data Redundancies, is the storage of same set of data two or more times. Storing information several times leads to the waste of storage space and an increase in the total size of the data stored. Updates to the database with such redundancies have the potential of becoming inconsistent. Various anomalies may arise due to redundancy considering the table for example:

Below is the Structure of Sale_Item Table :

Customer_Name *Address* *Sale* *Item* *Price/Unit*

Update Anamolies :

Multiple copies of the same fact may lead to update inconsistencies when an update is made and only some of the multiple copies are updated. Thus, a change in Price/Unit must be made, for consistency, in all tuples pertaining to the Item.

Insertion Anamolies :

we can not insert new information in the database unless we get other information also to enter. We can not enter Price/Unit for an new Item added in store unless a Customer buys it.

Deletion Anamolies :

If any Customer returns purchased item then information for Price/Unit for that Item is lost.

Data redundancy be completely eliminated when the database approach is used depends on situation sometimes theoretically it is possible but practically not always. As when we develop large application software then we need to divide or normalize the database, but many times after normalization speed becomes an issue. So at that time it may not be possible or practical.

(c) Explain why first normal form is acceptable for data processing applications. [5]

The first normal form (INF) involves the removal of repeated groups. Examples of such repeating groups are contacts and categories. Thus for a given customer, one or more contacts and one or more categories can exist.

For each repeating group, the repeating group is moved to a separate table. Suppose our primary table is the customer table given below-

Customer Table :

Customer ID
Customer Name
Customer Type
Contact Table
Contact ID
Customer ID
Contact Name
Category ID
Category ID
Customer ID
Category Name

The customer table is a parent to the contact and category tables.

The two relations are one to many. This means each customer can have one or more contacts and can be associated with one or more categories.

If we do not create the child tables, the alternative is to add more columns to support multiple contacts and categories. Clearly, creating child tables is the easier, more flexible, and more cost-effective solution.

Why the first normal form is acceptable for data processing applications is now obvious. If we do not choose the 1NF, our database design would continuously be changing whenever a specific entity in the database, say customer, has exceeded the number of contacts the main table (Customer table, in our example) can support. A continuously changing database structure and model, can eventually proves harmful for a database application. A solid and stable database model is the foundation on which everything else depends.

After an application has been developed, changing the database structure can be very expensive and time consuming. The entire application has to be tested throughly to guarantee no bugs have been introduced due to the modifications. Use of 1NF at the very beginning avoids all the above troubles. Hence 1NF is always acceptable for data processing applications. Also, before the second normal form is taken up it is essential to complete the 1NF of the database.

(d)Consider the relational database:

EMPLOYEE (ENO, EName, Skill, Pay-Rate, Date)
POSITION (Posting_No, Skill)
DUTY_ALLOCATION (Posting_No, ENO, Shift)
Give expressions in SQL for the following: [6]

(i) Find the names of employees who are assigned to all positions that require a clerk's skill.
SELECT EName FROM EMPLOYEE WHERE Skill="Clerk"

(ii) Get employees who are working either on the date 19860419 or 19860420.
SELECT * FROM EMPLOYEE WHERE DATE IN (19860419, 19860420).

(iii) Find the names and rate of pay of all employees who are not allocated a duty.

SELECT ENAME, PAY_RATE FROM EMPLOYEE, DUTY_ALLOCATION WHERE (EMPLOYEE.ENO=DUTY_ALLOCATION.ENO AND SHIFT=NULL)

Q2. Write short notes on :
(i) Database administrator
<u>Database Administrator</u> :
A person or a group of persons, who manage the centralized control of the database, is referred to as the database administrator (DBA). He is responsible for creating, modifying and maintaining the database.

Following are the functions of DBA :

1. The DBA is the custodian of the data and controls the database structure.
2. It sets up the definition of the global view or conceptual level of the database.
3. It specifies the external view of the various users and applications and is responsible for the definition and implementation of the internal performance of the DBMS.
4. It maps between the internal and the conceptual levels, as well as between the conceptual and external levels.
5. It maintains the integrity of the database.
6. The DBA is responsible for granting permission to the users of the database and stores the profile of each user in the database.

It is responsible for defining procedures to recover the database from failures due to human, natural or hardware causes with minimal loss of data.

(ii) Metadata

Metadata is data about data or can be defined as *Metadata is data to describe other data.* e.g. definition of a class is metadata. Models are inherently metadata, since they describe the things being modeled (rather than being the things). Many real-world applications have metadata, such as parts catalogs, blue prints, and dictionaries. Computer language implementations also use metadata heavily. Metadata is frequently confusing because it blurs the normal separation between the model and the real world. With ordinary applications, the same terms can be used to refer to metadata, the context is not sufficient to distinguish the description from the thing being described, so a more precise distinction must be made.

(iii) 3-level architecture of DBMS

According to the approach of ANSI/SPARC (American National Standard Institute / Standards Planning and Requirements Committee), there are three views of data abstraction: external view, conceptual view and internal or physical view.

External View :

It is the highest level of the abstraction of data. Each external view is defined by means of an External schema, which consists of definitions of each of the various types of external record at that external view.

The external level is the view that the individual user of the database has. It determines how the data LOOK LIKE, irrespective of how they are stored. It represents a part of the database. The same database may provide different level of abstraction for different classes of users.

Conceptual view :

It is the next lower level of abstraction. The conceptual view is defined by means of the conceptual schema. This is also known as user's view that describes WHAT types of data are actually stored. It simply contains the information about structure (or type) of data stored in database. A database administrator, who must decide which information, is to be kept in the database, what are the relations among the tables at conceptual level. The conceptual schema is defined using Data Definition Language (DDL).

Internal or Physical View :

It is the lowest level of the data abstraction. The physical view is defined by the means of internal schema.

It is concerned with the physical storage of the information means what data are stored and how. It also specifies where indexes exist, how stored fields are represented. It gives complete internal structure of storage and their access paths (specification of primary – secondary keys, indexes, pointers and sequencing, data compression and optimization techniques.

Mapping between the three Levels :

Mapping corresponds one record of one level to record of the another level. There are two mappings in three levels architecture.

(1) Mapping between External and Conceptual level, which gives the correspondence among the records and the relationship of the external and conceptual levels.

(2) mapping between internal and conceptual level.

(3) Internal to physical database. This is not necessary that an internal record at internal level is stored at a physical record, it can be from multiple physical records on storage device. It provides the relevant mapping.

The figure shows the interrelationship among these three levels of abstraction :

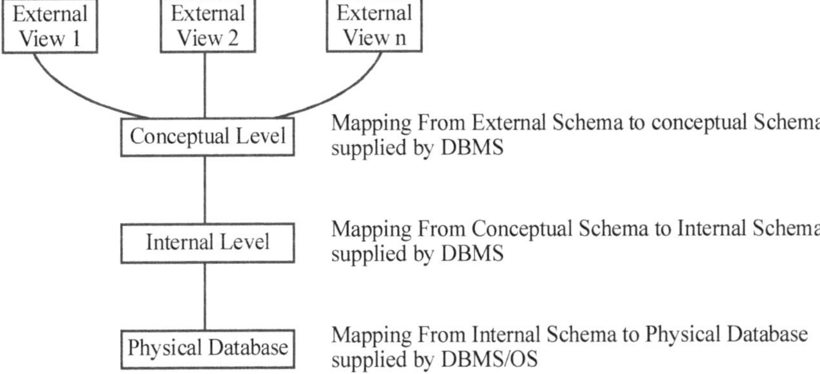

(iv) Data Independence

In a database system, the database management system provides the interface between the application programs and the data. When changes are made to the data representation, the metadata (data about data) maintained by the DBMS is changed but the DBMS continues to provide data to application programs in the previously used way. The DBMS handles the task of transformation of data wherever necessary.

This independence between the programs and the data is called **data independence**. Data independence is important because every time some change needs to be made to the data structure, the programs that were being used before the change would continue to work. To provide a high degree of data independence, a DBMS must include a sophisticated metadata management system.

(v) Abstraction

Abstraction means *representing the thing as much it is needed and hiding tedious details from the user* i.e. Abstraction consists of focusing on the essential, inherent aspects of an entity and ignoring its accidental properties. In system development, this means focusing on what an object is and does, before deciding how it should be implemented. Use of abstraction preserves the freedom to make decisions as long as possible by avoiding premature commitments to details. Most modern languages provide data abstraction but the ability to use inheritance and polymorphism provides additional power. Use of abstraction during analysis means dealing only with application-domain concepts, not making design and implementation decisions before the problem is understood. Proper use of abstraction allows the same model to be used for analysis high-level design, program structure, database structure, and documentation. A language-independent style of design defers programming details until the final, relatively mechanical stage of development.

3(a). Explain with respect to Distributed Databases:

1. Data Replication

Whenever a relation is to be stored in a database, then several parameters are supposed to be considered. Some among them are Data Replication and Data Fragmentation.

Data Replication :

The system maintains several identical copies (replicas) of the relation. Each copy is stored in a separate site, resulting in data replication. In case of full replication the copy is to be stored in every site. There are number of advantages and disadvantages of replications. Some among them are as follows :

(i) Availability :

In case of failure of one system, the copy of the relation can be picked up from another site. This reduces the failure of entire system.

(ii) Increased parallelism :

Whenever access to relation is increased then several sites can process the queries in parallel. This results in the fast response to the users.

(iii) Increased overhead on update :

To ensure that the system is having the relation at each site in updated position, the system is supposed to update the relation at several site whenever any changes is made to the relation. This increases the overhead.

For example, in a banking system, an account may be associated with the site in which the account has been opened.

2. Data Fragmentation

If a relation 'r' is fragmented, r is divided into a number of fragments r_1, r_2, ...r_n..... These fragments contain sufficient information to reconstruct the original relation "r". This can be done by union or join operation on these fragmentations. The fragmentation can be accomplished in two ways. The first is horizontal fragmentation and second is vertical fragmentation. The horizontal fragmentation splits the relation by assigning each tuple of "r" to one or more fragments. Vertical fragmentation splits the relation by decomposing the scheme "R" of relation "r" in a special way as similar to decomposition.

(i) Horizontal Fragmentation :

The relation 'r' is partitioned into a number of subsets, r_1, r_2.........r_n. Each subset consists of a number of tuples of relation r. Each of relation r must belong to one of the fragments, so that the original can be reconstructed, if needed. Consider a Customer relation as follows :

CUSTOMER

Name	City	Status	Turnover	Product
Naresh Enterprises	Raipur	30	300000	Colours
Mohan Kumar & Sons	Bikaner	50	450000	Chemicals
Nitin Enterprises	Bombay	60	500000	Bardana
Shubham Ltd.	Bombay	85	850000	Tea
Nikky Pvt. Ltd.	Raipur	90	900000	Coffee

The above relation can be fragmented horizontally with similar city in a separate relation. The resultant relation can be shown as follows :

CUSTOMER-Bombay

Name	City	Status	Turnover	Product
Nitin Enterprises	Bombay	60	500000	Bardana
Shubham Ltd.	Bombay	85	850000	Tea

CUSTOMER-Rajpur

Name	City	Status	Turnover	Product
Naresh Enterprises	Raipur	30	300000	Colours
Nikky Pvt. Ltd.	Raipur	90	900000	Coffee

CUSTOMER-Bikaner

Name	City	Status	Turnover	Product
Mohan Kumar & Sons	Bikaner	50	450000	Chemicals

Vertical Fragmentation :

The vertical Fragmentation is a process of decomposition. The vertical fragmentation of relation "r" involves the definition of several subsets r_1, r_2 ....r_n. Each fragmentation of relation "r" is defined by the following general relational algebraic expression :

Consider the following customer table ri = $\prod_i R(r)$

CUSTOMER

Cust-Id	Name	City	Status	Turnover	Product
11	Naresh Enterprises	Raipur	30	300000	Colours
22	Mohan Kumar & Sons	Bikaner	50	450000	Chemicals
33	Nitin Enterprises	Bombay	60	500000	Bardana
44	Shubham Ltd.	Bombay	85	850000	Tea
55	Nikky Pvt. Ltd.	Raipur	90	900000	Coffee

If the attributes Name, City and Status are projected then the resultant relation can be :

CUSTOMER-1

Cust-Id	Name	City	Status
11	Naresh Enterprises	Raipur	30
22	Mohan Kumar & Sons	Bikaner	50
33	Nitin Enterprises	Bombay	60
44	Shubham Ltd.	Bombay	85
55	Nikky Pvt. Ltd.	Raipur	90

If variables parameters like Turnover and Product is projected. Then the resultant relation becomes :

CUSTOMER-2

Cust-Id	Turnover	Product
11	300000	Colours
22	450000	Chemicals
33	500000	Bardana
44	850000	Tea
55	900000	Coffee

(b) List all functional dependencies satisfied by the following relation r : [7]

A	B	C	D
a_1	b_1	c_1	d_1
a_1	b_1	c_1	d_1
a_2	b_2	c_2	d_2
a_2	b_3	c_2	d_3
a_3	b_3	c_2	d_4

Below is the Functional dependencies satisfied by the relation r above :

I & II Rows

$\Rightarrow$ $B, D \rightarrow A, C$

II & IV Rows

$\Rightarrow$ $A, C \rightarrow B, D$

As $B,D \rightarrow A, C$

$A, C \rightarrow C,D$

$\Rightarrow$ $A,C \rightarrow C,D$

4(a). Compare and contrast RDBMS and OODBMS. [7]

RDBMS is Relational Database Management system which is based on establishing relationship among tables is purely based on mathematics. OODBMS is Object Oriented Database Management System which is based on the concept of object. RDBMSs were never designed to allow for the nested structure. These types of applications are extensively found in CAD/CAE, aerospace, etc. OODBMS can easily support these applications. Moreover, it is much easier and natural to navigate through these complex structures in form of objects that model the real world in OODBMS rather than table, tuples and records in RDBMS.

It is hard to confuse a relational database with an object-oriented database. The normalized relational model is based on a fairly elegant mathematical theory. Relational databases derive a virtual structure at run time based on values from sets of data stored in tables. Databases construct views of the data by selecting data from multiple tables and loading it into a single table (OODBs traverse the data from object to object).

Relational databases have a limited number of simple, built-in data types, such as integer and string, and a limited number of built-in operations that can handle these data types. You can create complex data types in a relational database, but you must do it on a linear basis, such as combing fields into records. And the operations on these new complex types are restricted, again, to those defined for the basic types (as opposed to arbitrary data types or subclassing with inheritance as found in OODMs).

The object model supports browsing of object class libraries, which allows the reuse, rather than the reinvention, of commonly used data elements. Objects in an OODB survive multiple sessions; they are persistent. If you delete an object stored in a relational database, other objects may be left with references to the deleted one and may now be incorrect. The integrity of the data thus becomes suspect and creates inconsistent versions.

In the relational database, complex objects must be broken up and stored in separate tables. This can only be done in a sequential procedure with the next retrieval replying on the outcome of the previous. The relational database does not understand a global request and thus cannot optimize multiple requests, OODBs can issue a single message that contains multiple transactions.

The relational model, however, suffers at least one major disadvantage, It is difficult to express the semantics of complex objects with only a table model for data storage. Although relational databases are adequate for accounting or other typical transaction-processing applications where the data types are simple and few in number, the relational model offers limited help when data types become numerous and complex.

Object-oriented databases are favoured for applications where the relationships among elements in the database carry the key information. That is, object-oriented models capture the structure of the data; relational models organize the data itself. If a record can be understood in isolation, then the relational database is probably suitable. If a record makes sense only in the context of other records, then an object-oriented database is more appropriate.

(b) Write short notes on and Suggest one application where each database is suited. **[8]**

(i) Knowledge databases

Definition :

A knowledge base management system is a computer system that manages the knowledge in a given domain or field of interest and exhibits reasoning power to the level of a human in this domain.

Database technology has already addressed the problems of improving system performance, concurrent access, distribution and friendly interface; these features are equally pertinent in a KBMS. There will be a continuing need for current DBMSs and their functionalities coexisting with an integrated KBMS. However, the reasoning power of a KBMS can improve the ease of retrieval of pertinent information from a DBMS.

(ii) Multimedia databases

Multimedia databases store multimedia data such as images, audio and video. Multimedia objects usually have descriptive attributes, such as their date of creation, name of the creator, and their categories. These days, multimedia data are typically stored outside database, in the file systems.

Thus a multimedia database is built-up for storing only the descriptive attributes and for keeping track of the files in which multimedia objects are stored.

Obviously, storing multimedia outside the database makes it difficult to provide database functionality, such as indexing on the strength of actual multimedia data content. It may also cause inconsistencies. It is thus desirable to store data in the database itself. Now, if multimedia data is to be stored in the database itself, the issues involved are-

Database must support large objects, because videos can occupy even gegabytes of storage. For example, Exodus provides this support.

In case of retrieval of some types of data like audio and video the data delivery must be at an assured steady rate. Such data are called synchronous data or continuous media data.

Multimedia data formats are usually JPEG and MPEG-1 and 2. The MPEX-2 stand and designed for digital broadcast systems and DVDs. It compresses 1 minute of video and audio to about 17 MB.

Application area suggested

Video-on-demand servers are popular systems today which store multimedia in file systems and consists of video server, view terminals and networks. These thus make a compromise between current systems based on file systems and video on demand.

A multimedia database contains image, spatial data, audio data, video data, and the like. Databases of this sort arise from the need to store photographs, and geographical data, and from voice-mail systems, graphics applications, and video-on-demand systems.

(iii) Design databases

Traditional database technology does not support the notions of complex objects, equivalent objects, or object versions. Engineering design databases are useful in computer aided design / manufacturing / software engineering (CAD/CAM/CASE) systems. In such systems, complex objects can be recursively partitioned into smaller objects. Furthermore, an object can have different representations at different levels of abstraction (equivalent objects). Moreover, a record of an object's evolution (object versions) should be maintained.

5(a). Compare and contrast index sequential file with B^+ tree file. **[6]**

Refer to Study material,Q2, Page No. -53

(b) What is normalization? What is its purpose? Mention different types of normal forms define them. **[9]**

Normalization theory is a useful aid in the design of database. This theory is built around the concept of normal form. It is a step method to refine the database design. Finally the database becomes available in the highest normal form. A relation is said to be in a normal form if it satisfies a certain specified set of constraints.

Following tables is in the Non-Normal form. A relation is said to be in non-normal form if and only if the underlying domains do not contain atomic values. Atomic value means of composite attribute overhere. In the example, order-details attribute contains the details about part-no and Qty. in single attribute. It is called non-atomic value.

Order-no	Order-date	Order-details	
1	12-12-2002	Part-no	Qty
		P1	10
		P2	30
2	01-10-2003	P5	10
		P6	16
		P7	52
3	12-05-2004	P6	52
		P3	44
		P8	40
		P3	15

First Normal Form (1 NF) :

A relation R is in first normal form (1 NF) if and only if all the underlying domain contains atomic values. The above table can be converted in to 1 NF as follows :

Order-no	Order-date	Order-details	
1	12-12-2002	Part-no	Qty
1	12-12-2002	P1	10
1	12-12-2002	P2	30
2	01-10-2003	P5	10
2	01-10-2003	P6	16
2	01-10-2003	P7	52
3	12-05-2004	P6	52
3	12-05-2004	P3	44
3	12-05-2004	P8	40
3	12-05-2004	P3	15

Hence all the tables of any databases are in 1 NF.

Second Normal Form (2NF) :

A relation R is in second normal form (2NF) if and only if it is in INF and every non key attribute is fully functionally dependent on the primary key.

To show how this constraint applies, let us turn to relation ORDERS as shown in above two tables. Here the relation key is { ORDER-NO, PART-ID}. The key attributes are ORDER-NO and PART-ID. The non key attributes are ORDER-DATE and QTY-ORDERED. The value of ORDER-DATE, however depends only on ORDER-NO. The relation is therefore not in 2NF.

Relations that are not in second normal form can always be decomposed into second normal form relations. To do this we can use a very simple rule that is : Remove the offending functional dependency.

This means that we take the functional dependency that violated the 2NF constraint and make a new relation out of all the attributes in this functional dependency. For example, the relation ORDERS is not in 2NF. The offending functional dependency is :

ORDER-NO ----------> ORDER-DATE

To make it in 2NF we make a new relation ORDERS from this functional dependency and remove ORDER-DATE from the original relation. Relation ORDERS now stores facts about orders only. The original relation is now replaced by relation ORDERS-CONTENTS, which stores facts about order lines. The relation key of relation ORDERS is ORDER-NO and ORDERS-CONTENTS is {ORDER-NO,PART-NO}. The newly generated relations are as shown in the following tables.

ORDERS

ORDER-NO	ORDER-DATE
1	12-12-2002
2	01-10-2003
3	12-05-2004

ORDER-CONTENTS

ORDER-NO	PART-NO	QTY-ORDERED
1	P1	10
1	P2	30
1	P5	10
2	P6	16
2	P7	52
2	P6	52
3	P3	44
3	P8	40
3	P3	15

Third Normal Form (3NF) :

A relation R is in third normal form (3NF) if and only if it is in 2NF and every non key attribute is non-transitively dependent on the primary key :

Relations in 2NF still contain redundancies and additional constraints must be satisfied to eliminate redundancies. Relations in third normal form (3NF) must satisfy yet another constraint. In such relations there should be no dependencies between non-key attributes.

Let us consider a relation VEHICLE, which is not in third normal form.

VEHICLE

Reg-no	**Owner**	**Model**	**Manf.**	**No-cyl.**
01	Ram	M1	Ford	4
77	Mary	M2	Maruti	6
30	Nalin	M3	Tata	4
37	George	M4	Ford	4
83	Ramesh	M1	Ford	4
99	Nutan	M6	Matiz	6
46	Niraj	M7	Bajaj	4
96	Ashish	M6	Matiz	6
74	Amit	M2	Maruti	6
92	Asha	M1	Ford	4

The vehicle stores informations regarding vehicles. Each vehicle is uniquely identified by reg-no and has one owner. The relation key is reg-no. The values for all the non key attributes can be determined easily by reg-no, therefore this relatin is in 2NF. But non key attribute are transitive. For example no_cyl is dependent on model and manf. Hence to make it in third normal form we decompose the relation in two relations REGISTRATION and VEHICLE. These are as follows :

REGISTRATION (Key : REG-no)

Reg-no	Owner	Model	Manf.
01	Ram	M1	Ford
77	Mary	M2	Maruti
30	Nalin	M3	Tata
37	George	M4	Ford
83	Ramesh	M1	Ford
99	Nutan	M6	Matiz
46	Niraj	M7	Bajaj
96	Ashish	M6	Matiz
74	Amit	M2	Maruti
92	Asha	M1	Ford

VEHICLE (Key : MODEL, MANF.)

Model	Manf.	No-cyl.
M1	Ford	4
M2	Maruti	6
M3	Tata	4
M4	Ford	4
M1	Matiz	6
M6	Bajaj	4

Boyce/Codd Normal Form (BCNF) :

A relation R is in BCNF if and only if every determinant is a candidate key. Following relation WORK is not in BCNF as it contains overlapping keys.

WORK

Relation key 2

Relation key 1

Project-ID	Person-ID	Manager	Time-Spent
1	J1	M1	30
2	J1	M2	20
1	J2	M1	11
2	J2	M2	50
3	J2	M3	15
1	J3	M2	5

This relation can be decomposed into further simpler relation which are now in BCNF.

PROJECTS- (Key : Project-ID)

Project-ID	Manager
1	M1
2	M2
3	M3

WORK

Project-ID	Person-ID	Time-Spent
1	J1	30
2	J1	20
1	J2	11
2	J2	50
3	J2	15
1	J3	5

Fourth Normal Form (4 NF) : A relation R is in fourth normal form (4NF) if and only if whenever there exists an Multi Valued dependency in R say A->B then all attributes of R are also functionally dependent on A. Hence a relation in 4NF should not contain independent Multi valued dependency.

Following two relations in context with the previous one are in 4 NF.

KNOWLEDGE :

Person-ID	Skill
J1	Computing
J2	Science
J3	Physics
J3	Maths
J2	Computer
J1	Chemistry

Assignments

Person-ID	Project-ID
J1	1
J1	2
J2	1
J2	2
J2	3
J3	1

6(a). Discuss rule based representation and Frame based representation schemes. [8]

RULE BASED

In this Scheme Knowledge is represented in an **IF [condition] THEN [action]** form and requires a control system to use the rules and a database to store the current input conditions and the outputs. Some simple examples are:

(i) IF [falling from aeroplane] **THEN** [open parachute]
(ii) IF [item is burning your hand] **THEN** [drop item]
(iii) IF [it is raining **AND** you are in the open] **THEN** [put up your umbrella]
(iv) IF [your nose is running **OR** you are about to sneeze] **THEN** [use your handkerchief]

Now lets look at a more complex example :

Rule 1:
IF X HAS A RISK OF HEART ATTACK
AND X HAS HAD A PREVIOUS HEART ATTACK
THEN give X the drug Digitalis

These form what is commonly known as the **Production Rules**. If the conditions on the left-hand side are met then the rule becomes applicable and is ready to be fired by the Control System. This set forms the system's Long Term Memory as the rules are generally hard and fast and do not change, though they may be added.

The Facts:

A: Smith has raised intraocular pressure

B: Smith has had a previous heart attack

These form what is called the **Global Database** which is a structure of facts known to the system. Each fact may be relevant only to the current enquiry or useful for general enquiries.

This database is dynamic in that it is constantly being updated as new knowledge is inferred by the system. This is sometimes referred to as the system's Short Term Memory.

The Queries :

Two questions need answering:

(i) Does Smith need digitalis?

(ii) Does Jones need digitalis?

So we now have some of the fundamental parts needed for our system and these can be described as **The Global Database**, **The Production Rules**, and now we need a **Control System**.

The **Control System** is the interpreting program that runs through the rules with the facts to determine which rules are applicable. Once it has checked all the rules it may be that there is more than one rule applicable and so it has to decide which rule is *fired*.

The relationship between the three components of a production system can be shown pictorially :

So going back to our example:

With the rules set up and the initial facts in place we start the ball rolling by asking "Does Smith need digitalis". In doing this we define a structure for the reply - either "Yes" or "No". The Control System must now attempt to manipulate the Global Database so that an answer is retrievable.

FRAME BASED

Frames are structures that represent a chunk of knowledge about a small domain of the world. For example, a hotel room: the typical hotel room has a bed, wardrobe, chair, telephone etc. A frame representation of the hotel room would contain all these elements, but not much else, it would not contain any information about average French cuisine or any other topic except what you would expect to see in the average hotel room. Frames are rather like a stereotype of a situation or thing. If you walk into a restaurant you *expect* to see tables and chairs and are surprised if there aren't any. Frames therefore set up the expected items in a given situation although these may easily be modified.

A powerful feature is the use of defaults in the slot-fillers which give the stereotypical style of frames. There are a number of different types of slot possible, the most basic being the simple name-value slots which have a name and a value. We have two types of information here: default information slots and new instance information slots. The former is passed to a new instance of the type on that instance's creation whereas the later must be determined on creation of the instance and put into the slot-filler. For example in a frame describing a motorcycle there might be a slot with name **colour** and value **silver/grey**. Now this would obviously be specific to an individual bike and must be determined upon the creation of the bike. Another slot **number_of_wheels** has value **2** would be a default value for all motorbikes and as such would be placed immediately in the slot-filler of a new bike.

Another type of slot is the frame identification slot which gives the frame its name. Closely related is the relationship slot which shows how the frame relates to others. For example the frame called **YAMMHA RX 2004** may be a special instance of **motorcycle** which in turn may be an instance of **vehicle**. There might also be slots that specify the requirements for a given frame to match this one. For example, a motorcycle is expected to have only two wheels, a set of handlebars, an engine and an exhaust pipe (to list a few!), if these requirements are met by a frame then it's quite likely that the frame is describing a motorcycle. A motorcar would not fit these requirements.

(b) Discuss the components of client/server computing. Also mention the advantages of client/server computing. [7]

Refer to JUNE03,Q4(a),Page No. -103

CS-06: DATABASE MANAGEMENT SYSTEM
DEC-2002

Note: *Question 1 is* ***compulsory****. Answer any* ***three*** *from the rest.*

1(a). Design a Relational database to the E - R diagram given below: [7]

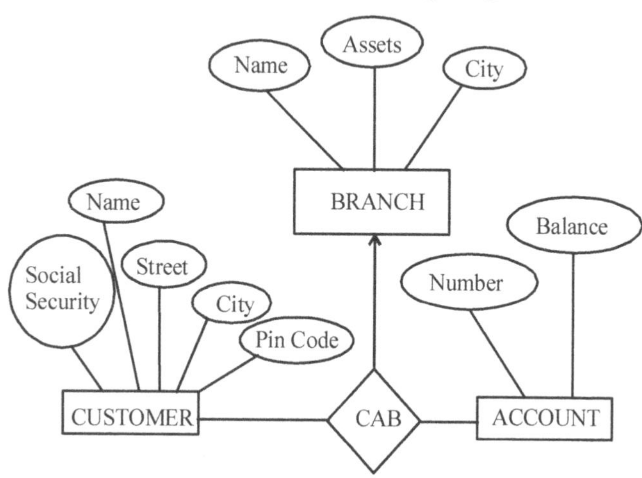

RDBMS of a Given ER Diagram

CUSTOMER TABLE

SOCIAL_SECURITY *NAME* *STREET*
CITY *PIN_CODE*

BRANCH TABLE

NAME *ASSETS* *CITY*

ACCOUNT TABLE

NUMBER *BALANCE*

CAB

SOCIAL_SECURITY *BRANCE NAME* *ACCOUNT NUMBER*

(b) Describe the following relational operators with examples: [10]
(i) UNION
(ii) DIFFERENCE

(iii) INTERSECTION
(iv) CARTESIAN PRODUCT
(v) PROJECTION

We will describe all these concepts on the basis of these tables :

id	Name
106	Kishan

id	Name
101	Ram
107	Ravi
112	Rahul

(i) Union :

The union operation of two relational tables is formed by appending rows from one table with those of a second table to produce a third. Duplicate rows are eliminated. The notation for the union of Tables A and B is A UNION B.

The relational tables used in the union operation must be union compatible. Tables that are union compatible must have the same number of columns and corresponding columns must come from the same domain. Below is the figure shows the union of P and Q.

Note that the duplicate rows has been removed.

id	Name
101	Ram
103	Krishna
104	Kishore
106	Kishan
107	Ravi
110	Varun
112	Rahul

Figure : P UNION Q

(ii) Difference :

The *difference* of two relational tables is a third that contains those rows that occur in the first table but not in the second. The Difference operation requires that the tables be union compatible. As with arithmetic, the order of subtraction matters. That is, P - Q is not the same as Q - P. Figure below shows the different results.

id	Name
106	Kishan

id	Name
101	Ram
107	Ravi
112	Rahul

Figure : The Difference Operator

(iii) Intersection

The intersection of two relational tables is a third table that contains common rows. Both tables must be union compatible. The notation for the intersection of P and Q is P [intersection] Q = R or P INTERSECT Q. Figure below shows the single rows in P and Q.

id	Name
103	Krishna
104	Kishore
110	Varun

Figure : Intersection

(iv) Product

The product of two relational tables, also called the Cartesian Product, is the concatenation of every row in one table with every row in the second. The product of table P (having m rows) and table Q (having n rows) is the table R (having m x n rows). The product is denoted as P X Q or P TIMES Q.

P id	P name	Q id	Q name
101	Ram	103	Krishna
101	Ram	104	Kisore
101	Ram	106	Kishan
101	Ram	110	Varun
103	Krishna	103	Krishna
103	Krishna	104	Kisore
103	Krishna	106	Kishan
103	Krishna	110	Varun
104	Kisore	103	Krishna
104	Kisore	104	Kisore
104	Kisore	106	Kishan
104	Kisore	110	Varun
107	Ravi	103	Krishna
107	Ravi	104	Kisore
107	Ravi	106	Kishan
107	Ravi	110	Varun
110	Varun	103	Krishna
110	Varun	104	Kisore
110	Varun	106	Kishan
110	Varun	110	Varun
112	Rahul	103	Krishna
112	Rahul	104	Kisore
112	Rahul	106	Kishan
112	Rahul	110	Varun

Figure : Product

(v) Projection :

The PROJECT operation selects certain columns from the table & discards the other columns.

For example, the following operation

$\Pi_{Sex,\,Salary}$ (EMPLOYEE)

will result the following table

Sex	Salary

from table

Name	Dept	Sex	Salary

(c) Write short notes on the following: **[10]**

(i) Distributed databases

Distribution database can be defined as consisting of a collection of data with different parts under the control of separate DBMSs, running on independent computer systems. All the computers are interconnected and each system has autonomous processing capability, serving local applications. Each system participates, as well, in the execution of one or more global applications. Such applications require data from more than one site.

A database server is the software managing a database, and a client is an application that requests information from a server. Each computer in a system is a node. A node in a distributed database system can be a client, a server or both.

A Distributed database must also provide the ability to hide the location of the data and the complexity of accessing it. The primary benefits of a distributed database is that the data of physically separate database can be logically combined and potentially made accessible to all users on a network. The database to which a user is directly connected is called the local database. Any additional databases accessed by this user are called remote database.

(ii) Object Oriented databases

An Object-oriented programming language (OOPL) provides facilities to create classes for organising objects, to structure an inheritance hierarchy, to organise classes so that subclass may inherit attributes and methods from superclasses, and to call methods to access specific objects. Similarly, an object-oriented database system (OODB) should provide facilities to create classes for organising objects, to create objects, to structure an inheritance hierarchy, to organise classes so that subclasses may inherit attributes and methods from superclasses, and to call methods to access specific objects. Beyond these, an today's relational database system must provide standard database facilities found in today's relational database systems (RDBs), including nonprocedural query facility for retreiving objects, automatic query optimisation and processing. Dynamic **schema changes** (changing the class definition and inheritance structure), **automatic management of access methods** (e.g., B+-tree index, extensible hashing, sorting, etc.) to improve **query processing performance, automatic transaction management, concurrency control, recovery from system crashes,** and **security and authorisation**, Programming languages, including OOPLs, are designed with one user and a relatively small database in mind. Database systems are designed with many users and very large databases in mind; hence performance, security and authorisation, concurrency control, and dynamic schema changes become important issues. Further, transaction systems are used to maintain critical data accurately; hence, transaction management, concurrency control, and recovery are important facilities.

(iii) Data Redundancy

The same piece of information may be stored in two or more files. For example, the particulars of an individual who may be a customer or an employee may be stored in two or more files. Some of these information may be changing, such as the address, the pay drawn, etc. It is therefore quite possible that while the address in the master file for one application has been updated the address in the master file for another application may have not been. It may not also be easy for the computer-based system to even find out that in how may files the repeating items such as the address is occurring.

(iv) Query Processor

Query processing is the procedure of selecting the best plan or strategy to be used in responding to a database request. The plan is then executed to generate a response. The component of the DBMS responsible for generating this strategy is called a **query processor.**

Query processing is also referred as **query optimization**. However, bear in mind that optimization here is mostly in the form of improvement in light of the inexact knowledge of the status of the database. The optimization done in practical systems is not necessarily the best. The optimal strategy may be too difficult to evaluate and could require much more computing to improve on it which on average may not be dramatically different from the one afforded through a heuristic strategy.

Query processing is a stepwise process. The first step is to transform the query into a standard form. For instance, a query expressed in QBE is translated into SQL and subsequently into a relational algebraic expression. During this transformation process, the **parser** portion of the query processor checks the syntax and verifies if the relations and attributes used in the query are defined in the database. Having translated the query into a given form such as a relation algebraic expression, the optimization is performed by substituting equivalent expressions for those in the query. Such equivalent expressions, are more efficiently evaluated than the ones in the transformed query. Substitution of such expressions also depends on factors such as the existence of certain database structures, whether or not a given file is sorted, the presence of different indexes, and so on. In the next step a number of strategies called **access plans** are generated for evaluating the performed query. The physical characteristics of the data and any supporting access methods are taken into account in generating the alternate access plans. The cost of each access plan is estimated and the optimal one is chosen and executed.

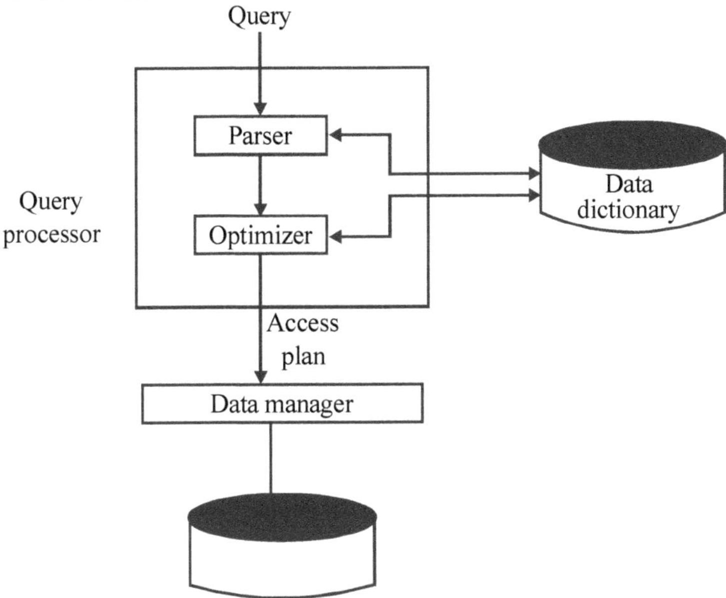

(d) Explain the difference between the physical and logical data independence. [3]

Database independence, is usually considered from two points of view: physical independence and logical independence. Physical data independence allows changes in the physical storage devices or organisation of the files to be made without requiring changes in the conceptual view or any of the external views and hence in the application programs using the database. Thus, the files may migrate from one type of physical media to another or the file structure may change without any need for changes in the application programs. Logical data independence implies that application programs need not be changed if fields are added to an existing record' nor do they have to be changed if fields not used by application programs are deleted. Logical data independence indicates that the conceptual schema can be changed without affecting the existing external schemas. Data independence is advantageous in the database environment since it allows for changes at one level of the database without affecting other levels. These are absorbed by the mappings between the levels.

Logical data independence is more difficult to achieve than physical independence. Since application programs are heavily dependent on the logical structure of the data they access.

2(a). Discuss why navigation is simpler in the Relational data model than in the Hierarchical data model. [4]

Refer to Study material, Q1,Page No. -5

(b) ABC Ltd. is a software company involved in the design, development and marketing of S/W products for personal computers. What entities are of interest to such an enterprise? Draw the E - R diagram giving the list of entities and the relationships among them. [8]

Below is the E-R Diagram of the following situation : -

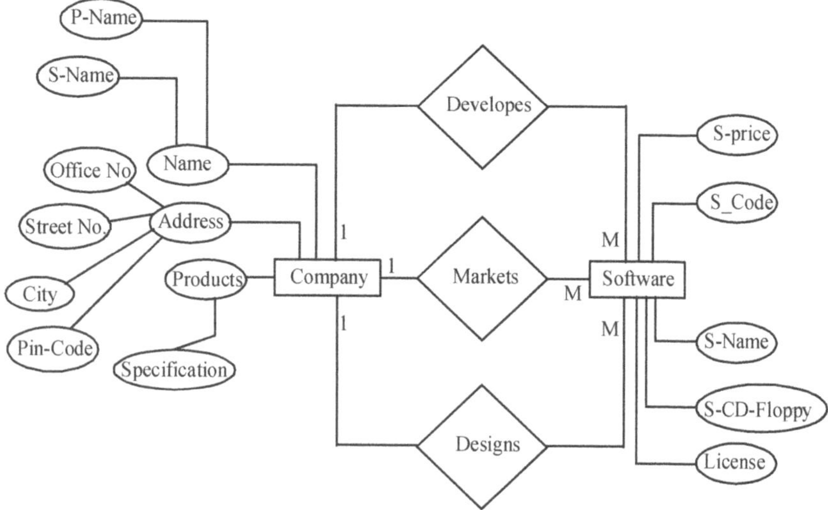

Following are the entities of interest to such an enterprise : -

Company :- This is basically a software company.
Software : - This is the product a company designs, develops and markets.

Following are the relationship among different entities :-
Entities : - Company, Software
Relationship : - Develops

Entities : - Company , Software
Relationship : - Designs

Entities : - Company , Software
Relationship : - Markets

(c) Explain the differences between the File-Oriented system and a Database-Oriented system. **[3]**

Keeping Organizational information in a typical file-processing system has number of major disadvantages and those are improved in a Database System.

Redundancy and Inconsistency :

In a typical file-processing system has own private files. This can often lead to considerable, redundancy (duplication of same information) in stored data. With resultant waste in storage space and raise many problems for managing a file containing department information for employees.

In a database system, however, redundancy should be controlled-that is, the system should be aware of the redundancy and should assume responsibility for propagating updates. While in a DBMS as it has a centralized system avoid unnecessary duplication of record means **redundancy is record.**

Inconsistency :

Data inconsistencies are often encountered in everyday life. For an example consider a situation when an organization changes its address and accordingly informs every one to communicate to the new address, but we find that some of the communications are received at the new address. But we find that some of mailed to the address. Combining all data in a database would involve redundancy as well as inconsistency. So, as DBMS has centralized storage, **inconsistency is avoided.**

Shared data :

In a typical file-processing system data are scattered in various files and different format, it is difficult to share data with the same format. While in a Database system, its centralized storage allows the sharing of data to multiple applications and to various users also.

Integrity Problem :

Data Integrity means that data maintained in a database should both accurate and consistent. Inconsistency between two representing the same "fact" is an example of lack of integrity (which of course can occur only if redundancy exists in the stored data). That it should ensure that if there is a reference to certain object, *that object must have existed.*

Even if redundancy is eliminated, however, the database may still contain incorrect data. Therefore, data being inserted for storage must be checked to ensure that they fall within a specified range and are of the correct format. For an example, Amount to be deposited must be greater than 0. This **Integrity is maintained** in a Database System.

Security Problem :

Having complete jurisdiction over the operational data, the DBA (a) can ensure that the only means of access to the database is through the proper channels, and hence (b) can define authorization checks to be carried out whenever access to sensitive data is attempted. Different checks can be established for each type of access (retrieve, modify, delete, etc.) to each piece of information in the database. [Note that without such checks the security of the data may actually be more at the risk in a database system than in a traditional (dispersed) filing system.]

In a typical file-processing system, to provide each such security separate function or program must be written and it is difficult. While in a Database System **Security restrictions can be applied** easily.

Concurrent-access problem :

In a multi-user system multiple users can update the data simultaneously, which can lead to problem of inconsistency. For an example, If two customers withdraw an amount of Rs. 100 from an Account (having balance Rs. 150) at a same time, the result of the concurrent execution may leave the account in an incorrect state. While in a database system solution for the concurrent access is provided.

3(a). Describe the methodologies used in the evaluation of a DBMS. What are the merits and demerits of each of these? [7]

Earlier, organizations followed the fragmented approach to data processing by designing files to specifically suit different application systems. Since the different functional units (departments) in an organization have large amounts of data to share, this approach, inevitably leads to some major disadvantages as discussed below :

1. Data Redundancy :

Since the files and application programs are written over a long period of time, data in the files is likely to get repeated. This may also lead to inconsistency that is, the various copies of the same data may contain different information. Data redundancy could also occur due to duplication of data at different locations – the need for the same data at physically different locations.

2. Risk to data integrity :

The data values stored, must satisfy certain integrity constraints. These constraints can be enforced in the system, by adding appropriate code in the application programs. The problem is compounded when constraints involve several data items from different files.

3. Data isolation :

since data is scattered in various files, and files may be in different formats, it is difficult to write new application programs to retrieve the appropriate data.

4. Difficult access to data :

Whenever there is a new request that was not anticipated earlier, there are two possible solutions. Either extract the records manually, or have the system programmer write the necessary application.

5. Unsatisfactory security measures :

Every user of the system should be allowed to view only that part of the data that is relevant to his department. Since application programs are added to the system in an ad hoc manner, it is difficult to enforce such integrity constraints.

6. Concurrent access :

many systems allow multiple users to update the data simultaneously to improve the overall performance of the system and obtain a faster response. But in such an environment interaction of concurrent updates my result in inconsistent data. Since the application programs which have not been previously coordinated are used to access data, supervision is very difficult to provide.

Database management addressed all these problems, though at the price of increased overhead and costs.

However, with the advancement of technology and the all-round development made in Hardware, Software, Networking and Operation Systems, the drawbacks of Data Management have been eliminated to a great extent.

(b) Create a B-Tree structure of the order 3 for the following relation (CUSTOMER): [8]

CUSTOMER :

Customer_No.	Customer_Name	Location
C1	N1	L1
C2	N2	L2
C9	N3	L2
C10	N4	L3
C11	N5	L3
C15	N6	L3
C19	N7	L4
C23	N8	L3
C25	N9	L4
C37	N10	L2
C32	N11	L2
C34	N12	L1

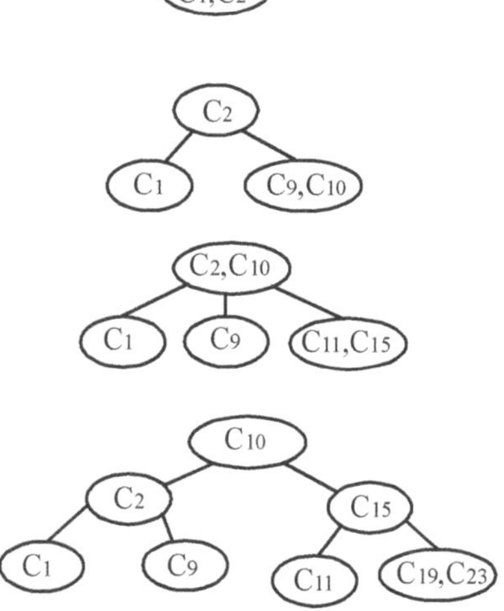

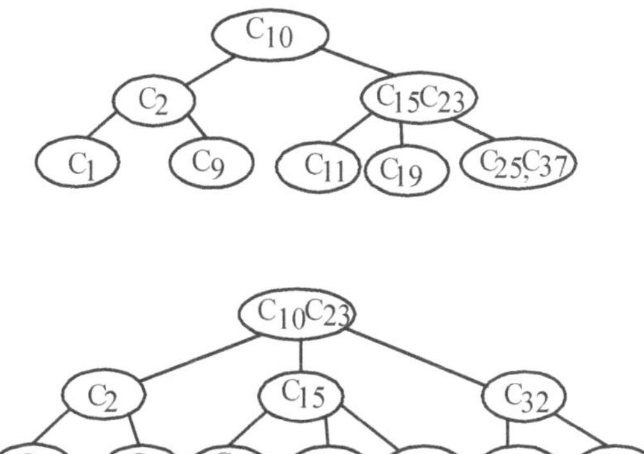

4. Write short notes on : [15]

(i) API

An acronym for Application Programming Interface, the set of commands that an application uses to request and carry out lower-level services performed by a computer's operating system.

A set of routines used by an application to direct the performance of procedures by a computer's operating system. For computers running a graphical user interface, an API manages an application's windows, icons, menus, and dialog boxes. The Window Installer provides an application programming interface (API) that developers can use to build complex installation programs, such as the installation program for Office 2000 itself. Developers can also use the Windows Installer API to build programs that aid other users in creating their own custom installation programs.

As an Office solution developer, you don't need to call the Windows Installer API to create a setup program for your solution. You can use existing tools, such as the Package and Deployment Wizard included in Microsoft Office 2000 Developer, to create a setup program that installs the solution onto the user's computer You can extend the language capabilities of the toolkit by calling procedures included in the Windows CE API. The Windows CE API, a subset of the Microsoft Win32 API, is a collection of DLLs containing many of the procedures used by Windows-based desktop platforms. You can use these DLLs to accomplish a variety of tasks, such as displaying windows and graphics, managing memory and power, and accessing persistent storage.

(ii) Dynamic Data Exchange (DDE)

An interprocess communication method that allows two or more applications running simultaneously to exchange data and commands.

The Microsoft Win32 application programming interface (API) provides several methods for transferring data between applications. One method is to use the Win 32 dynamic data exchange (DDE) protocol. The DDE protocol is a set of messages and guidelines. It sends messages between applications that share data and uses shared memory to exchange data between applications. Applications can use the DDE protocol for one-time data transfers and for continuous exchanges in which applications send updates to one another as new data becomes available.

The Win32 API also includes the Dynamic Data Exchange Management Library (DDEML). The DDEML is a dynamic-link library (DLL) that Win32-based applications are used to share data. The DDEML provides functions and messages that simplify the task of adding DDE capability to a win32-based application. Instead of sending, posting and processing DDE messages directly, an application uses the DDEML functions to manage DDE conversations. (A DDE conversation is the interaction between client and server applications.)

(iii) Semantic Nets

Refer to JUNE03,Q6(iii),Page No.-109

5(a). What is a Knowledge Based system? Compare and contrast Knowledge Based system with a Database system. [JUNE2002,Q6(a)] [8]

Using the analogy of a DBMS, Knowledge base management system can be defined as a computer system used to manage and manipulate shared knowledge. A knowledge base system's manipulation facility includes reasoning facility, usually including aspects of one or more of the following forms of reasoning : deductive, inductive or objective. **Deductive reasoning** implies that a new fact can be inferred from a given set of facts or knowledge using known rules of inference. For instance, a given proposition can be found to be true or false in the light of existing knowledge in the form of other propositions believed to be either true or false. **Inductive reasoning** is used to prove something by first providing a base fact and then the increment step; having proved these, we can prove a generalized fact. **Abductive reasoning** is used in generating a hypothesis to explain observations. Like deductive reasoning, it points to possible inferences from related concept, however, unlike deductive reasoning, the number of inferences could be more than one. The likelihood of knowing which of these inferences corresponds to the current state of the system can be gleaned from the explanations generated by the system. These explanations can facilitate choosing among these alternatives and arriving at the final conclusion.

In addition to the reasoning facility, a knowledge base system may incorporate an

explanation facility so that the user can verify whether the reasoning used by the system is consistent and complete. The reasoning facility also offers a form of tutoring to the uninitiated user. The so-called expert systems and the associated expert system generation facilities are one form of knowledge base systems that have emerged from research labs and are being marketed commercially. Since a KBMS includes reasoning capacity, there is a clear benefit in incorporating this reasoning power in database application programs in languages such as COBOL andPascal.

Database	Knowledge
1. In DBMS, data models are used to show data and relationship between them.	1. In KBMS, knowledge representation schemes are used to show knowledge.
2. Data independence, is the ability to modify a schema definition in one level affecting in next higher level.	2. A knowledge independence signifies that the knowledge stored in system must be insulated from changes in usage in its physical or logical structure.
3. DBMS, handles large amount of shared data.	3. KBMS, handles small amount of knowledge.
4.In DBMS, emphasis is placed on a efficient access and management of the data that model a portion of real work.	4. In KBMS, emphasis is placed on a robust knowledge representation scheme and extensive reasoning capability. Robust signifies that the scheme is rich in expressive power and at the same time it is efficient.
5.DBMS concerned with information contained in data.	5.KBMS concerned with meaning of information

(b) What does VSAM stand for? Briefly describe the VSAM indexing and also, mention the advantages and disadvantages. [7]

Refer to Study material,Q2, Page No. -55

6(a). Explain why Project - Join Normal form is more desirable than 4NF. [6]

FOURTH NORMAL FORM

When attributes in a relation have multivalued, further Normalisation to 4NF are required. We will illustrate this with an example. Consider a vendor supplying many items to many projects in an organisation. The following are the assumptions :

1. A vendor is capable of supplying many items
2. A project uses many items
3. A vendor supplies to many projects.
4. An item may be supplied by many vendors.

Vendor code	Item code	Project no.1
V1	11	P1
V1	12	P1
V1	11	P3
V1	12	P3
V2	12	P1
V2	13	P1
V3	11	P2
V3	11	P2

The relation given in table has a number of problems. For example:

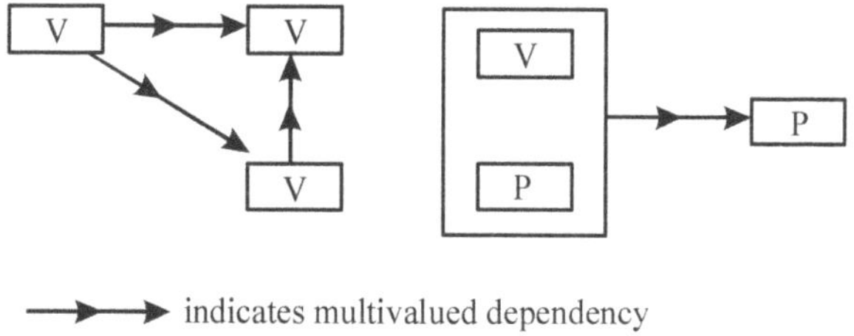

indicates multivalued dependency

1. If vendor V1 has to supply to project P2, but the item is not yet decided, then a row with a blank for item code has to be introduced.
2.The information about item 1 is stored for vendor V3.

Observe that the relation given in Table is in 3NF and also in BCNF. It still has the problems mentioned above. The problem is reduced by expressing this relation as two relations in the Fourth Normal Form (4NF). A relation is in 4NF if it has no more than one independent multivalued dependency with a functional dependency. Table can be expressed as the two 4NF relations given in Table. The fact that vendors are capable of supplying certain items and that they are assigned to supply for some projects are independently specified in the 4NF relation.

(a) Vendor Supply	
Vendor code	Item code
V1	11
V1	12
V2	12
V2	13
V3	11

(b) Vendor project	
Vendor code	Project no.
V1	P1
V1	P3
V2	P1
V3	P1
V3	P2

Any relation can be nonloss-decomposed into an equivalent collection of 5NF relation; 5NF is always achievable.

5NF is guaranteed to be free of anomalies that can be eliminated by taking projections.

From the above, it is seen that Project-Join Normal form is more desirable than 4NF.

(b) Show that every 3NF scheme is in 2NF. Illustrate with an example.
As per the definition for 3NF schema, 3NF : A relation R is in third normal form (3NF) if and only if it is in 2NF and every nonkey attribute is nontransitively dependent on the primary key it proves that the schema is in 3NF is already in 2NF.

According to definition of 3NF, every Functional dependency should be satisfy atleast one of the follows :

1. FD should be trivial
2. Determinant A of FD A→ B should be candidate key
3. B-A should be part of candidate key.

And in accordance to the definition of 2NF, Relation is in 2NF as it does not have any partial dependency. It should satisfy at least one of the following :

1. FD should be trivial
2. Every FD A→B should be Full functional dependent, that means Determinant of FD(A) should not be a part of Key.

Now, let us see that how a 3NF scheme is already in 2NF.
Let us check from a sample scheme :
R1(City, Area, Pincode) with F1 = {City→City, {City, Area}→Pincode,}

First rule for 3NF says FD should be trivial. If it is trivial in 3NF, it is also in 2NF and that is the first rule of the 2NF. So all the trivial FD are satisfied 2NF. The only FD City → City satisfy the 1st rule for 3NF and 2 NF also.

Second rule 3NF says that IF first rule is not satisfy by any FD, it should satisfy the 2nd rule that is Determinant A of FDA→B should be candidate key.

If any FD satisfy this rule, then determinant of this FD is a key not a partial key and it satisfy the 2nd Option rule for 2NF that Every FD A→B A should be complete key not partial key. So it proves that All the FDs that satisfy rule of 3NF also satisfy the 2nd rule for 3NF also satisfy the 2nd rule for to be in 2NF.

The only FD {City, Area} → Pincode from rest of the FDs satisfies the 2nd rule of the 3NF. It also satisfy the 2nd rule of the 2NF.

Third optional rule for 3NF says that each rest of FD A→B, B-A should be part of key. But, this rule will be optional to 1st and 2nd rule of the 3NF. This means for FD A→B, dependent key can be partial key not the dependent of FD.

So, the 3rd rule also satisfy the 2nd rule for the 2NF
The FD Pincode City satisfy the 3rd rule for the 3NF. It also satisfies 2nd rule of the 2NF as Determinant is not partial key.

The FD area → City does not satisfy rule for the 3NF as (City area) is not candidate key. It also not satisfy the 2nd rule of the 2NF as Determinant is a partial Key.

Hence, proved that a 3NF schema is already in 2NF schema

(c) Discuss any six important Codd's rules. **[3]**
Rule 1: The information rule
All information is explicitly and logically represented in exactly one way by - data values in tables.

In simple terms this means that if an item of data doesn't reside somewhere in a table in the database then it doesn't exist and this should be extended to the point where even such information as table, view and column names to mention just a few, should be contained somewhere in table form. This necessitates the provision of an active data dictionary, that is itself relational, and it is the provision of such facilities that allow the relatively easy additions to RDBMS's of programming and CASE tools for example. This rule serves on its own to invalidate the claims of several databases to be relational simply because of their lack of ability to store dictionary implement their dictionary information systems in some native file structure, and thus set themselves up for failing at the first hurdle.

Rule 2: The rule of guaranteed access

Every item of data must be logically addressable by resorting to a combination of table name, primary key value and column name.

While it is possible to retrieve individual items of data in many different ways, especially in a relational/SQL environment, it must be true that any item can be retrieved by supplying the table name, the primary key value of the row holding the item and the column name in which it is to be found. If you think back to the table like storage structure, this rule is saying that at the intersection of a column and a row you will necessarily find one value of a data item (or null).

Rule 3: The systematic treatment of null values.

It may surprise you to see subject on the list of properties, but it is fundamental to the DBMS that null values are supported in the representation of missing and inapplicable information. This support of null values must be consistent through out the DBMS, and independent of data type (a null value in a CHAR field must mean the same as null in an INTEGER field for example).
We may for example define four permissible values for a column SEX as :

M Male
F Female
X No data available
Y Not applicable

Such a solution requires careful design, and must decrease productivity at every level. This solution is particularly undesirable when very high-level languages such as SQL is used to manipulate such data, and if such a solution is used for numeric columns all sorts of problems can arise.

Rule 4: The database description rule

A description of the database is held and maintained using the logical structures used to define the data, thus allowing users with appropriate authority to query such information in the same ways and using the same language as they would for any other data in the database.

Put into easy terms, Rule 4 means that there must be a data dictionary within the RDBMS that is constructed from tables and/or views that can be examined using SQL. This rule states that a dictionary is mandatory, and it taken in conjunction with Rule1, there can be no doubt that the dictionary must also consist the combination of tables and views.

Rule 5: The comprehensive sub-language rule

There must be at least one language whose statements can be expressed as character strings conforming to some well defined syntax, that is comprehensive in supporting the following :

1. Data definition
2. View definition
3. Data manipulation
4. Integrity constraints
5. Authorisation
6. Transaction boundaries

Again in real terms, this means that the RDBMS must be completely manageable through its own dialect of SQL, although some products still support SQL-Like language (Ingress support of Quel for example). This rule also sets out to scope the functionality of SQL - you will detect an implicit requirement to support access control, integrity constraints and transaction management facilities for example.

Rule 6: The view updating rule
All views that can be updated in theory, can also be updated by the system.

This is quite a difficult rule to interpret, and so a word of explanation is required whilst it is possible to create views in all sorts of illogical ways, and with all sorts of aggregate and virtual columns, it is obviously not possible to update through some of them. As a very simple example, if you define a **virtual column** in a view as A*B where A and B are columns in a base table, then how can you perform an update on that virtual column directly? The database cannot be possible to break down any number supplied, into its two component parts, without more information being supplied. To delve a little deeper, we should consider that the possible complexity of a view is almost infinite in logical terms, simply because a views. Particular vendors restrict: the complexity of their own implementations, in some cases quite drastically.

Even in logical terms it is often incredibly difficult to tell whether a view is theoretically updatable, let alone delve into be practicabilities of actually doing so. In fact there exists another set of rules that, when applied to a view, can be used to determine its level of logical complexity, and it is only realistic to apply Rule 6 to those views that are defined as **simple** by such criteria.

CS-06: DATABASE MANAGEMENT SYSTEM
JUNE-2003

Note: *Question 1 is* ***compulsory****. Answer any* ***three*** *from the rest.*

1(a). XYZ Bank offers 5 types of accounts, namely Savings, Recurring, Loan, Current and Money market. It operates a number of branches and a client of the Bank can have any number of accounts, can be individual and joint. Identify the entities of your interest and show their attributes. What relationships exist among these entities? Draw the corresponding E-R diagram. Also design a relation data base to the relational database to the above E-R diagram.

[10]

Below are the Entities, attributes, relationship among different entities, E-R Diagram and Relational Database Structure:-

Entities of Interest :

(i) Customer (or account holder)
(ii) Branch
(iii) Account of five types (savings, recurring, loan, current, money)

Attributes of the above Entities :

(i) Entity:- Customer
Attributes:- Name
Address
House Number.
Street Number.
City
Pin Code.

(ii) Entity:- Branch
Attribute:- Name
B.no.
Assets
City

(iii) Entity:- Account
Attribute:- Number
Street

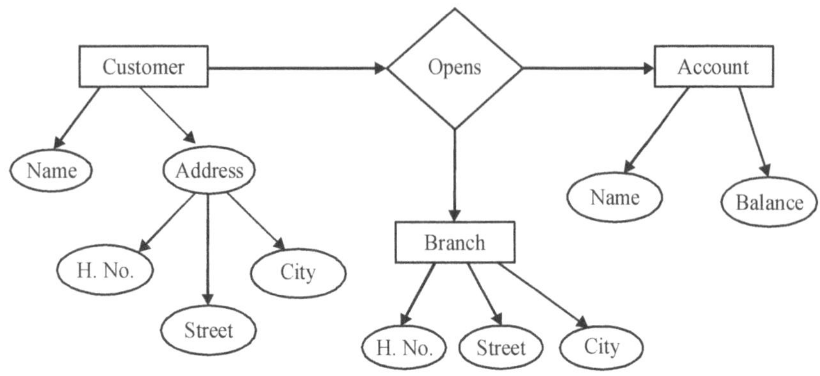

E-R Diagram for the given situation

Customer Table

Account_Number Name Address Branch_Name

Branch Table

Name Assets B_city

Account Table

Number Balance

(b) Discuss the differences between the following file organisations : [10]
(i) Sequential
(ii) Indexed sequential
(iii) Relative file organisation
(iv) Multikey file organisation

Compare their storage and access efficiencies. Also mention what kind of application is best suited for the above file organisations.

(i) Sequential and Indexed Sequential file :

In a sequential files, records are stored in some specific order e.g.:- order of arrival, value of key field etc.

In Indexed sequential file an index is added to the sequential file to provide random access. It supports both sequential access by key value and direct access to a particular record given its key value.

Following are the points of difference:

1. Sequential file supports access by key value, whereas index sequential file supports both sequential access and direct access to a particular record.

2. In index sequential file updates are easily accommodated whereas in sequential files update cannot be easily handled.

3. In Sequential file random access is not possible whereas, in index sequential file, random access of records is possible.

Sequential & Relative File Organisation : - Relative file offers an effective way to organize data when there is a need to access individual records directly.

Following are the points of difference : -

1. Sequential file are used in application areas where batch processing is there where interactive processing is used.

2. Sequential files are simple to use and can be stored on inexpensive media. Whereas, a direct file must be stored on a direct access device.

3. Sequential files cannot access particular records directly, whereas direct file provides effective way to access particular record directly through various hashing algorithms, while no hashing techniques are required in sequential file.

Sequential & Multikey file :
Multikey file offers support for several different kinds of access to a collection of data records to have one data file with multiple access paths. If there is only one copy of any data record to be updated, so update synchronization problem caused by record duplication is avoided. This approach is called Multikey organization.

Following are the points of difference : -

1. The concept of Multikey access generally is implemented by building multiple indexes to provide different access paths to the data records.

2. There may also be multiple linked lists through the data records.

3. The most appropriate method of implementing a particular Multikey is dependent upon the actual uses to be made of the data and the kinds of Multikey file support available.

Applications for Sequential files: It is more convenient and economical for holding large file. It is required in applications where records are processed sequentially in batch mode such as examination result or electricity billing system. It is simple to implement requires very low Software/Hardware support. Its efficiency of processing is also good. Sequential files are good to implement particularly, when file size is large.

(c) Define 3NF. Explain why the "employee" relation in the following database does not satisfy 3NF and decompose it into relations that satisfy 3NF. What are the advantages gained by this decomposition ? [10]

EMPLOYEE

E_No	E_Name	Address	Dept	Dept_Head
E1	N1	A1	D1	E1
E2	N2	A2	D1	E1
E3	N3	A3	D1	E1
E4	N4	A4	D2	E5
E5	N5	A5	D2	E5

Third Normal Form (3NF)

Third normal form is based on the concept of *transitive dependency.* A functional dependency X->Y in a relation is a **transitive dependency** if there is a set of attributes Z that is *not a subset* of any key of the relation, and both X->Z and Z->Y hold. In other words, a relation is in **3NF** if, whenever a functional dependency X->A holds in the relation, either (a) X is a superkey of the relation, or (b) A is a prime attribute of the relation.

Practical Rule : *"Eliminate Columns not Dependent on Key,"* i.e., if attributes do not contribute to a description of a key, remove them to a separate table.
Formal Definition: A relation is in **third normal form** (3NF) if and only if it is in 2NF and every nonkey attribute is nontransitively dependent on the primary key.
In this employee table DEPT & DEPT NAME should be in different table to comply the 3NF. Because as per the 3NF every nonkey attribute is nontransitively dependent on the primary key and here DEPT & DEPT NAME is functionally depend on each other.
So, 3NF Table structure is following:

Employee Table

EMPNO	*NAME*	*ADDRESS*	*DEPT*

Dept Table

DEPTT	*DEPTTNAME*

Q2. Write short notes on:

(i) Updation, Insertion, Deletion anomalies

Update Anomalies :

Multiple copies of anomalies are the problem occurred during management of database it can be insertion, deletion, updation anomalies. The same fact may lead to update anomalies or inconsistencies when an update is made and only some of the multiple copies are in all tuples pertaining to the particular student. If one of the three tuples(assuming for this particular student) is not changed to reflect the new Phone_No. of that particular student, there will be an inconsistency in the data.

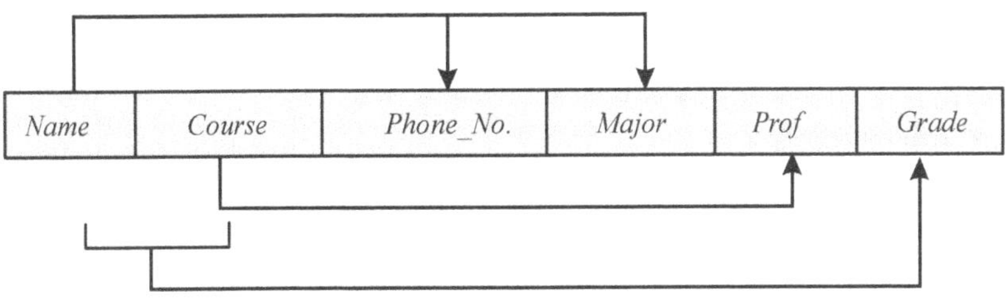

Insertion Anomalies :

If this is the only relation in the database showing the association between a faculty member and the course he or she teaches, the fact that a given processor is teaching a given course cannot be entered in the database unless a student is registered in the course. Also, if another relation also establishes a relationship between a course and a processor who teaches that course the information stored in these relations to be consistent.

Deletion Anomalies :

If the only student registered in a given course discontinues the course, the information as to which professor is offering the course will be lost if this is the only relation in the database showing the association between a faculty member and the course she or he teaches.

(ii) Views

A view is a virtual table, that is one that does not actually exist. It is made up of a query on other tables in the database. It could only be consisting columns or rows from a table or from many tables. A view which restricts the user to certain rows is called a horizontal view and a vertical restricts the user to certain columns. We are not restricted to purely horizontal or vertical view of data.

A view can be as complicated as we like. We can have grouped views where the query contains a GROUP BY clause. This makes the view a summary of the data in a table or tables.

If in the list column names is omitted the columns in the view the same as in the underlying tables. You must specify column names if the query includes calculated columns or two columns with the same name. There are several advantages to views, including:

✓ ***Security*** :

User can be given access to only the rows/columns of tables that concern them. The table may contain data for the whole firm but they only see data for their department.

✓ ***Data integrity*** :

The WITH CHECK OPTION clause is used to enforce the query conditions on any updates to the view. If the view shows data for a particular office the user can only enter data for that office.

✓ ***Simplicity*** :

Even if a view is a multi-table query, querying the view still looks like a single-table query.

✓ ***Protection from change*** :

If the structure of the database changes, the user's view of the data can remain the same.

There are two **disadvantages to views :**

✓ ***Performance :***

A view may look like a single table but underneath the DBMS is usually still running multi-table queries. If the view is complex then even simple queries can take a long time.

✓ ***Update restrictions :***

Updating the data through a view may or may not be possible. If the view is complex the DBMS may decide it can't perform updates and make the view read-only.

The format of view statement is as follows:

create view <view name> as <query expression>

Example

(a) For reasons for confidentiality, not all users are permitted to see the Pay_Rate of an employee. For such users the DBA can create a view, for example, EMP_VIEW defined as:

```
create view EMP_VIEW as
(select Empl_No, Name, Skill
from EMPLOYEE)
```

(b) A view can be created for a subset of the tuples of a relation, as in this example. For assigning employees to particular jobs, the manager requires a list of the employees who have not been assigned to any jobs.

```
create view FREE as
(select Empl_No
from EMPLOYEE
minus
(select Empl_No
from DUTY_ALLOCATION))
```

(iii) Boyce-Code Normal Form (BCNF)

***Boyce-Code Normal Form (BCNF)* :**

Assume that a relation has more than one possible key. Assume further that the composite keys have common attribute. If an attribute of a composite key is dependent on an attribute of the other composite key, a normalization called BCNF is needed. Consider, as an example, the relation **Professor :**

Professor (**Professor code,** Dept., Head of Dept., Parent time)

It is assume that

1. A professor can work in more than one department.

2. The percentage of the time has spends in each department is given.

3. Each department has only one Head of Department.

Below given the relation attributes. The two possible composite keys are professor code and Dept. or Professor code and Head of Dept. Observe that department as well as Head of Dept. are not non-key attributes. They are a part of composite key.

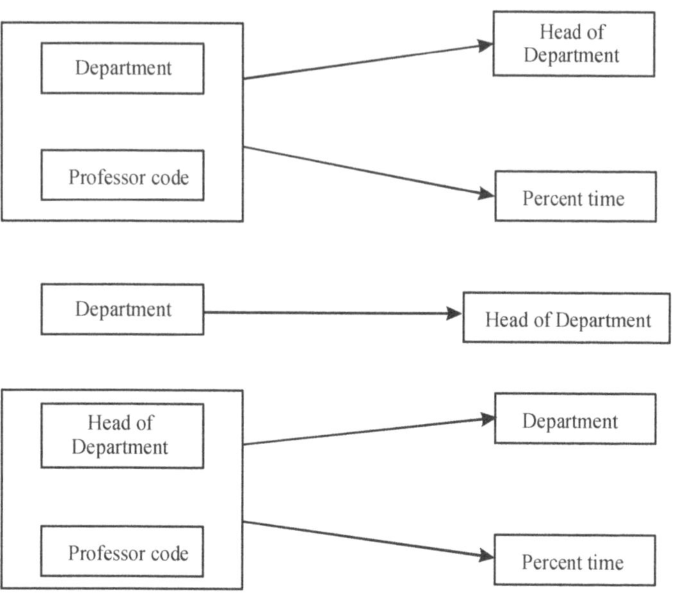

Professor Code	Department	Head of Dept.	Parent
P1	Physics	Ghosh	50
P1	Mathematics	Krishnan	50
P2	Chemistry	Rao	25
P2	Physics	Ghosh	75
P3	Mathematics	Krishnan	100

3(a). What is Data Replication? Explain with the help of example. Discuss the advantages/disadvantages of data replication in the distributed data base system. [5]

Data Replication

Replication is the process of maintaining several identical replicas (copies) of the relation. Each replica is stored at a different site, resulting in data replication. Replication allows for increased local data availability. The advantages of local data availability are :

1. Access of a non update type of information is cheaper.
2. Even if access to a remote site is not possible, access to local data is still available.

There are a number of advantages and disadvantages to replication.

Availability:
If one of the sites containing relation r fails, then the relation r may be found in another site. Thought the system may continue to process queries involving r despite the failure of the one site.

Increased Parallelism:
In the case where the majority of access to the relation r results in only the reading of the relation, the several sites can process queries involving r in parallel. The more replicas of r there are, the greater the chance that the needed data is found in the site where the transaction is executing. Hence, data replication minimizes movement of data between sites.

Increased Overhead on Update:
The system must ensure that all replicas of a relation r are consistent since otherwise erroneous computations may results. This implies that whenever r is updated, this update must be propagated to all sites containing replicas, resulting in increased overhead. For example, in a banking system, where account information is replicated in various sites, it is necessary that transaction assure that the balance in a particular account accessible in all sites.

In general, replication enhances the performance of read operations and increases the availability of data to read transaction. However, update transactions incur greater overhead. The problem of controlling concurrent updates by several transactions to replicated data is more complex than the centralized approach to concurrency control. We may simplify the management of replicas of relation r by choosing one of them as the primary copy of r. For example, in a banking system, an account may be associated with the site in which the account has been opened. Similarly, in an airline reservation system, a flight may be associated with the site at which the flight originates.

(b) Discuss the different approaches to design of object oriented database system. [6]

There are at least six approaches to design of object oriented database system :

1. Novel database data model/data language approach :
The most aggressive approach is to develop entirely new database language and database management system with object orientation capabilities. Most of the

research project in object-oriented databases has pursued this approach. In the industry introduces novel DML (Data Manipulation Language) and DDL (Data Definition Language) constructs for a data model based on semantic and functional data models.

2. Extending an existing database language with object orientation capabilities : A number of programming languages have been extended with object-oriented constructs. C++ flavors (an extension of LISP), and Object Pascal are examples of this approach in programming languages. It is conceivable to follow a similar strategy with database languages. Since SQL is a standard and the most popular database language, the most reasonable solution is to extend this language with object-oriented constructs, reflecting the object orientation capabilities of the underlying database management system. This approach being pursued by most vendors of relational systems, as they evolve the next generation products. There have been many such attempts incorporating inheritance, function composition for nested entities, and even some support of encapsulation in an SQL framework.

3. Extending an existing object :
Object oriented programming language with database capabilities: Another approach is to introduce database capabilities to an existing object-oriented language. The object orientation features abstract data type, inheritance, object identity—will already be supported by the object-oriented language. The extensions will incorporate database features (querying, transaction support, persistence, and so on).

4. Embedding object : oriented database language constructs in a host (conventional) language: Database languages can be embedded in host programming languages. For examples, SQL statements can be embedded in PL/I C, Fortran and Ada. The types of SQL (that is relations and rows) are quite different from the type systems of these host languages. Some object-oriented databases have taken a similar approach with a host language and an object-oriented database language.

4(a). What is client/server computing ? Why do we need it ? Discuss its advantages. [7]

Client/Server model is an application software in which one application (the client) asks for and receives information from another application (the server). Client/server is a concept of computing as seen from the end user's view point that of the system or application. In client/server environment, data are manipulated at the user level. Client/server computing can be envisioned as a multi-vendor, multi-product, multi-application implementation. Client/server computing is software based architecture that enables distributed computing resources on a network to share common resources among groups of users at intelligent workstations.

The Block structure of client server computing is as shown in the figure.

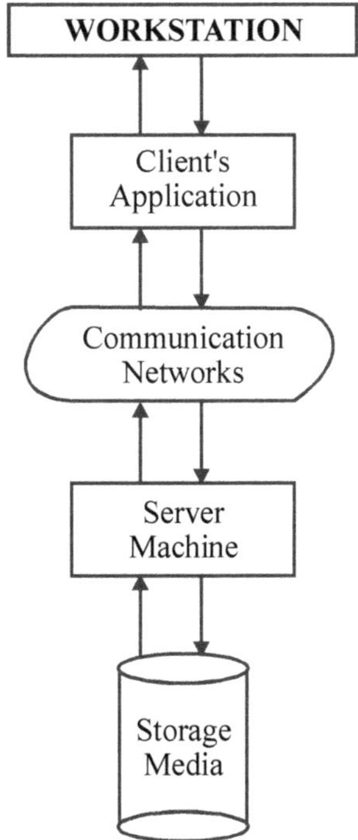

Client is an application that initiates peer to peer communication and users usually involve client software when they use network services. Most client software consists of conventional Application programs each time when an client application executes it requests to server, awaits for response and when response arrives it continues processing. Generally clients are easier to build than server is and not require some special system privileges to operate.

On the other hand server is any program that services the clients. It waits for a request and when request arrives it performs necessary computation but it does not send information to client until it tells to do so. It also manages synchronization of services.

In this association of client/server computing, client is a more active partner it requests to specific functions, receives result and acknowledging for completions of request, but it doesn't manages synchronization like server because server has special system privileges. For example a file server has a special code to check whether a client has the permission to access a particular file or not. Similarly server has several check codes to determine the issue of :

Authentication : Verify the identify of each client.

Authorization : Check the permission of client to access the services issued by a server.

Data Security : Secure client's data from unintentionally revealed or compromised.

Privacy : Keep separates, data of clients with each other.

Protection : Product system resources from application programs

Advantages -

Client/server is an open system. It offers organizations ability to distribute processing and data across network using powerful graphical workstations, servers, and mainframes. The client/server model enables rightsizing, the selection and location of computing resources according to the needs of individuals and work groups. Some of the Basic advantages of client-server computing are listed below :

1. Provides low cost and user friendly environment.
2. Increased productivity.
3. It can be used to develop highly complex database application that can be solved by a mainframe computer until about 5 years back.
4. It offers expandability and ensure that performance degradation is not so much while connecting more client.
5. Since clients are PCs or workstation, various application such as spreadsheet, can be connected through Dynamic Data Exchange (DDE) and Object Linking and Embedding(OLE).
6. Inter-operability-key components viz. Client, server, network work together.
7. Scalability-any of the key elements may be replaced when the need to either grow or reduce processing for that element dictates, without major impact on the other elements.
8. Adaptability : new technology may be incorporated into the system
9. Affordability : Cost effectiveness is insured by using less expensive MIPS available on each platform.
10. Data integrity : entity, domain and referential integrity are maintained on the database server.
11. Accessibility : data may be accessed from WANs and multiple client applications.
12. Performance : performance may be optimized by hardware and process..
13. Security : data security is centralized on the server.

(b) Discuss the various components involved in the client/server computing. **[8]**

Components of Client Server Computing are described as follows :
The definition of client/server highlights the four fundamental building components in the client/server architecture. Each component has its own unique characteristics. There are :

(i) Server
(ii) Clients
(iii) Networks
(iv) Applications

(i) Server :
A server performs a set of special tasks for any other device requesting their services. A server is a reactive process activated by requests sent from clients. The server performs requested transactions and does not interact with any other servers. Server can broadly divided into transaction servers and data servers. Here, transaction server provide an interface to which clients can send requests to perform an action, in responds to which they execute the action and send back results to the client while data server allow clients to interact with the server by making requests to read or update, in units such as files or pages.

For example, File servers provide a file systems interact where clients can create update, read and delete files.
The server machine could be running NOVELL LAN or INTEL based server or UNIX from SCO or AT&T or UNIX being run on RISC machines like HP, SUN microsystem, IBM compac etc.

There are server machines should be running on RDBMS engine like Sybase, Oracle, Informix etc. The server machine takes care of data storage, backup, recovery and database services.

(ii) Client :
The client acts as the user entry point into the client/server environment. To be a client a workstation must be intelligent because it must have processing capabili-

ties and make requests to common resources. In the client/server relationship, the client uses the services provided by one or more server processors. It is the proactive member of the relationship, issuing requests to the server and receiving responses. A client is dedicated to an individual user. It comes into existence at the beginning of a user session and ends when the user session ends.

(iii) Network :

The essence of a client/server system network is connectivity in a multi-product, multi-vendor environment. A network connects the workstations with common resources and is a system within which information is transferred. Networks can be classified according to their geographic coverage. LAN serves a single building or a campus of several buildings. MAN serves the entire city or metropolitan area. WAN serves larger geographically spread areas.

(iv) Applications :

Software applications tie the other three components together to form the client/server architecture. The feature that distinguishes client/server from other technology architecture is that it contains cooperative processing capabilities, which physically split the processing performed by the client from that performed by the server while presenting a single logical picture to the user.

5(a). Discuss key features of B-Trees and B+ Trees. Also comment on the relative advantages and disadvantages. Mention the use of them by giving an example for each. [8]

B Trees :

B Trees are multi-way trees. That is each node contains a set of keys and pointers. A B Tree with four keys and five pointers represents the minimum size of a B Tree node. A B Tree contains only data pages. B Trees are dynamic. That is, the height of the tree grows and contracts as records are added and deleted.

B+ Trees :

B+ trees are related to two data structures: ISAM Trees and B-Trees.

ISAM stands for indexed sequential access method. As the name implies, the data is maintained in sorted order. A set of index pages provides fast access to the data pages. ISAM is a relatively static approach. Although it can accommodate additions and deletions, the index pages do not change. Additions are handled through overflow pages. Thus, the efficiency of this access method can degrade if there is a lot of data movement.

A B+ Tree combines features of ISAM and B Trees. It contains index pages and data pages. The data pages always appear as leaf nodes in the tree. The root node and intermediate nodes are always index pages. These features are similar to ISAM. Unlike ISAM, overflow pages are not used in B+ trees.

The index pages in a B+ tree are constructed through the process of inserting and deleting records. Thus, B+ trees grow and contract like their B Tree counterparts. The contents and the number of index pages reflects this growth and shrinkage.

(b) List 4 responsibilities of Database Manager. For each responsibility, explain those problems that would arise if the responsibilities were not met. [7]

Database Manager :

A Database Manager is a program module, which provides an interface between the low level data stored on disk and various application programs/queries. It converts user's request in form of queries into the physical file system. It establishes synchronization between simultaneous operations of concurrent users and also responsible for backup, recovery and security purpose. Some of the important responsibilities of Database managers are given as :

(i) Interaction with file manager :

As low-level commands are understood by operating system to get different access of physical record. It translates the various DML statements into low-level file system commands.

(ii) Integrity enforcement :

The data values stored in the database must satisfy certain types of consistency constraints. For example an entry for a date field can not exceed the value 31 or for a month it would be 12. Such a consistency constraints are checked by database manager. If any constraints are not entertained or not checked at the time of storing or manipulation of the data, there are lot of chances for getting database of incorrect data. So, constraints enforcement are required for data validity.

(iii) Security :

Not every user of the database system should be able to access every part of database. Different level of users, same level of user can have different authentication on different data. So, to prevent user for invalid operation each user may assign different rights on different types of access. For a security, authentication must be checked before processing data request.

(iv) Backup and Recovery :

Since the database is a valuable asset, it is its responsibility to ensure that the asset is not lost or damaged. During failure of system, the information stored in database may lost. It is the responsibility of database manager to detect such failures and put the database into an existing state prior to failure. This can be furnished by Backup and Recovery procedures.

Concurrency Control :

As DBMS is multi user, multiple user can fire different transactions on the same data, which can arise the problem of data inconsistency. So, it is necessary to control interaction among several concurrent users and maintain consistency.

6. Discuss the following knowledge Representation Schemes: [15]

(i) Rule-based Representation

Production-based system consists of a set of production rules, a data structure that models the system's current state, and a control subsystem or interpreter that interprets the current state and controls its activity by initiating appropriate action. A rule is said to be enabled or triggered when the condition part of the rule is satisfied by the current state of the system. An enabled rule is said to be fired if the action part of a rule is executed. If the system status is such that more than one rule is triggered, the interpreter may be required to fire one or more of these simultaneously enabled rules; this is referred to as a conflict resolution. The conflict resolution can be enacted using its own set of productions. It uses criteria such as priority or ranking, prior selection, arbitrary or random choice, or doing all actions in parallel. The order in which the conditions are examined can be determined and priority could be adjusted dynamically. The action part can be a single action or a set of procedures that will change the status of the system. The latter change can include disabling a subset of the existing productions and enabling other productions.

An example of a rule-based system is given below. This system examines the causes and the corrective actions to be performed after failing to start a car. The execution of each action will modify the state of the starting system under consideration and if there is more than one problem, all the corrective actions will have to be taken.

```
if starter cranks the engine very slowly
   then problem may one or more of: extreme cold
            temperature, battery, cables, connections, voltage
            regulator, alternator; use jumper cable to start
if starter does not crank but solenoid operates
    then check cables and tighten and clean terminals and
            check battery voltage
if problem is low battery voltage
```

then problem may be battery: check specific gravity and replace if not acceptable;
problem may be loose, worn, or broken alternator belt: do a visual inspection and if belt is okay, tighten belt, otherwise replace it;
problem may be cables: visual inspection, clean and tighten connections, and replace broken connectors or cables;
problem may be voltage regulator: check and replace;
problem may be alternator: check and repair or replace alternator;
problem may be shorts in electrical system: locate and correct

if problem loose or worn alternator belt
then tighten or replace alternator belt

if problem is battery
then check specific gravity and if acceptable charge otherwise replace battery

if problem is voltage regulator
then replace voltage regulator

if problem is alternator
then repair or replace alternator

if battery, cables and connections are good, solenoid operates, but starter does not crank or cranks slowly
then replace the starter

if battery, cables, and connections are good but solenoid does not click
then check ignition switch to solenoid circuit and correct malfunctions

if battery, cables, connections, and ignition switch to solenoid circuit are good but solenoid does not click
then replace solenoid

if starter spins but does not crank the engine
then replace starter

if starter cranks the engine, smell of gas in the exhaust, but the engine does not fire
then check and dry ignition circuit and replace faulty parts

if starter crank the engine but engine does not fire and no smell of gas
then check and correct problems with fuel lines, fuel pump, fuel filter, carburetor, fill tank

Since the action part of a rule can modify the state of the system, additional rules may have to be fired. There are two methods of matching rules to the current state of a system: forward chaining and backward chaining. In **forward chaining**, the initial set of facts are used to determine the rules that apply. If more than one rules applies, one of these is chosen. The search proceeds by firing this rule and arriving at a new set of facts. This procedure is repeated until a solution is reached. In **backward chaining**, all rules that have to be fired are first determined for the desired solution. These rules are then fired sequentially in the forward direction.

In a large system, the production rules limit the interaction between rules and lead to inefficiencies. These inefficiencies become evident when a number of production rules have to be fired, but can only be executed one at a time. Each such firing is proceeded by an interpretation of the current state of the system against the production rules. On average, half of these production rules have to be tested before each firing.

(ii) Frame-based Representation

FRAME BASED

Frames are structures that represent a chunk of knowledge about a small domain of the world. For example, a hotel room: the typical hotel room has a bed, wardrobe, chair, telephone etc. A frame representation of the hotel room would contain all these elements, but not much else, it would not contain any information about average French cuisine or any other topic except what you would expect to see in the average hotel room. Frames are rather like a stereotype of a situation or object.

A frame is a data structure representing the collection of the expected and/or predicted description of a stereotype object, action or event. Each important feature of the object is held in a slot. An optional procedure can be attached to a slot to introduce procedural information or specify consistency constraints. The frame also contains the object's relationship to other objects, these being represented by frames as well. The description of the object includes a number of important features of the object and the relationships between other descriptors.

In addition to the predicted description of the various features of the object being represented, the frame may contain information such as the level of confidence assigned to the descriptor, the default values, alternate values (or their range) for descriptors, and variations in the descriptors that can be associated with the frame. The descriptors or slots can allow the inheritance of properties from a related frame.

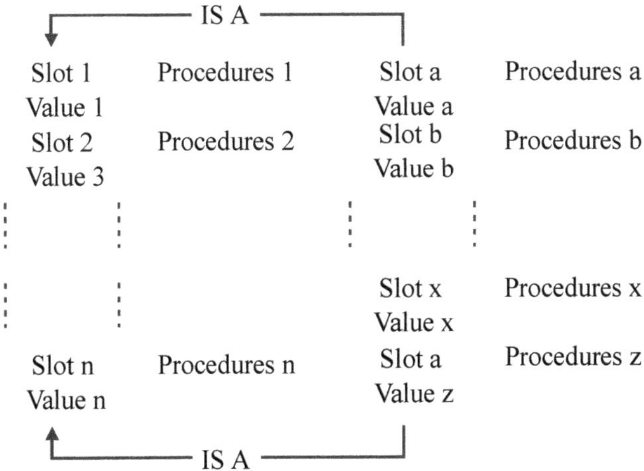

The frame Bungalow(assume) is a specialization of the frame Building and inherits from Building descriptors such as walls, doors, windows, roof. The slot or descriptor itself can be a frame. Thus, the descriptor window can have descriptors of its own, for example size and type.

In addition, descriptors could have appropriate reasoning or inferencing procedures attached. These procedures are triggered or executed whenever the descriptors are filled in, modified, or matched to clean precompiled knowledge. Frames have been used extensively to represent visual knowledge and knowledge about natural languages.

(iii) Semantic Nets **[DEC2002,Q4(iii)]**

A lot of knowledge is default knowledge such as birds can fly. You don't want to have to list every attribute of every object, you'd end up with a large amount of data, it would surely be more sensible to create a hierarchy or information. If an entity is a bird you want to make certain assumptions automatically and this results in an inheritance hierarchy. For example : Tweetie is a canary, canary is a bird, bird is an animal, etc.

We would plug in the attributes at the highest possible level e.g. Animal : Has skin, bold. Can move.

Bird : Is a type of animal. Has feathers. Can fly.
Canary : Is a type of bird. Is Yellow and Small.
Tweetie : Is a canary. Has a toe missing.

Semantic nets work along these lines and all semantic nets are constructed from two basic components :

Nodes and ARC's

Nodes :

These represent the objects, concepts, the things of the domain. Nodes are usually represented by a circle or oval diagrammatically.

ARCs :

These represent the relationship between nodes. These can be action between objects, abstract interaction between concepts, or any number of things in between! Arcs are drawn as arrows connecting the nodes.

(Semantic nets were initially created to demonstrate a theory of long term memory structure in humans by Ross Quillian. His initial aim was to build a program that could understand language but, surprisingly enough, this turned out to be a little too ambitious so he dropped his specification down to comparing two word concepts. The results were to be expressed in a pseudo-English language.)

CS-06: DATABASE MANAGEMENT SYSTEM
DEC-2003

Note: *Question 1 is* ***compulsory****. Answer any* ***three*** *from the rest.*

1(a). Construct an ER diagram (including important attributes) for a car insurance database that includes data about customer (car owners), cars, accidents, drivers involved in accidents and injured drivers and/or passengers. Note that any customer can insure many cars, each car may have different drivers at different times and accidents typically involve one or more cars.

[10]

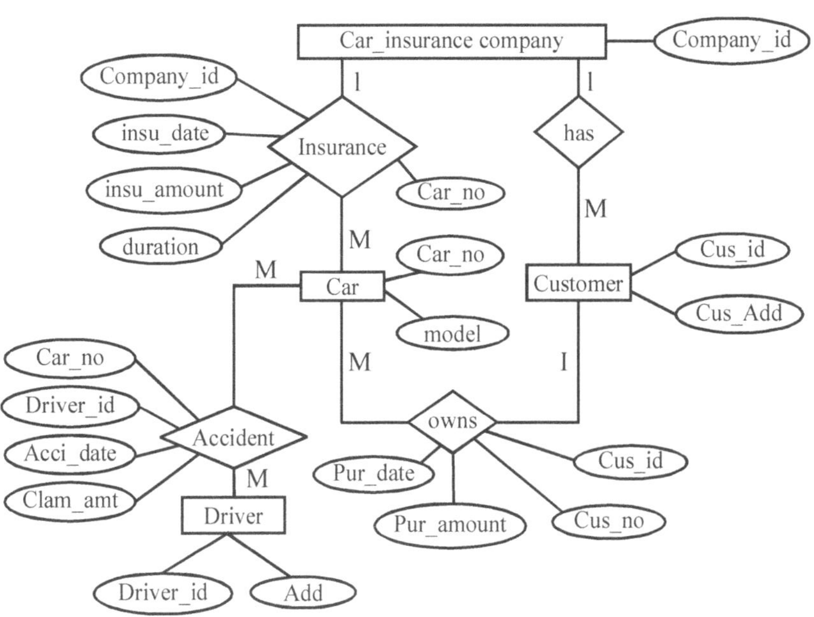

entity set CAR_INSURANCE COMPANY

company_id : string ; (**PK**)

entity set CAR

car_no : string ; (**PK**)
mode : string ;

entity set CUSTOMER
cus_id : string ; (*unique indentification)
cus_add : string ;
company_id : string ;

entity set DRIVER
driver_id : string ; (*unique identification)
Add : string ;

relationship set OWNS
cus_id : string ;
car_no : string ;
pur_date : date ;
pur_amount : integer ;

relationship set ACCIDENT
car_no : string ;
dri_id : string ;
acc_date : date ;
dam_amt ; integer ;

relationship set INSURANCE
car_no : string ;
company_id : string ;
insu_date : date ;
duration : date ;
insu_amount : integer ;

Date structure :

(1) Company

company_id : char(9)

PK(Primary Key) ⇒ company_id

(2) Customer

cus_id : char(9) cus_Add : varchar(100) company_id : char(9)

PK(Primary Key) ⇒ cus_id
FK(Foreign Key) ⇒ company_id reference (company)

(3) Car

car_no : char(9) model : char(9)

PK ⇒ car_no

(4) Driver

Driver_id : char(9) Add : varchar(100)

PK ⇒ Driver_id

(5) Owns

cus_id : char(9) cus_no : char(9) pur_date : date pur_amount : integer

FK ⇒ company_id references
(company)
FK ⇒ car_no references
(car)

(6) Accident

car_no : char(9) Driver_id : char(9) Acci_date : date dam_amt : integer

FK ⇒ car_no references
(car)
FK ⇒ Driver_id references
(Driver)

(7) Insurance

car_no : char(9) company_id : char(9) insu_date : date insu_amount : integer duration : date

FK ⇒ company_id references
(company)
FK ⇒ car_no references
(car)

(b) Explain the 3 levels of the database architecture. Also discuss the advantages of having the 3 levels. **[8]**

According the approach of ANSI/SPARC (American National Standard Institute / Standards Planning and Requirements Committee). There are three views of data abstraction : external view, conceptual view and internal or physical view.

1. External View

It is the highest level of the abstraction of data. Each external view is defined by means of an External schema. Which consists basically definitions of each of the various types of external record found at that external view.
The external level is that the view that the individual user of the database has. It determines How the data LOOK LIKE, irrespective of how they are stored. It represents a part of the database. The same database may provide different classes of users.

2. Conceptual view

It is the next lower level of abstraction. The conceptual view is defined by means of the conceptual schema. This is also known as user's view that describes WHAT type of data are actually stored. It simply contains the information about structure (or type) of data stored in database. A database administrator, who must decide which information, is to be kept in the database, what are the relations among the tables at conceptual level. The conceptual schema is defined using Data definition Language(DDL).

3. Internal or Physical View

It is the lowest level of the data abstraction. The Physical view is defined by the means of Internal schema.

It is concerned with the physical storage of the information means what data are stored and How. It also specifies what indexes exist, how stored fields are represented . It gives complete internal structure of storage and their access paths (specification of primary, secondary keys ,indexes, pointers and sequencing , data compressions and optimization techniques.

Mapping Between the three Levels :

Mapping corresponds one record of one level to record of the another level. There are two mappings in three levels architecture .

(1) Mapping between External and Conceptual level.
(2) Mapping between internal and conceptual level.
(3) Internal to physical database. There is not necessary that an internal record at internal level is stored at a physical record, it can be from multiple records on storage device. It provides the relevant mapping.

The figure shows the interrelationship among these three levels of abstraction.

Figure : Illustrating the three-schema architecture

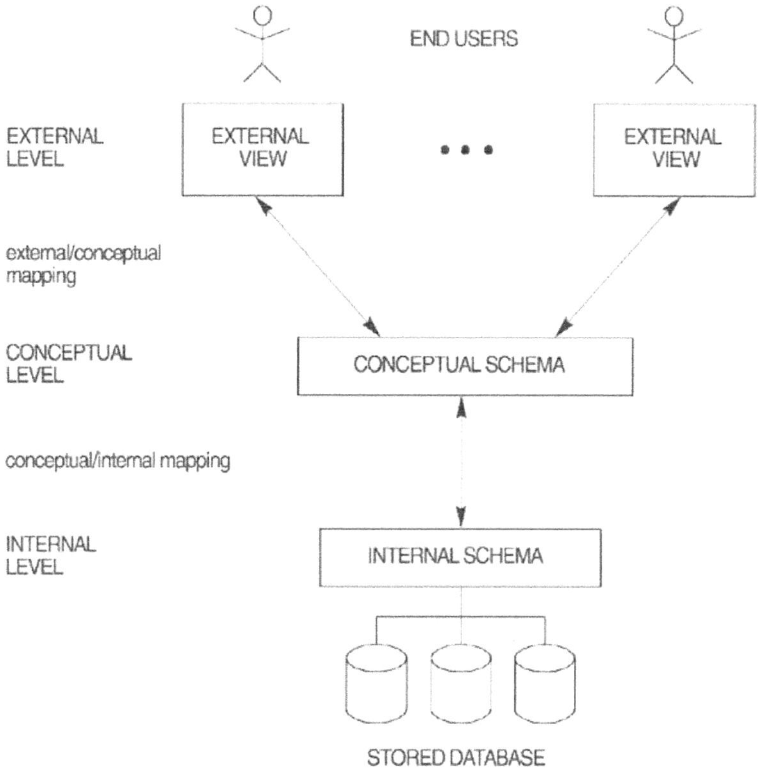

(c) What are functional dependencies? With a suitable example explain the importance of functional dependencies in database design and data modelling. **[7]**

Functional dependencies are constraints on the set of legal relations. They allow us to express facts about the enterprise that we are modeling with our database. Consider a relation schema R, and let $\alpha \subseteq R$ and $\beta \subseteq R$. The **functional dependency**

$$\alpha \rightarrow \beta$$

holds on schema R if, in any legal relation r(R), for all pairs of tuples t and t_2 in r such that $t_1 [\alpha] = t_2 [\alpha]$, it is also the case that $t_2[\beta] = t_2[\beta]$.

Functional dependencies allow us to express constraints that we cannot express with superkeys. Consider the schema

Loan-info-schema = (loan-number, branch-name, customer-name, amount)

Which is simplification of the lending-schema that we saw earlier. The set of functional dependencies that we expect to hold on this relation schema is

loan-number → amount
loan-number → branch-name

We would not, however, expect the functional dependency

loan-number → customer-name

to hold, since, in general, a given loan can be made to more than one customer (for example, to both members of a husband-wife pair).

In the loan relation (on Loan-schema), we see that the dependency loan-number → amount is satisfied. In contrast to the case of customer-city and customer-street in customer-schema, we do believe that the real-world enterprise that modeling requires each loan to have only one amount therefore, we want to require that loan-number → amount be satisfied by the loan relation at all times. In other words. We require that the constraints loan-number → amount hold on Loan-schema.

(d) Discuss the Boyce-Codd Normal Form (BCNF) with the help of an example. **[JUNE03,Q2,(iii)]** **[5]**

Boyce-Code Normal Form (BCNF)

Assume that a relation has more than one possible key. Assume further that the composite keys have common attribute. If an attribute of a composite key is dependent on an attribute of the other composite key, a normalization called BCNF is needed.

Refer to JUNE04,Q1(c),Page No. - 60

2(a). Consider the following Relational schema. An employee can work in more than one department: [10]

Emp (Eid, Ename, Salary)
Works (Eid, did)
Dept (did, dname, managerid, floornum)

Write the following in SQL:
(i) Print the names of all employees who work on the 10th floor and earn salary less than Rs. 50,000.
(ii) Print the names of the departments that employee Santa works in.
(iii) Print the names of all managers who manage three or more departments on the same floor.
(iv) Print the names of all employees who work on floor(s) where Jane Donald works.
(v) Give every employee who works in the toys dept. a 10% raise in the salary.

(i) Select E.ENAME from EMP E, DEPT D, WORKS W where D.DID=W.DID and E.EID=W.EID and E.SALARY<50000 AND D.FLOORNUM = 10

(ii) Select D.DNAME from EMP E, DEPT D, WORKS W where E.ENAME = 'SANTA' and E.EID = W.EID and W.DID = D.DID

(iii) Select distinct E.ENAME, D.FLOORNUM from EMP E, DEPT D where D.FLOORNUM= (Select FLOORNUM from DEPT D group by D.FLOORNUM having COUNT(D.DID)>=3)and E.EID = D.MANAGERID

(iv) Select E.ENAME from DEPT D, EMP E, WORKS W where D.floornum =(SELECT D.FLOORNUM from DEPT D, EMP E, WORKS W where ENAME = 'JANE DONALD' and E.EID = W.EID and D.DID = W.DID) and E.EID = W.EID and D.DID = W.DID

(v) Select E.ENAME, 'SALARY'='E.SALARY+(E.SALARY*10/100)' from EMP E, DEPT D, WORKS W where D.DNAME = 'TOY' and D.DID = W.DID and E.EID = W.EID

(b) Compare and contrast primary key, candidate key and foreign key by giving a suitable example. [JUNE01,Q1(b)] [5]

Primary key

A column or combination of columns that uniquely identifies a row in a table. It cannot allow null values and must always have a unique index. A primary key is used to relate a table to foreign keys in other tables.

Example : In a relation Dept (Dept_no, Dept_name, Head_of_Dept) the primary key is Dept_no. There can be only one primary key in a relation(table).

Candidate key

A unique identifier for a row within a database table. A candidate (or surrogate) key can be made up of one or more columns. By definition, every table must have at least one candidate key (in which case it automatically becomes the primary key for a table), but it is possible for a table to have more than one candidate key (in which case one of them must be designated as the primary key). Any candidate key that is not the primary key is called an **alternate key**.

Example : In previous example dept_no and head_of_dept both can be primary key of this relation so both are candidate keys now any one can be choose as a primary key.

Foreign key

A column or combination of columns whose values match the primary key of some other table. A foreign key does not have to be unique; in fact, foreign keys are often in a many-to-one relationship to a primary key. Foreign key values should be copies of the primary key values; no value in the foreign key except NULL should ever exist unless the same value exists in the primary key. A foreign key may be NULL; if any part of a composite foreign key is NULL, the entire foreign key must be NULL.

Example : Consider two relation Dept(Dept_no, Dept_name, Head_of_Dept) and Employee (Emp_no, Ename, Dept_no) here dept_no is primary key in relatio dept and dept is called parent table and dept_no is made foreign key in relationn employee. This is called child table. Foreign key is made for data consistency that means for avoiding invalid dept_no in employee table.

3. Explain the following: **[15]**

(i) Hashing

A process whereby an item is placed into a structure based on a key-to-address transformation.

Hashing is a way of performing optimal searches and retrievals. Essentially, it increases speed, betters ease of transfer, improves retrieval, optimizes searching of data, reduces overhead. Thus, one objective of hashing is to optimize disk

accesses and packing density. The packing density, roughly equivalent to a load factor, is simply how much of the table is filled (normally, 70% is sufficient). The ultimate goal, however, is to minimize disk space and access time by inserting and retrieving a record from the table in only one seek. One way to minimize this time is to use small table sizes (say m < 10).
There are 4 key components involved in hashing :

1. the hash table
2. the hashing method
3. collisions
4. collision resolution techniques

(ii) Indexing
An index is a set of y, address pairs. Indexing associates a set of objects to a set of orderable quantities, which are usually smaller in number or their properties provide a mechanism for faster search. The purpose of indexing is to expedite the search process. Indexes created from a sequential (or sorted) set of primary keys are referred to as index sequential. Although the indices and the data blocks are held together physically, we distinguish between them logically. We shall use the term index file to describe the indexes and data file to refer to the data records. The index is usually small enough to be read into the processor memory.

(iii) B^+ tree indexes
The most powerful DBMSs allow a great deal of implementation detail to be defined for the relations. The more common but less powerful DBMSs (mostly on microcomputers) allow very simple definitions, for example, indexing on certain attributes (this is usually a B+-tree index).

(iv) Specialization
Refer to JUNE04,Q5(b),Page No. -71

(v) Generalization
Refer to JUNE04,Q5(b),Page No. -71

4(a). Discuss the features of OODBMS. Also mention the advantages. [8]
Four basic features of OODBMS :
1. Reduced maintenance
The primary goal of object-oriented development is the assurance that the system will enjoy a longer life while having far smaller maintenance costs. Because most of the processes within the system are encapsulated, the behaviours may be reused and incorporated into new behaviours.

2. Real-world modelling

Object-oriented systems tend to model the real world in a more complete fashion than do traditional methods. Objects are organised into classes of objects, and, objects are associated with behaviours. The model is based on objects rather than on data and processing.

3. Improved reliability

Object-oriented systems promise to be far more reliable than traditional systems, primarily because new behaviours can be built from existing objects.

4. High code reusability

When a new object is created, it will automatically inherit the data attributes and characteristics of the class from which it was spawned. The new object will also inherit the data and behaviours from all super classes in which it participates .

Four advantages of OODBMS :

(i) Providing a database that can store the objects between runs of a program offers both increased flexibility and increased security. The ability to store the objects also allows the objects to be shared in a distributed environment. An object-oriented database can allow only the actively used objects to be loaded into memory and thus minimizes or preempts the need for virtual memory paging. This is especially useful in large-scale systems.

(ii) Performance, always a significant issue in system implementation, may be significantly improved by using an object-oriented model instead of a relational model. The greatest improvement can be expected in applications with high data complexity and large number of inter-relationships.

(iii) Object-oriented databases can store not only complex application components but also larger structures.

(iv) Since objects contain direct references to other objects, complex data set can be efficiently assembled using these direct references. The ability to search by direct references significantly improves navigational access.

(b) Discuss the following and also list the area of application : **[7]**

(i) Multimedia Database

Multimedia databases store multimedia data such as images, audio and video. Multimedia objects usually have descriptive attributes, such as their date of creation, name of the creator, and their categories. These days, multimedia data are typically stored outside database, in the file systems.

Thus a multimedia database is built-up for storing only the descriptive attributes and for keeping track of the files in which multimedia objects are stored. Obviously, storing multimedia outside the database makes it difficult to provide database functionality, such as indexing on the strength of actual multimedia data content. It may also cause inconsistencies. It is thus desirable to store data in the database itself.

Database must support large objects, because videos can occupy even gegabytes of storage. For example, Exodus provides this support.

In case of retrieval of some types of data like audio and video the data delivery must be at an assured steady rate. Such data are called synchronous data or continuous media data.

Multimedia data formats are usually JPEG and MPEG-1 and 2. The MPEX-2 stand and designed for digital broadcast systems and DVDs. It compresses 1 minute of video and audio to about 17 MB. Now with more and more advancement in the technology it can be further compressed upto much higher extent than this.

Application area suggested

Video-on-demand servers are popular systems today which store multimedia in file systems and consists of video server, view terminals and networks. These thus make a compromise between current systems based on file systems and video on demand.

A multimedia database contains image, spatial data, audio data, video data, and the like. Databases of this sort arise from the need to store photographs, and geographical data, and from voice-mail systems, graphics applications, and video-on-demand systems.

(ii) Knowledge Database

Refer to JUNE04,Q1(d),Page No. -63

5 Explain the following: [15]

(i) Multithreaded Processes

A single process can have multiple threads of execution. This simply means that a single multithreaded process can do the work of multiple single-threaded processes. The advantage of a multithreaded process is that it can do the work of many single-threaded processes but requires far less system overhead. If a database server uses multithreaded server processes, it can support large number of clients with minimal system overhead. The user processes and server processes are different and one server process can serve multiple user processes. This configuration is called Multithreaded Architecture.

(ii) Object Linking

Linking is one way of attaching information from one application to another. Link can be locked, broken or reconnected. Linked information is stored in source application. Concept of linking is used in application which support OLE(Object Linking and Embedding), which is designed to let users focus on data rather than on the software required to manipulate the data. A document becomes a collection of objects, rather than a file. Applications that are OLE- capable provide an API that passes the description of the object to any other application that requests the object. OLE is perhaps the most powerful way to share information between documents. In order to link an object created in another application to another file, but applications need to be running in the same environment i.e., either DDE or OLE.

(iii) Client/Server Computing

[JUN2002,Q6(b);JAN2001,Q5(b);JUN2003,Q4(a)]

Client/server computing defines an architecture in which program logic is distributed between client systems and server systems. Client/server computing is a result of trends in the 1980s to populate desktops with powerful computers that were connected via LANs to back-end database servers or application servers. It was a model designed to replace the mainframe computing model in which all the processing was done by a centralized system.

Interestingly, the old centralized model was resurrected in the form of the thin client, in which applications run on back-end megaservers, not on desktop computers.

With the rise of the Internet, the client/server computing model has evolved from a two-way relationship (usually called a two-tiered model) to a three-tiered or multitiered model in which clients communicate with intermediate application servers or Web servers, which in turn communicate with back-end data servers and/or legacy systems. The intermediate servers then return the results of database queries back to clients.

6(a). Consider the relation R with 5 attributes A, B, C, D, E. You are given the following dependencies: **[9]**

$A \rightarrow B$

$BC \rightarrow E$

$ED \rightarrow A$

(i) List all keys of R.

(ii) Is R in 3NF or BCNF?

(iii) Design the normalised tables.

(i)

(ABCDE)+ = (ABCDE)
(BCDE)+ = (ABCDE) A can be dropped
(CDE)+ = (ABCDE) B can be dropped
(DE)+ = (ABDE) C cannot be dropped
(CE)+ = (CE) D cannot be dropped
(CD)+ = (CD) E cannot be dropped
So, CDE is a key, but that is just one of them…
CDE is one key
It is obvious that C and D must be part of the key, but (CD)+ = (CD) … not a key…
(BCD)+ = (ABCDE) so BCD is another key
(ACD)+ = (ABCDE) so ACD is another key

Thus, the keys are :
CDE, BCD, ACD

(ii)

Yes, the given relation is in 3NF.
Reason : even though none of the FD's left-hand sides are superkeys, all the FD's right hand sides are "primary attributes."
No, the given relation is not in BCNF.
Reason : None of the left-hand sides are superkeys…

(iii) Below is the **normalized tables** for the given relation :
AB
EDA
CDE

(b) Explain the trade offs in distributing the database in the context of Distributed database. [6]

There are several reasons for building distributed database systems, including sharing of data, reliability and availability, and speedup of query processing. However, along with these advantages come several disadvantages, including software development cost, greater potential for bugs, and increased processing overhead.

Advantages of Data Distribution:

The primary advantage of distributed database systems is the ability to share and access data in a reliable and efficient manner.

1. Data sharing and Distributed Control

If a number of different sites are connected to each other, then a user at one site may be able to access data that is available at another site. For example, in the distributed banking system, it is possible for a user in one branch to access data in another branch. Without this capability, a user wishing to transfer funds from one branch to another would have to resort to some external mechanism for such a transfer. This external mechanism would, in effect, be a single centralized database.

The primary advantage to accomplishing data sharing by means of data distribution is that each site is able to retain a degree of control over data stored locally. In a centralized system, the database administrator of the central site controls the database. In a distributed system, there is a global database administrator responsible for the entire system. A part of these responsibilities is delegated to the local database administrator for each site. Depending upon the design of the distributed database system, each local administrator may have a different degree of autonomy is often a major advantage of distributed databases.

2. Reliability and Availability

If one site fails in distributed system, the remaining sites may be able to continue operating. In particular, if data is replicated in several sites, transaction needing a particular data item may find it in several sites. Thus, the failure of a site does not necessarily imply the shutdown of the system.

The failure of one site must be detected by the system, and appropriate action may be needed to recover from the failure. The system must no longer use the service of the failed site. Finally, when the failed site recovers or is repaired, mechanisms must be available to integrate it smoothly back into the system.

Although recovery from failure is more complex in distributed systems than in centralized system, the ability of most of the systems to continue to operate despite failure of one site results in increased availability. Availability is crucial for database systems used for real-time applications. Loss of access to data, for example, an airline may result in the loss of potential ticket buyers to competitors.

3. Speedup Query Processing

If a query involves data at several sites, it may be possible to split the query into subqueries that can be executed in parallel by several sites. Such parallel computation allows for faster processing of a user's query. In those cases in which data is replicated, queries may be directed by the system to the least heavily loaded sites.

Disadvantages of Data Distribution :

The primary disadvantage of distributed database systems is the added complexity required to ensure proper coordination among the sites. This increased complexity takes the form of :

Software development cost: **It is more difficult to implement a distributed database system and, thus, more costly.**
Greater potential for bugs: Since the sites that comprise the distributed system operate in parallel, it is harder to ensure the correctness of algorithms. The potential exists for extremely subtle bugs. The art of constructing distributed algorithms remains an active and important area or research.

Increased processing overhead: **The exchange of messages and the additional computation required to achieve intersite coordination is a form of overhead that does not arise in centralized systems.**

In choosing the design for a database system, the designer must balance the advantages against the disadvantages of distribution of data design ranging from fully distributed designs to designs which included large degree of centralization.

CS-06: DATABASE MANAGEMENT SYSTEM
JUNE-2004

Note: *Question 1 is **compulsory**. Answer any **three** from the rest.*

1(a). What are the advantages of DBMS over a traditional file system? [7]

Major advantages of Database Management over a File Management System are as under :

1. Time required in maintaining record is reduced.
2. Computer does calculations, hence human error is over.
3. Generally data redundancy not occurs.
4. The data may be used in proportional to its sequence or physical presence.
5. Lack of duplication.
6. Assured backup system.
7. Data storage at single place.
8. Data manager enforces central and concurrent control and enforces integrity among the users.
9. Granting of authorization for data access.
10. The data in the database is stored in tables, each table contains number of records and each record in a table is a unique set of related fields.
11. A DBMS can create a file, add data to it, delete data from it or modify data in a file.
12. The stored data can be indexed at user's will.
13. A selective or collective retrieval of data is possible.
14. DBMS gives selective view of data to its users.

DBMS provides a facility termed as DDL whereby one can define conceptual scheme and give details of how to implement conceptual scheme in physical device.

(b) What is ISAM? How are records stored in ISAM? Show this with diagrams. [8]

ISAM stands for indexed sequential access method. As the name implies, the data is maintained in sorted order. A set of index pages provides fast access to the data pages. ISAM is a relatively static approach. Although it can accommodate additions and deletions, the index pages do not change. Additions are handled through overflow pages. Thus, the efficiency of this access method can degrade if there is a lot of data movement.

Records Storage : When a record is stored by ISAM, its record key must be one of the fields in the record. The records themselves are first sorted by record key into ascending order before they are stored on one or more disk drives. ISAM will always maintain the records in this sorted order. Each record is stored on one of the tracks of a disk. Those records that follow it in sorted sequence are placed directly after it on the same track or, if room does not permit, are spilled over onto the next track in the same cylinder. In other words, they are dropped down to the next platter surface. The arm does not move; looking downward, the next head is selected electronically. Since the tracks on a cylinder are labelled 0, 1, 2. .... the records that follow those on track 1 are placed on track 2. Track 0 is the next file cylinder. The cylinders are also labelled 0,1,2,............

Figure below shows two cylinders of records, but only their keys are shown. Note that the keys are in ascending sequence throughout their storage on both cylinders. We have not shown record 0 on either cylinder, as this is used by ISAM for control. Of course, the number of tracks on each cylinder is a function of the size of the disk pack.

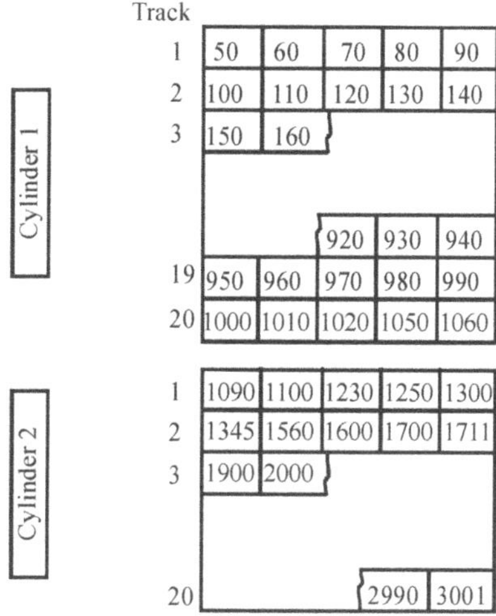

Record Storage

(c) Define BCNF. How does it differ from 3NF? Explain them through an example. [7]

Formal Definition: A relation is in **Boyce/Codd normal form** (BCNF) if and only if every determinant is a candidate key. [A determinant is any attribute on which some other attribute is (fully) functionally dependent.]

Boyce-Codd normal form is stricter than **3NF**, meaning that every relation in BCNF is also in 3NF; however, a relation in 3NF is *not necessarily* in BCNF. A relation schema is an **BCNF** if whenever a functional dependency X->A holds in the relation, then X is a superkey of the relation. The only difference between BCNF and 3NF is that condition of **3NF** (i.e 3NF also require prime attribute), which allows A to be prime if X is not a superkey, is absent from BCNF.

Consider, as an example, the relation **Professor:**
Professor (**Professor code,** Dept., Head of Dept., Parent time)
Assuming that

1. The percentage of the time spent in each department is given.
2. A professor can work in more than one department
3. Each department has only one Head of Department

The relationship diagram for the above relation is given below. The two possible composite keys are professor code and Dept. or Professor code and Head of Department. Observe that department as well as Head of Department are not non-key attributes. They are a part of composite key.

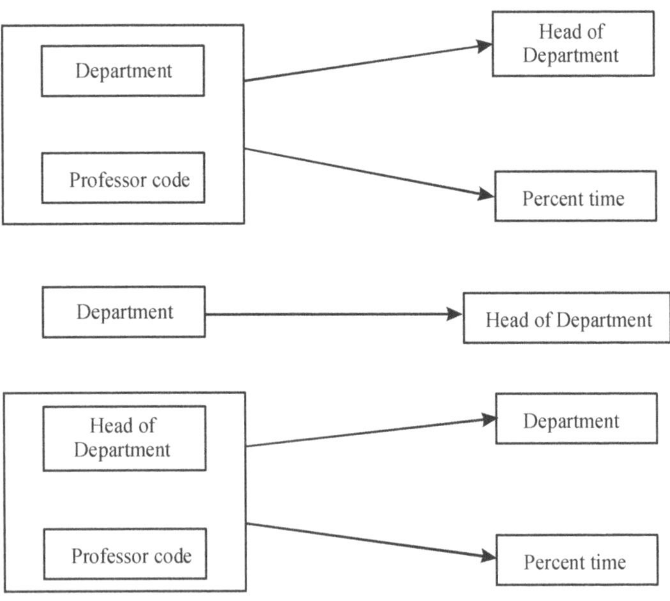

Dependency Diagram of Professor Relation

Professor Code	Department	Head of Dept.	Parent
P1	Physics	Ghosh	50
P1	Mathematics	Krishnan	50
P2	Chemistry	Rao	25
P2	Physics	Ghosh	75
P3	Mathematics	Krishnan	100

The relation given in above table is in 3NF. Observe, however, the names of Dept. and Head of Dept. are duplicated. Further, if professor P2 resigns, rows 3 and 4 are deleted. We lose the information that Rao is the Head of Department in Chemistry. The normalization of the relation is done by creating a new relation for Dept. and Head of Dept. and deleting Head of Dept. from Professor relation. The normalized relations are shown in the following table.

(a)

Professor Code	Departme-nt	Percent time
P1	Physics	50
P1	Mathemat ics	50
P2	Chemistry	25
P2	Physics	75
P3	Mathemat ics	100

(b)

Department	Head of Dept.
Physics	Ghosh
Mathematics	Krishnan
Chemistry	Rao

And the dependency diagrams for these new relations in figure 8. The dependency diagram gives the important clue to this normalization step as is clear from the figure below.

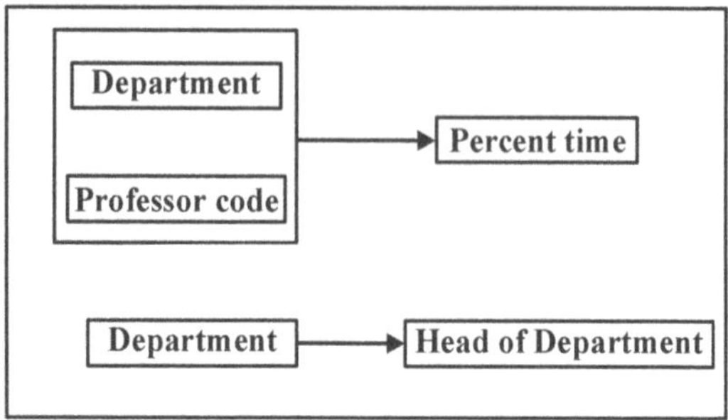

Figure : Dependency diagram of Professor relation

(d) What is a knowledge-base system? Differentiate between a knowledge base system and a database system. [8]

Using the analogy of a DBMS, Knowledge base management system can be defined as a computer system is used to manage and manipulate shared knowledge. A knowledge base system's manipulation facility includes reasoning facility, usually including aspects of one or more of the following forms of reasoning : deductive, inductive or obductive. **Deductive reasoning** implies that a new fact can be inferred from a given set of facts or knowledge using known rules of inference. For instance, a given proposition can be found to be true or false in the light of existing knowledge in the form of other propositions believed to be either true or false. **Inductive reasoning** is used to prove something by first providing a base fact and then the increment step; having proved these, we can prove a generalized fact. **Abductive reasoning** is used in generating a hypothesis to explain observations. Like deductive reasoning, it points to possible inferences from related concept, however, unlike deductive reasoning, the number of inferences could be more than one. The likelihood of knowing which of these inferences corresponds to the current state of the system can be gleaned from the explanations generated by the system. These explanations can facilitate choosing among these alternatives and arriving at the final conclusion.

In addition to the reasoning facility, a knowledge base system may incorporate an **explanation facility** so that the user can verify whether the reasoning used by the system is consistent and complete. The reasoning facility also offers a form of tutoring to the uninitiated user. The so-called expert systems and the associated expert system generation facilities are one form of knowledge base systems that have emerged from research labs and are being marketed commercially. Since a KBMS includes reasoning capacity, there is a clear benefit in incorporating this reasoning power in database application programs in languages such as COBOL and Pascal.

Database	Knowledge
1. In DBMS, data models are used to show data and relationship between them.	1. In KBMS, knowledge representation schemes are used to show knowledge.
2. Data independence, is the ability to modify a schema definition in one level affecting in next higher level.	2. A knowledge independence signifies that the knowledge stored in system must be insulated from changes in usage in its physical or logical structure.
3. DBMS, handles large amount of shared data.	3. KBMS, handles small amount of knowledge.
4.In DBMS, emphasis is placed on a efficient access and management of the data that model a portion of real work.	4. In KBMS, emphasis is placed on a robust knowledge representation scheme and extensive reasoning capability. Robust signifies that the scheme is rich in expressive power and at the same time it is efficient.
5.DBMS concerned with information contained in data.	5.KBMS concerned with meaning of information

2(a). Make an ER diagram of a warehouse. The warehouse has two type of items: low risk items and high risk items. The low risk items are issued on receipt of a simple challan but the high risk items are issued only if the challan is verified and authenticated by proper authorities. The issues are made only to a valid employee of the company. Make necessary assumptions. [7]

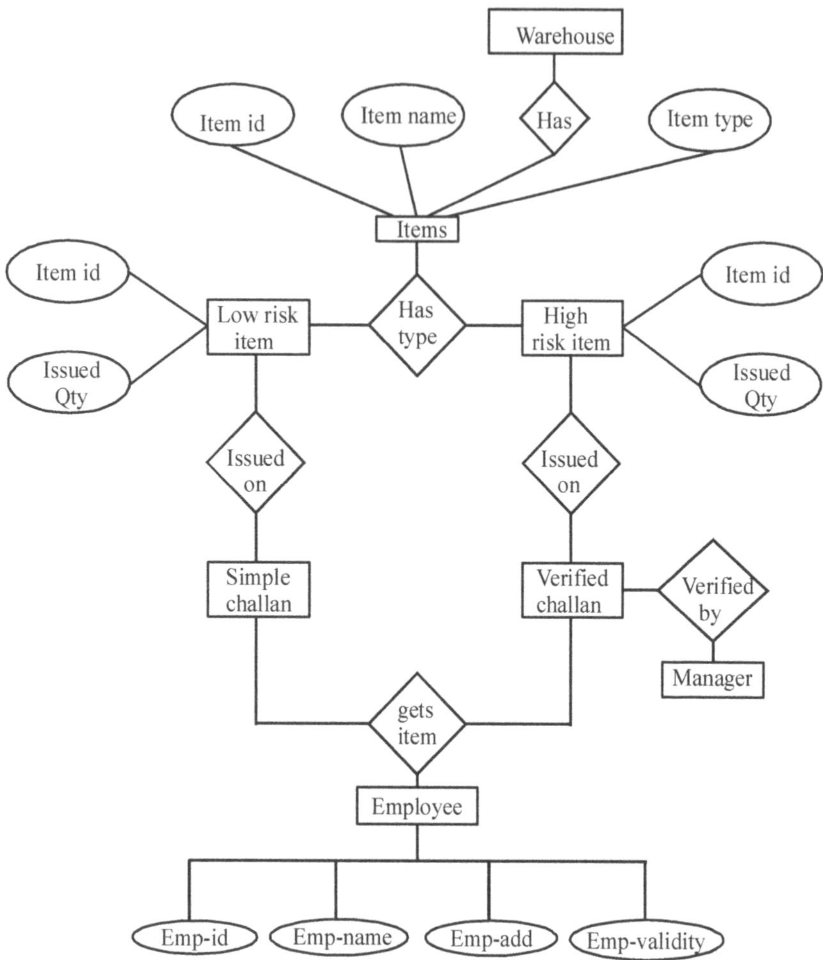

(b) Briefly explain three advantages and three disadvantages of distributed database. [6]

The primary **advantage** of distributed database systems is the ability to share and access data in a reliable and efficient manner.

(i) Data sharing and Distributed Control

If a number of different sites are connected to each other, then a user at one site may be able to access data that is available at another site. For example, in the distributed banking system , it is possible for a user in one branch to access data in another branch. Without this capability, a user wishing to transfer funds from one branch to another would have to resort to some external mechanism for such a transfer. This external mechanism would, in effect, be a single centralized database.

The primary advantage to accomplish data sharing by means of data distribution is that each site is able to retain a degree of control over data stored locally. In a centralized system, the database administrator of the central site controls the database. In a distributed system, there is a global database administrator responsible for the entire system. A part of these responsibilities is delegated to the local database administrator for each site. Depending upon the design of the distributed database system, each local administrator may have a different degree of autonomy is often a major advantage of distributed databases.

(ii) Reliability and Availability

If one site fails in distributed system, the remaining sites may be able to continue operating. In particular, if data are replicated in several sites, transaction needing a particular data item may find it in several sites. Thus, the failure of a site does not necessarily imply the shutdown of the system.

The failure of one site must be detected by the system, and appropriate action may be needed to recover from the failure. The system must no longer use the service of the failed site. Finally, when the failed site recovers or is repaired, mechanisms must be available to integrate it smoothly back into the system.

Although recovery from failure is more complex in distributed systems than in centralized system, the ability of most of the systems to continue to operate despite failure of one site results in increased availability. Availability is crucial for database systems used for real-time applications. Loss of access to data, for example, an airline may result in the loss of potential ticket buyers to competitors.

(iii) Speedup Query Processing

If a query involves data at several sites, it may be possible to split the query into subqueries that can be executed in parallel by several sites. Such parallel computation allows for faster processing of a user's query. In those cases in which data is replicated, queries may be directed by the system to the least heavily loaded sites.

Disadvantages of Data Distribution :

The primary disadvantage of distributed database systems is the added complexity required to ensure proper coordination among the sites. This increased complexity takes the form of :

(i) Software development cost

It is more difficult to implement a distributed database system and, thus, more costly.

(ii) Greater potential for bugs

Since the sites that comprise the distributed system operate in parallel, it is harder to ensure the correctness of algorithms. The potential exists for extremely subtle bugs. The art of constructing distributed algorithms remains an active and important area of research.

(iii) Increased processing overhead

The exchange of messages and the additional computation required to achieve intersite coordination is a form of overhead that does not arise in centralized systems.

In choosing the design for a database system, the designer must balance the advantages against the disadvantages of distribution of data design ranging from fully distributed designs to designs which included large degree of centralization.

(c) Describe data fragmentation. **[2]**

If a relation 'r' is fragmented, r is divided into a number of fragments $r_1, r_2, \ldots\ldots r_n \ldots$ These fragments contain sufficient information to reconstruct the original relation "r". This can be done by union or join operation on these fragmentations. The fragmentation can be accomplished in two ways. The first is horizontal fragmentation and second is vertical fragmentation. The horizontal fragmentation splits the relation by assigning each tuple of "r" to one or more fragments. Vertical fragmentation splits the relation by decomposing the scheme "R" of relation "r" in a special way as similar to decomposition.

Horizontal Fragmentation

The relation 'r' is partitioned into a number of subsets, $r_1, r_2 \ldots\ldots r_n$. Each subset consists of a number of tuples of relation r. Each of relation r must belong to one of the fragments, so that the original can be reconstructed, if needed.

Vertical Fragmentation

The vertical Fragmentation is a process of decomposition. The vertical fragmentation of relation "r" involves the definition of several subsets $r_1, r_2 \ldots\ldots r_n$. Each fragmentation of relation "r" is defined by the following general relational algebraic expression :

$$ri = \prod_{R_i}(r)$$

3(a). Consider the relation R which has attributes that hold schedules of courses and sections at a university; R = { Course No., Section No., Offering_dept, Credit hrs, Course level, Semester, Instructor SSN, year, Days_hrs, Room No., No. of students)
Suppose that the following functional dependencies hold on R
{Course No.} → {Offering dept, Credit hrs, Course level}
{Course No., Section No., Semester, year} →
{Days_hrs, Room No., No. of students, Instructor SSN}
{Room No., Days_hrs, semester, year} →
{Instructor SSN, Course No., Section No.}

(i)Which sets of attributes form keys of R?
(ii)Show how you would normalize the relation above. Also give the final tables.
[10]

(i) As per given relation R :
{course No, section No, semester, years} is the set of Attribute which form the keys of R on which all the elements of the relation depend.

(ii) In case of Ist Normalization :
There is no composite attributes, and every attribute is single and describe one property. And needs further normalization to higher levels.

Course No	Section no	Offering dept.	Credit hrs	Course level	Semester	Instructors SSN	Year	Day hrs	Room No	No of Students

In case of 2nd Normalization :
A function is said to be 2nd NF of it is INF and non-key attribute key are functionally dependent on the key attribute here {course No, section no, semester, year} is the key attribute on which al the non - key attributes are depend.

Course No	Offering dept.	Credit hrs	Course level

Course No	Section no	Semester	Year	Day hrs	Room No	No of Students	Instructors SSN

In case of 3rd Normalization :
A third Normal form will be needed where all attribute in relation tuple are not functionally dependent. Only on the key attribute.

Course No	Offering dept.	Credit hrs	Course level

Course No	Section no	Semester	Year	Day hrs	Room No	No of Students	Instructors SSN

Semester	Year	No of Students	Day hrs

(b) Define the two principle integrity rule for the relational model. In which situations would you need to apply these rules? [5]

The relational model includes two general integrity rules. These integrity rules implicitly or explicitly define the set of consistent database states, or changes of state, or both. Other integrity constraints can be specified, for example, in terms of dependencies during database design. In this answer we define the integrity rules formulated by Codd.

Integrity Rule 1

Integrity rule 1 is concerned with primary key values. Before we formally state the rule, let us look at the effect of null values in prime attributes. A null value for an attribute is a value that is either not known at the time or does not apply to a given instance of the object. It may also be possible that a particular tuple does not have a value for an attribute; this fact could be represented by a null value.

If any attribute of a primary key (prime attribute) were permitted to have null values, then because the attributes in the key must be non-redundant, the key cannot be used for unique identification of tuples. This contradicts the requirements for a primary key.

Integrity rule 2

: is concerned with foreign keys, i.e., with attributes of a relation having domains that are those of the primary key of another relation.

Relation (R) , may contain references to another relation (S). Relations R and S need not be distinct. Suppose the reference in r is via a set of attributes that forms a primary key of the relation S. This set of attributes in R is a foreign key. A valid relationship between a tuple in R to one in S requires that the values of the attributes in the foreign key of R correspond to the primary key of a tuple in S.

This ensures that the reference from the tuple of the relation R is made unambiguously to an existing tuple in the S relation. The referencing attribute(s) in the R relation can have null value(s); in this case, it is not referencing any tuple in the S relation. However, if the value is not null, it must exist as the primary attribute of a tuple of the S relation. If the referencing attribute in R has a value that is nonexistent in S, R is attempting to refer a nonexistent tuple and hence a nonexistent instance of the corresponding entity. This cannot be allowed.

4(a). Consider the following relations:
supplier (sid, sname, add)
parts (pid, pname, color)
catalog (sid, pid, cost)
(i)Find the parts supplied by Acme Widgets supplier only.
(ii)Find all the supplied who supply red or green parts.
(iii)Find the supplier who charges the most for any part. [9]

(i)
Select P.name from suppliers S, parts P, catalog C where S.sid=c.sid and P.pid=C.pid and S.name='Acne Widgets'.

(ii)
Select S.sname from suppliers S, parts P, catalog C where S.sid=C.sid and P.pid=C.pid and (P.color='Red' or P.color='Green')

(iii)
Select S.sname from suppliers S, catalog C where S.sid=C.sid and C.cost=(select max(cost) from catalog)

(b) Two relations R1 and R2 are given in the tables below.

Student_ID	Course_Code	Marks
I_1	C_1	70
I_2	C_2	50
I_3	C_3	40
I_4	C_4	20
I_5	C_5	75
I_6	C_6	90

Course_ID	Course_Name
C_1	DBMS
C_2	DS
C_3	DCN

Use the relational algebraic operation to answer the following queries.
(i) Course taken by student I_1.
(ii) List all the students who have got more than 40 marks in course C_1. [6]

(i) π Course_Name (σ (Student_Id) = '1_1'^R_2.Course_id(temp)).
(ii) π Marks (σ (Student_Id) (Marks>40^Course_Code= 'C_1')).

5(a). Explain five basic functions of a database administrator. [5]

Database Administrator

A person or a group of persons, who manage the centralized control of the database, is referred to as the database administrator (DBA). He is responsible for creating, modifying and maintaining the database.

Following are the functions of DBA :

1. The DBA is the custodian of the data and controls the database structure.
2. It sets up the definition of the global view or conceptual level of the database.
3. It specifies the external view of the various users and applications and is responsible for the definition and implementation of the internal performance of the DBMS.
4. It maps between the internal and the conceptual levels, as well as between the conceptual and external levels.
5. It maintains the integrity of the database.
6. The DBA is responsible for granting permission to the users of the database and stores the profile of each user in the database.
It is responsible for defining procedures to recover the database from failures due to human, natural or hardware causes with minimal loss of data.

(b) Explain, with a suitable example, generalization and specialization. [5]

Generalization is the abstracting process of viewing sets of objects as a single general class by concentrating on the general characteristics of the constituent sets while suppressing or ignoring their differences. It is the union of a number of lower-level entity types for the purpose of producing a higher-level entity type.

For example, student is a generalization of graduate or undergraduate, full-time or part-time students. Similarly, employee is a generalizaion of the classes of objects cook, waiter, cashier. Generalization is an IS_An relationship; therefore, manager IS_An employee, cook IS_An employee, waiter IS_An employee, and so forth.

Specialization is the abstracting process of introducing new characteristics to an existing class of object to create one or more new classes of objects. This involves taking a higher-level entity and, using additional characteristics, generating lower-level entities. The lower-level entities also inherit the characteristics of the higher-level entities. In applying the characteristic size to car we can create a full-size, mid-size, compact, or subcompact car. Specialization may be seen as the reverse process of generalization: additional specific properties are introduced at a lower level in a hierarchy of objects. **For example** FULL-TIME-EMPLOYEE is a specialization of the entity set EMPLOYEE which can be differentiated by the additional attribute Salary.

(c) Explain briefly about distributed computing environment. [5]

Distributed computing environment integrates computers in geographically distant location and underlying applications. These computers could be of different types with different operating systems, even the RDBMSs. It can also utilize heterogeneous client environment like VB.

This also includes the following :

1. Global Dictionary

The data dictionary of these geographically separate database is stored centrally to take action on distributed transactions. This caters to location transparency e.g. if the salary of all the people in a corporation belonging to grade G2 is higher by 25 %, the transaction statement need not specify the location name where G2's data has to be changed. A statement similar to increase salary of G2 by 25 % globally will do.

2. Two Phase Commit (2PC)

In 2PC, the commit server in phase one checks out the availability of participating servers in all the locations. In phase two, after sending the transactions to the individual participating servers and receiving OK from them on updation, the commit server sends END COMMIT status to all the participating servers.

3. Replicated Server/Table

In this method, the tables required for distributed transaction are copied/replicated to all participating servers sites. The replication server ensures that when there is a change in the replicated table, the change transmitted to all the locations. This enables reduced network traffic and lays prone to application storage owing to network failure.

6(a). Discuss 4 basic features of OODBMS. Give 4 advantages of OODBMS. [8]

Four basic features of OODBMS :

1. Reduced maintenance

The primary goal of object-oriented development is the assurance that the system will enjoy a longer life while having far smaller maintenance costs. Because most of the processes within the system are encapsulated, the behaviours may be reused and incorporated into new behaviours.

2. Real-world modelling

Object-oriented systems tend to model the real world in a more complete fashion than do traditional methods. Objects are organised into classes of objects, and, objects are associated with behaviours. The model is based on objects rather than on data and processing.

3. Improved reliability

Object-oriented systems promise to be far more reliable than traditional systems, primarily because new behaviours can be built from existing objects.

4. High code reusability

When a new object is created, it will automatically inherit the data attributes and characteristics of the class from which it was spawned. The new object will also inherit the data and behaviours from all super classes in which it participates .

Four advantages of OODBMS :

(i) Providing a database that can store the objects between runs of a program offers both increased flexibility and increased security. The ability to store the objects also allows the objects to be shared in a distributed environment. An object-oriented database can allow only the actively used objects to be loaded into memory and thus minimizes or preempts the need for virtual memory paging. This is especially useful in large-scale systems.

(ii) Performance, always a significant issue in system implementation, may be significantly improved by using an object-oriented model instead of a relational model. The greatest improvement can be expected in applications with high data complexity and large numbers of inter-relationships.

(iii) Object-oriented databases can store not only complex application components but also larger structures.

(iv) Since objects contain direct references to other objects, complex data set can be efficiently assembled using these direct references. The ability to search by direct references significantly improves navigational access.

(b) Explain hashing. Show how it is used in direct file organization. Give two advantages and two disadvantages of hashing. **[7]**

A process whereby an item is placed into a structure based on a key-to-address transformation.

Hashing is a way of performing optimal searches and retrievals. Essentially, it increases speed, betters ease of transfer, improves retrieval, optimizes searching of data, reduces overhead. Thus, one objective of hashing is to optimize disk accesses and packing density. The packing density, roughly equivalent to a load factor, is simply how much of the table is filled (normally, 70% is sufficient). The ultimate goal, however, is to minimize disk space and access time by inserting and retrieving a record from the table in only one seek. One way to minimize this time is to use small table sizes (say m < 10).

There are 4 key components involved in hashing :

1. the hash table
2. the hashing method
3. collisions
4. collision resolution techniques

Files which are stored on a direct access storage medium are called direct access files as they have a unique address through which they can be accessed directly.

* A portion of disk space is reserved
* A "hashing" algorithm computes record address

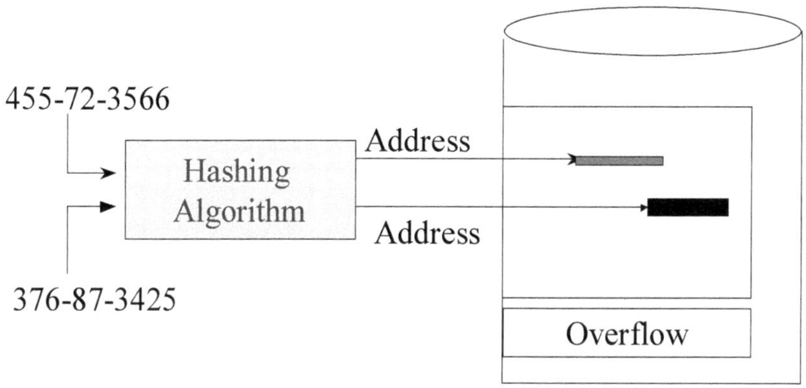

Figure : How hashing is used in Direct file organization.

The Advantages and Disadvantages of Hashing

Advantages

(i) One **advantage** of hashing is that no index storage space is required, whereas inserting into other structures such as trees does normally require an index. Such an index could be in the form of a queue.

(ii) Second **advantage** of hashing is it provides the advantage of rapid updates.

Disadvantages

(i) One **disadvantage** to using hashing as an insert and retrieval tool is that it usually lacks locality and sequential retrieval by key. Consequently, insertion and retrieval are more random.

(ii) Second **disadvantage** is the inability to use duplicate keys. This is a problem when key values are very small (i.e. one or two digits).

CS-06 : DATABASE MANAGEMENT SYSTEM
DEC 2004

Note : *There are six questions in this paper. Question no. 1 is* ***compulsory.*** *Attempt any* ***three*** *from the rest.*

1(a) Explain the various components of a database management system with the help of a diagram. [7]

Below is the diagram of various components of DBMS :

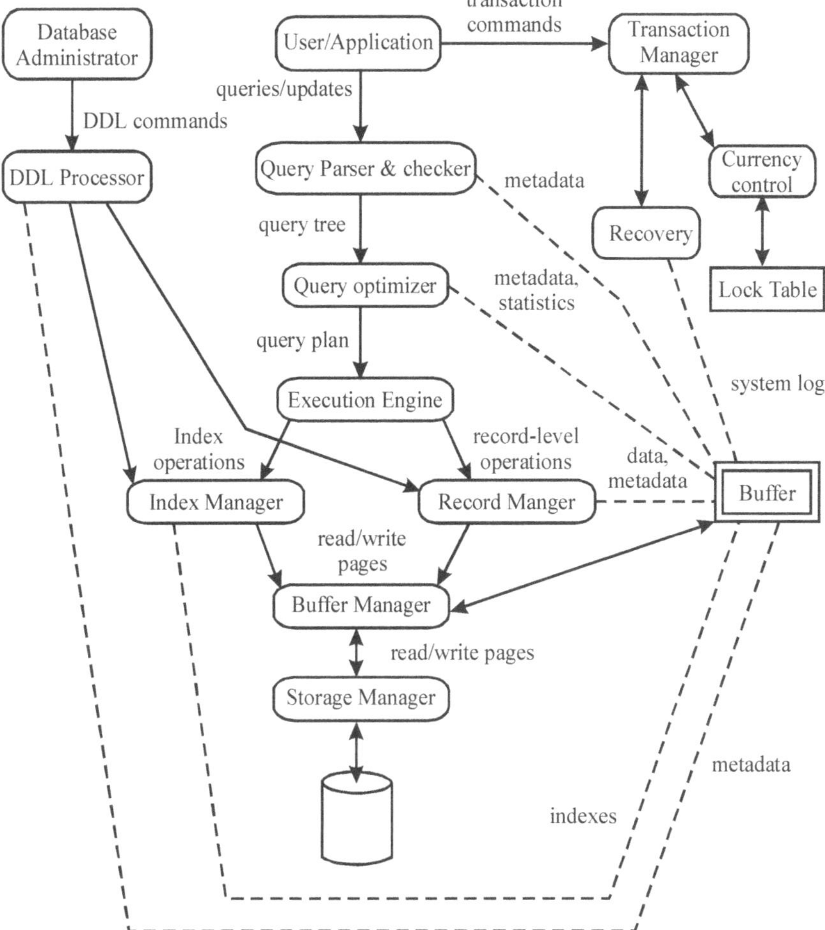

Database Management System is a system to manage database (a organised collection of data), here organised means data will be in the form of tables(collection of rows and columns). Following are the major Six components of Database Management System.

(i) Data :- Data stored in a database include numerical data which may be integers (whole numbers only) or floating point numbers (decimal), and non-numerical data such as characters (alphabetic and numeric characters), date or logical (true or false). More advanced systems may include more complicated data entities such as pictures and images as data types.

(ii) Standard operations :- Standard operations are provided by most DBMS. These operations provide the user basic capabilities for data manipulation. Examples of these standard operations are sorting, deleting and selecting records.

(iii) Data definition language (DDL) **:-** DDL is the language used to describe the contents of the database. It is used to describe, for example, attribute names (field names), data types, location in the database, etc.

(iv) Data manipulation and query language :- Normally a query language is supported by a DBMS to form commands for input, edit, analysis, output, reformatting, etc. Same degree of standardisation has been achieved with SQL (Structured Query Language).

(v) Programming tools :- Besides commands and queries, the database should be accessible directly from application programs through function calls (subroutine calls) in conventional programming languages.

(vi) File structures :- Every DBMS has its own internal structures used to organise the data although some common data models are used by most DBMS.

(b) Define 2NF and 3NF. Normalize the following table to 3NF. [8]

Id_No	Name	Department	Course	Hostel
2010	Harjee	Chemistry	BSc	Block-I
2050	Arshdeep	Physics	BSc	Block-I
3015	Simran	Mathematics	MA	Block-III
3020	Mulkti	English	MA	Block-III
4005	Pawan	Punjabi	BA	Block-II
5010	Lov!een	Computer Sc	BCA	Block-IV

Second Normal Form (2NF)

Second normal form ⇒ is based on the concept of *fully functional dependency.*

A functional X->Y is a **fully functional dependency** is removal of any attribute A from X means that the dependency does not hold any more. A relation schema is in **2NF** if every nonprime attribute in relation is *fully functionally dependent* on the primary key of the relation. It also can be restated as: a relation schema is in **2NF** if every nonprime attribute in relation is not partially dependent on *any key* of the relation.

Practical Rule ⇒ *"Eliminate Redundant Data,"* i.e., if an attribute depends on only part of a multivalued key, remove it to a separate table.

Formal Definition: A relation is in **second normal form** (2NF) if and only if it is in 1NF and every nonkey attribute is fully dependent on the primary key.

Third Normal Form (3NF)

Third normal form ⇒ is based on the concept of *transitive dependency.* A functional dependency X->Y in a relation is a **transitive dependency** if there is a set of attributes Z that is *not a subset* of any key of the relation, and both X->Z and Z->Y hold. In other words, a relation is in **3NF** if, whenever a functional dependency X->A holds in the relation, either (a) X is a superkey of the relation, or (b) A is a prime attribute of the relation.

Practical Rule ⇒ *"Eliminate Columns not Dependent on Key,"* i.e., if attributes do not contribute to a description of a key, remove them to a separate table.

Formal Definition: A relation is in **third normal form** (3NF) if and only if it is in 2NF and every nonkey attribute is nontransitively dependent on the primary key.

The following is the 3NF Structure

Id_NO	**Name**	**Department**	**Course**

The table further divided into another table for course and Hostel.

Course	**Hostel.**

(c) Design an E-R diagram for an Airlines Reservation System consisting of flights, airports, fares, reservations, tickets, crew and passengers. Clearly indicate the entities, relationships and the key constraints. [7]

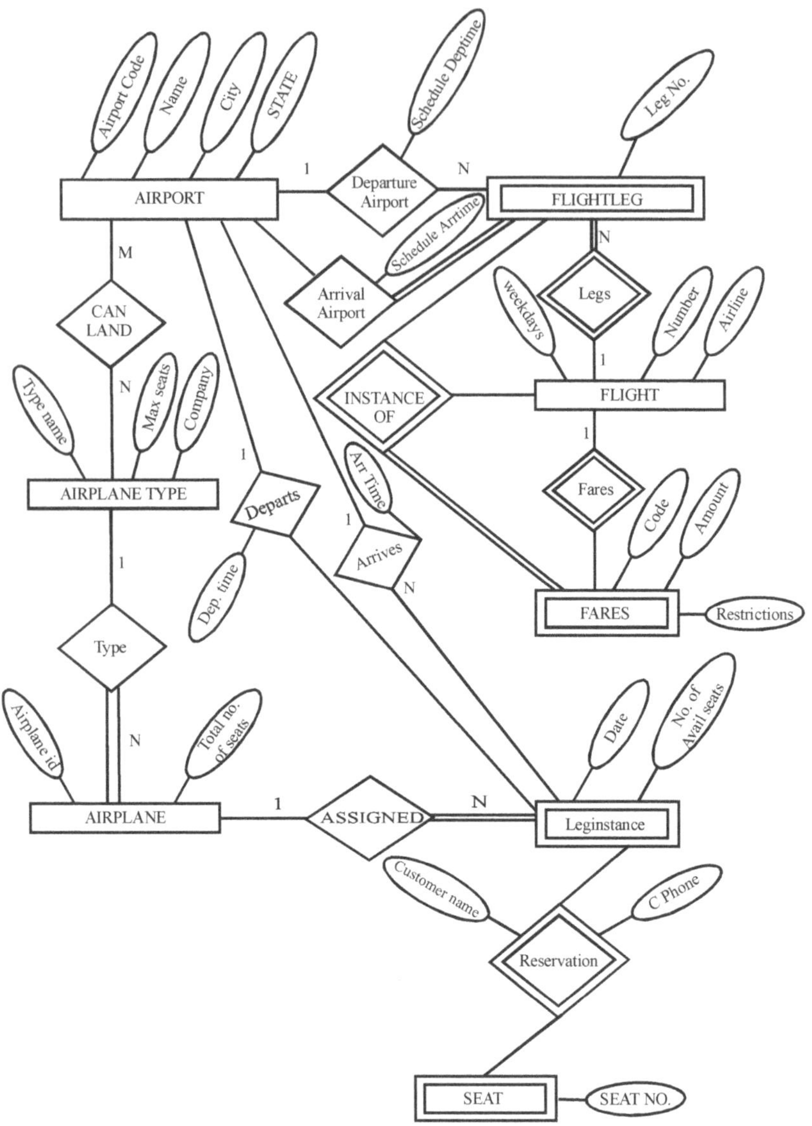

(d) Explain three levels of architecture of a DBMS with the help of a diagram. **[5]**

Repeated in JUNE05, 1(c)

(e) Explain the concept of frame based representation with the help of an example showing the frames and facts/slots. [3]

Frame-based Representation ⇒ Frames are structures that represent a chunk of knowledge about a small domain of the world. For example, a hotel room: the typical hotel room has a bed, wardrobe, chair, telephone etc. A frame representation of the hotel room would contain all these elements, but not much else, it would not contain any information about average French cuisine or any other topic except what you would expect to see in the average hotel room. Frames are rather like a stereotype of a situation or object.

A frame is a data structure representing the collection of the expected and/or predicted description of a stereotype object, action or event. Each important feature of the object is held in a slot. An optional procedure can be attached to a slot to introduce procedural information or specify consistency constraints. The frame also contains the object's relationship to other objects, these being represented by frames as well. The description of the object includes a number of important features of the object and the relationships between other descriptors.

In addition to the predicted description of the various features of the object being represented, the frame may contain information such as the level of confidence assigned to the descriptor, the default values, alternate values (or their range) for descriptors, and variations in the descriptors that can be associated with the frame. The descriptors or slots can allow the inheritance of properties from a related frame.

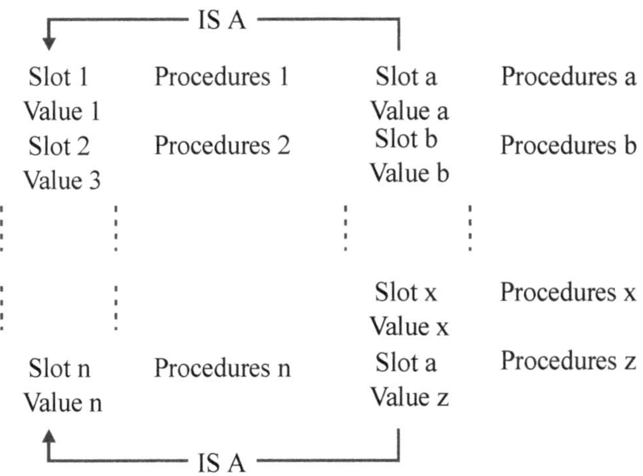

The frame Bungalow(assume) is a specialization of the frame Building and inherits from Building descriptors such as walls, doors, windows, roof. The slot or descriptor itself can be a frame. Thus, the descriptor window can have descriptors of its own, for example size and type.

In addition, descriptors could have appropriate reasoning or inferencing procedures attached. These procedures are triggered or executed whenever the descriptors are filled in, modified, or matched to clean precompiled knowledge.

Frames have been used extensively to represent visual knowledge and knowledge about natural languages.

2(a) Explain the evolution of client/server computing. Also describe its components. [5]

Refer in JUNE05, Q1(d)

(b) Give the structure of a distributed database system with the help of a diagram. Also give its trade-offs. List two distinct applications where we can use the distributed databases. [10]

Structure of distributed database system ⇒ Access to various data items in a distributed system is usually accomplished through transactions, which must preserve the ACID Properties. There are two types of transaction that we need to consider. The local transactions are those that access and update data in only one local database, the global transactions are those that access and update data in several local databases. However, in the case of global transactions, this task is much more complicated, since several sites may be participating in execution. The failure of one of these sites, or the failure of a communication link connecting these sites, may result in erroneous computations.

Each site has its own local transaction manager, whose function is to ensure, the ACID at that site. The various transaction manager cooperate to execute global transactions. Each site of the system contains two subsystems:

- The transaction manager manages the execution of those transactions (or sub transactions) that access data stored in a local site. Note that each such transaction may be either a local transaction (that is, a transaction that executes at only that site) or part of a global transaction (that is, a transaction that executes at several sites).
- The transaction Co-ordinator Coordinates the execution of the various transactions (both local and global) initiated at that site.

The overall system architecture is depicted in Figure.

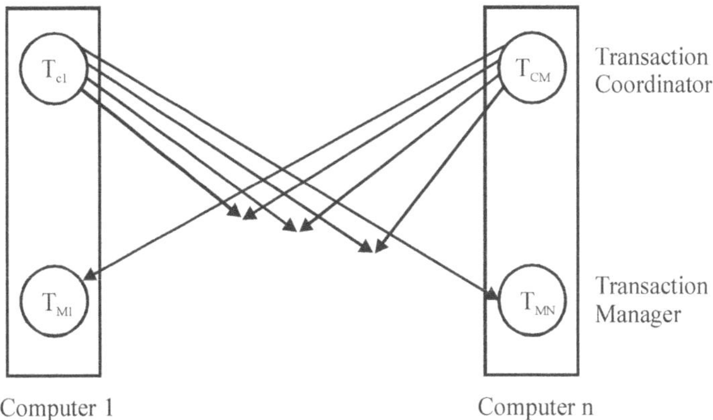

Distributed System Architecture

Each Transaction manager is responsible for:-
(i) Maintaining a log for recovery purposes.
(ii) Participating in an appropriate concurrent execution of the transactions executing at that site.

The Co-ordinator is responsible for
(i) Starting the execution of the transaction.
(ii) Breaking the transaction into a number of sub transactions, to the appropriate sites for execution.
(iii) Co-ordinating the termination of the transactions, which may result in the transaction being committed at all sites or aborted at all sites.

The system failure mode types are
(i) Failure of a site
(ii) Loss of message
(iii) Failure of a communication
(iv) Network Partition

Now Refer in JUNE05, 5(a)

Distributed databases applications ⇒ There is no doubt that there is great demand for distributed database applications. Indeed, tremendously expensive special-purpose distributed systems have been applied and today are used extensively in the banking, airline, and telecommunication industries.

3(a) Explain an Object Oriented Database Management System. What are its applications? Also list the alternatives OODB strategies. [8]
(**O**bject-**O**riented **R**elational **DBMS**) A relational database management system that has object-oriented capabilities.

Object Oriented databases ⇒ An Object-oriented programming language (OOPL) provides facilities to create classes for organising objects, to structure an inheritance hierarchy, to organise classes so that subclass may inherit attributes and methods from superclasses, and to call methods to access specific objects. Similarly, an object-oriented database system (OODB) should provide facilities to create classes for organising objects, to create objects, to structure an inheritance hierarchy, to organise classes so that subclasses may inherit attributes and methods from superclasses, and to call methods to access specific objects. Beyond these, an today's relational database system must provide standard database facilities found in today's relational database systems (RDBs), including nonprocedural query facility for retreiving objects, automatic query optimisation and processing. Dynamic **schema changes** (changing the class definition and inheritance structure), **automatic management of access methods** (e.g., B+-tree index, extensible hashing, sorting, etc.) to improve **query processing performance, automatic transaction management, concurrency control, recovery from system crashes,** and **security and authorisation**, Programming languages, including OOPLs, are designed with one user and a relatively small database in mind. Database systems are designed with many users and very large databases in mind; hence performance, security and authorisation, concurrency control, and dynamic schema changes become important issues. Further, transaction systems are used to maintain critical data accurately; hence, transaction management, concurrency control, and recovery are important facilities.

Alternative Object Oriented Database Strategies:

(i) Extending an existing database language with Object Orientation Capabilities: A number of programming languages have been extended with object-oriented constructs. C++ flavours (an extension of LISP), and object Pascal are example of this approach in programming languages. It is conceivable to follow a similar strategy with database languages. Since SQL is a standard and the most popular database language, the most reasonable solution is to extend this language with object-oriented constructs, reflecting the object orientation capabilities of the underlying database management system. This approach being pursued by most vendors of relational systems as they evolve the next generation products. There have been many such attempts incorporating inheritance, function composition for nested entities, and even some support of encapsulation in an SQL frame work.

(ii) Novel database data model / data language approach: The most aggressive approach is to develop entirely new database language and database management system with object orientation capabilities. In the Industry introduces novel DML and DDL constructs for a data model based on semantic and functional data models.

(iii) Extending an existing object-oriented Programming language with database capabilities to an existing object-oriented language. The object orientation features abstract data typing, inheritance, object identity – will already be supported by the object – oriented language.

(iv) Embedding object-oriented database language constructs in a host (conventional) language:

Database languages can be embedded in host programming languages. For example, SQL statements can be embedded in FORTRAN, ADA etc. The types of SQL (that is relations and rows in relations) are quite different from the type systems are quite different from the type systems of these host language: Some object oriented database have taken a similar approach with a host language and an object-oriented database language.

(b) Discuss the Relational Model of DBMS. How is it different from other models? List at least two types of applications which suit this model. [7]

The relational data base approach is relatively recent and begun with a theoretical paper of Codd. Which proposed that by using a technique called normalization the entanglement observation in the tree and network structure can be replaced by a relatively neater structure. Codd principles relate to the logical description of the data and it is important to bear in mind that this is quite independent and feasible way in which the data is stored. The attractiveness of the relational approach arouse from the simplicity in the data organization and the availability of reasonably simple to very powerful query languages. The size of the relational database approach is that all the data is expressed in terms of tables and nothing but tables. Therefore, all entities and attributes have to be expressed in rows and columns. In the PC world also the availability of DBASE III and its later versions have encouraged the greater use of relational databases. The immense popularity of spreadsheets also arouse because of the inherent simplicity of expressing information in terms of rows and columns.

The differences that arise in the relational approach is in setting up relationships between different tables. This actually makes use of certain mathematical operations on the relation such as projection, union, joins, etc. Similarly in order to achieve the organization of the data in terms of tables in a satisfactory manner, a technique called normalization is used.

Relational model is different from Other models :

1. Implementation independence :- The relational model logically Represents all relationships implicitly, and hence, one does not know what associations are or are not physically represented by an efficient access path (without looking at the internal data model).

2. Logical key pointers :- The relational data model uses primary (and secondary) keys in records to represent the association between two records. Because of this models implementation independence, however, it is conceivable that the physical database (totally masked from the user of a relational database) could use address pointers or one of many other methods.

3. Normalization theory :- Properties of a database that make it free of certain maintenance problems have been developed within the context of the relational model (although these properties can also be designed into a network data model database).

4. High-level programming languages :- Programming languages have been developed specifically to access databases defined via the relational data model; these languages permit data to be manipulated as groups or files rather than procedurally: one record at a time.

These are well suited for commercial applications, and where data is very large and requires greater security(like military operations).

4(a) Consider the relations : **[8]**

BRANCH (Branch_Name, City, Branch_Amount)

ACCOUNT (Branch_Name, Account_No, Balance)

CUSTOMER (Account_No, Customer_Name)

Write the SQL statements for the following :

(i) Find all the customers who have an account of all the branches located in "Chandigarh".

(ii) Find accounts of the "Model Town" branch having a balance greater than Rs. 50,000.

(iii) Find Branch_Name and Amount of city "Delhi".

(iv) Find Account_No, Customer_Name and Balance of the branch name "Model Town".

```
(a) SELECT Customer, Customer_Name
            FROM Customer, Branch
            WHERE City = "Chandigarh"

(b) SELECT Account_No
            FROM Account
            WHERE Brach_Name = "Model Town" AND Balance >
            50,000;

(c) SELECT Branch_Name; Branch_Amount
            FROM   Branch
            WHERECity = "Delhi";
```

(d) SELECT A Account_No, C. Customer_Name
A Balance
FROM Account A, Customer C
WHERE (A Account_No = C. Account_No)
AND Brnach_Name = "Model Town";

(b) Give the step by step procedure for the implementation of Indexing through M-Way search tree with the help of an example. [7]

M-Way Search Trees ⇒ The performance of an index can be enhanced significantly by increasing the branching factor of the tree. Rather than binary branching, m-way(m2) branching can be used. For expository purposes, we ignore for the moment pointers out of the structure to data record and consider only the internal structure of the tree. An m-way search tree is a tree in which each node has out- degree <= m. When an m-way search tree is not empty, it has the following properties.

1. Each node of the tree has the structure shown in figure

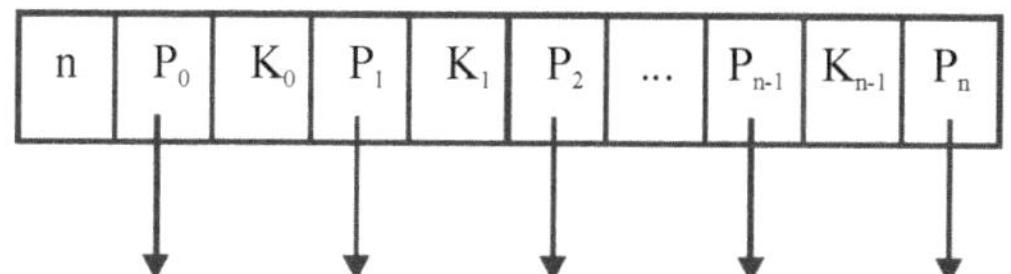

The P_0, P_1, ...P_n are pointers to the node's subtrees and the K_0, ...,K_{n-1} are key values. The requirement that each node have out-degree <= m forces n = m – 1.

2. The key values in a node are in ascending order:

$K_i < K_{i+1}$

Fori = 0, ... n – 2.

3. All key values in nodes of the subtree pointed to by Pi are less than the key value Ki for i = 0, ... N – 2.

4. All key values in nodes of the subtree pointed to by Pi are less than the key value Ki for i = 0, ..., n – 1.

5. The subtree pointed to by the P_i = i = 0, ..., n are also m – way search trees.

Note that the arrangement of key values in nodes is analogous to their arrangement in binary search trees. A five-way search tree has a maximum of five pointers out of each node, i.e., n 4. Some nodes of the tree may contain fewer than five pointers.

Example :- Coming Figure illustrates a three-way search tree. Only the key values and the non-null subtree pointers are shown. In the figure, leaf nodes have been depicted as containing just key values. Each internal node of the search tree has the structure, here with a maximum of three subtree pointers.

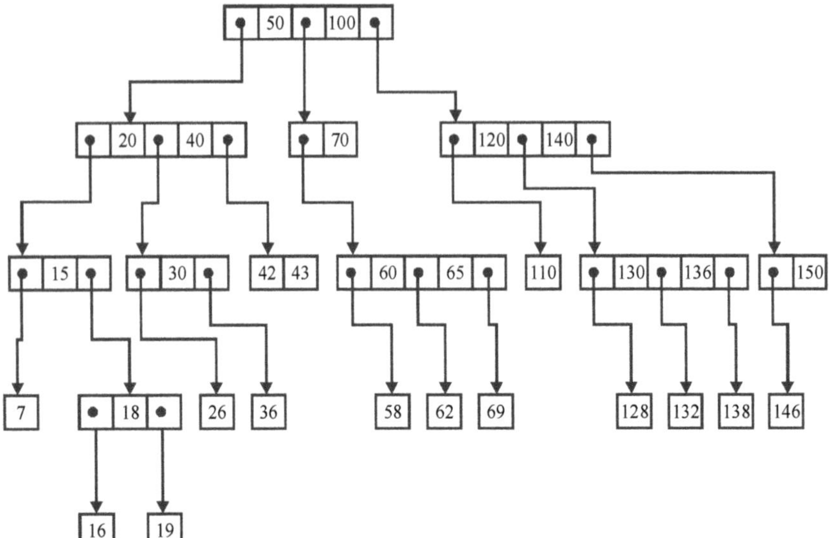

M-Way Search Trees as Indexes ⇒ When an m-way search tree is used as an index, each key-pointer pair (Ki, Pi) becomes a triplet Pi, Ki, Ai where Ai is the address of the data record associated with key value Ki. Thus, each tree node not only points to its child nodes in the tree, but also points into the collection of data records. If the index is dense, every record in the collection will be pointed to by some node in the index.

We can define the node type for an m-way search tree index as follows in Pascal.

```
type nodeptr = ↑ nodetype;
        Recptr =↑ rectype;
        N1, keytype = integer;
        nodetype = record
                n : integer
                keyptrs : array [0..n1] of record
                        ptr : nodeptr;
                        key : keytype;
                        addr: recptr
                    end;
            keyptrn:nodeptr
        end;
```

Again key's type need not be integer, $n \leq m - 1$ and $n1 = n - 1$.

5(a) Explain the difference between Cartesian Product and Natural Join Operations with examples. [7]

The Cartesian-Product operation, denoted by a cross (X), allow us to combine information from any two relations.

Recall that a relation is defined to be a subset of a Cartesian product of a set of domains.

Example :- borrower (Customer_name, loa no)

Loan (branch_name, loan no, amount)

So the Cartesian Product of two borrower and loan schema.

r = borrower × loan is

(borrower.Customer_name, borrower. loan no, loan. branch_name, loan. loan_no, loan. amount)

The natural join is a binary operation that allows us to combine certain selections and a Cartesian product into one operation. It is denoted by the join symbol. The natural-join operation forms a Cartesian product of its two arguments, performs a selection forcing equality on those attributes that appear in both relation schemas, and finally removes duplicate attribute.

(b) Explain Multilist file organization and Inverted file organization with examples. Also give the comparison and trade off in the design of Multikey file. [8]

Multilist file organisation ⇒ Before defining multilist file organisation, let us understand the difference between linked oranisation and sequential file organisation. Linked organisations differ from sequential organisations essentially in that the logical sequence of records is generally from the physical sequence. In a sequential organisation, if the i'th record of the file is at location li then the i + 1'st record is in the next physical position li + c where c may be the length of the i'th record or some constant that determines the inter-record spacing. In a linked organisation the next logical record is obtained by following a link value from the present record. Linking records together in order of increasing primary key value facilitates easy insertion and deletion once the place at which the insertion or deletion to be made is known. Searching for a record with a given primary key value is difficult when no index is available, since the only search possible is a sequential search. To facilitate searching on the primary key as well as on secondary keys it is customary to maintain several indexes, one for each key. An employee number index, for instance, may contain entries corresponding to ranges of employee numbers. One possibility for the example of **figure (a)** would be to have an entry for each of the ranges 501-700, 701-900 and 901-1100. All records having E# in the same range will be linked together as in **figure (b).** Using an index in this way reduces the length of the lists and thus the search time. This idea is very easily generalized to allow for easy secondary key retrieval. We just set up indexes for each key and allow records to be in more than one list. This leads to the multilist structure for file representation. Figure (c) shows the indexes and lists corresponding to multilist representation of the data of **figure (b).** It is assumed that the only fields designated as keys are: E#, Occupation, Sex and Salary, Each record in the file, in addition to all the relevant information fields, has 1 link field for each key field.

Record	E#	Name	Occupation	Degree	Location	MS	MS
A	800	HAWKINS	programmer	B.S.	Los Angeles	S	10,000
B	510	WILLIAMS	analyst	B.S.	Los Angeles	M	15,000
C	950	FRAWLEY	analyst	M.S.	Minneapolis	S	12,000
D	750	AUSTIN	programmer	B.S.	Los Angeles	S	12,000
E	620	MESSER	programmer	B.S.	Minneapolis	M	9,000

Figure (a) : Sample data for Employee File

The logical order of record in any particular list may or may not be important depending upon the application. In the example file, lists corresponding to E#, Occupation and Sex have been set up in order of increasing E#. The salary lists have been set up in order of increasing salary within each range (record A precedes D and C even though E#(C) and E#(D) are less than E#(A)).

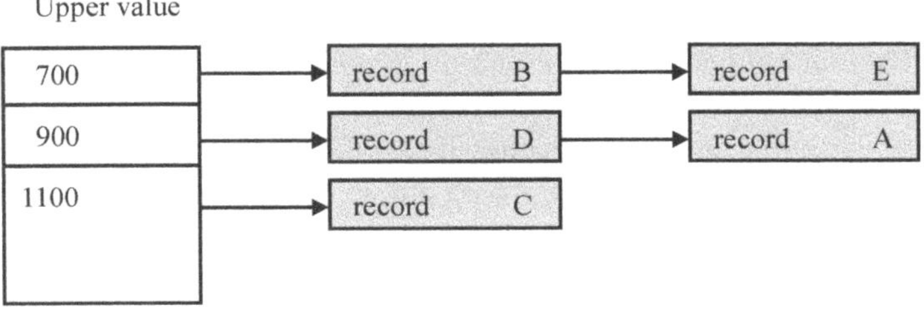

Figure (b) : Linking together all seconds in the same type.

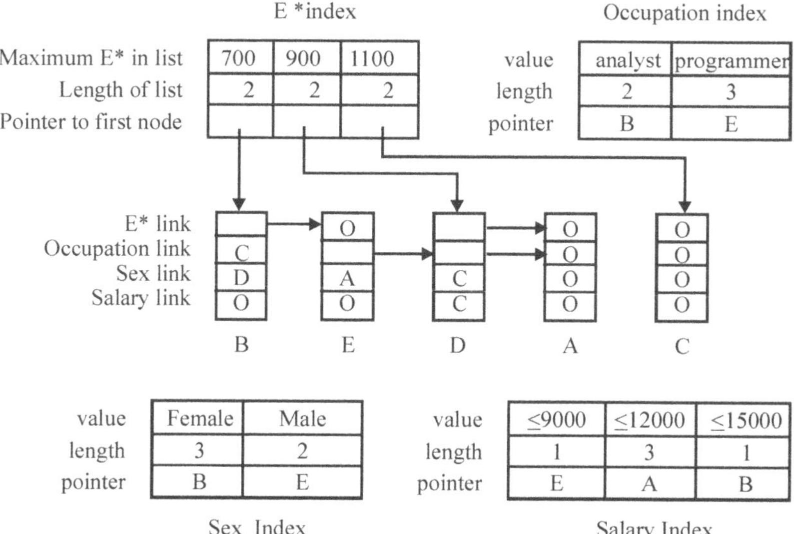

Figure (c) : Multilist representation for figure (a)

Notice that in addition to key values and pointers to lists, each index entry also contains the length of the corresponding list. This information is useful when retrieval on boolean queries is required. In order to meet a query of the type, retrieve all records with Sex = female and Occupation = analyst, we search the Sex and Occupation indexes for female and analyst respectively. This gives us the pointers B and B. The length of the list of analysts is less than that of the list of females, so the analyst list starting at B is searched. The records in this list are retrieved and the Sex key examined to determine if the record truly satisfies the query. Retaining list length enables us to reduce search time by allowing us to search the smaller list. Multilist structures provide a seemingly satisfactory solution for simple and range queries. When Boolean queries are involved, the search time may bear no relation to the number of records satisfying the query. The query K1 = XX and K2 and XY may lead to a XX list of length n and a K2 list of length m. Then, min{n,m} records will be retrieved and tested against the query. It is quite possible that none or only a very small number of these min {n, m} records have both K1= XX and K2 = XY. This situation can be remedied to some extent by the use of compound keys. A compound key is obtained by combining two or more keys together. We would combine the Sex and Occupation kesy to get a new key Sex-Occupation. The values for this key would be: female analyst, female programmer, made analyst and male programmer. With this compound key replacing the two keys Sex and Occupation, we can satisfy queries of the type, all male programmers or all programmers, by retreiving only as many records as actually satisfy the query. The index size, however, grows rapidly with key compounding. If we have ten keys K1, ...K10, the index for Ki having ni entries, then the index for the compound key K1 K2.......K10 will have $\pi_{i=1}^{10}$ ni entries while the original indexes, had a total of $\Sigma_{i=1}^{10}$ ni entries, handling simple queries becomes more complex if the individual key indexes are no longer retained.

Inserting a new record into a multilist structure is easy so long as the individual lists do not have to be maintained in some order. In this case the record may be inserted at the front of the appropriate lists. Deletion of a record is difficult since there are no back pointers. Deletion may be simplified at the expense of doubling the number of link fields and maintaining each list as a double linked list. When space is at a premium, this expense may not be acceptable. An alternative is the coral ring structure described below.

Inverted File Organisation ⇒ Conceptually, inverted files are similar to multilists. The difference is that while in multilists records with the same key value are linked together with link information being kept in individual records, in the case of inverted files this link information is kept in the index itself. Figure(e) shows the indexes for the file of figure. A slightly different strategy has been used in the E# and salary indexes than was used in figure though the same strategy could have been used here too. To simplify further discussion, we shall assume that the index for every key is dense and contains a value entry for each distinct value in the file. Since the index entries are variable length (the number of records with the same key value is variable), index maintenance becomes more complex than for multilists. However, several benefits acquired from this scheme. Boolean queries require only one access per record satisfying the query (Plus some accesses to process the indexes). Queries of the type K1 = XX and K2 = XY. These two lists are then merged to obtain a list of all records satisfying the query. K1 = XX and K2 = XY can be handled similarly by intersecting the two lists. K1 = not XX can be handles by maintaining a universal list. U, with the addresses of all records. Then, K1 = .not. XX is just the difference between U and the list for k1 = XX. Any complex boolean query may be handles in this way. The retrieval works in two steps. In the first step, the indexes are processes to obtain a list of records satisfying the query and in the second, these records are retrieved using the list, The number of disk accesses needed is equal to the number of records being retrieved plus the number to process the indexes.

Inverted files represent one extreme of file organisation in which only the index structures are important. The records themselves may be stored in any way (sequentially ordered by primary key. Random, linked ordered by primary key etc.

E# index

510	
620	
750	
800	
950	

Occupation index

analyst	B,C
programmer	A,D,E

Salary index

9,000	E
10,000	A
12,000	C, D
15,000	B

Sex Index

female	B, C, D
male	A, E

Figure (e) : Indexes for fully inverted file

Inverted files may also result in space saving compared with other file structures when record retrieval does not require retrieval of key fields. In this case, the key fields may be deleted from the records. In the case of multilist structures, this deletion of key fields is possible only with significant loss in system retrieval performance Insertion and deletion of records requires only the ability to insert and delete within indexes.

Comparison and trade off in the design of Multikey file;

Both inverted files and multi-list files have

➢ An index for each secondary key.

➢ An index entry for each distinct value of the secondary key.

➢ In either file organisation

The index may be tabular or tree-structured.

The entries in an index may or may not be sorted.

The pointers to data records may be direct or indirect.

➢ The indexes differ in that

An entry in an inversion index has a pointer to each data record with that value.

An entry in a multi-list index has a pointer to the first data record with that value.

Thus, an inversion index may have variable-length entries whereas a multi-list index has fixed-length entries. In either organization

➢ The data record pointers for a key value may or may not appear in some sorted order.

➢ Keeping entries in sorted order introduces overhead.

➢ The data record file

Is not affected by having an inversion index built on top of it.

➢ Must contain the linked lists of records with identical secondary key values in the multi-list structure.

➢Some of the implications of these differences are the following :

Index management is easier in the multi-list approach because entries are fixed in length.

The inverted file approach tends to exhibit better inquiry performance. Many types of queries can be answered by accessing inversion indexes without necessitating access to data records, thereby reducing I/O-access requirements. Inversion of a file can be transparent to a programmer who accesses that file but does not sue the inversion indexes, while a multi-list structure affects the file's record layout. The multi-list pointers can be made transparent to a programmer if the data manager does not make them available for programmer user and stores them at the end of each record.

Additionally, the multi-list structure has proven useful in linking together occurrences of different record types, thereby providing access paths based upon logical relationships. It is also possible to provide multiple sort orders through a single data collection, by linking the records together in order by various keys.

6(a) What is a view? What are the major advantages of views? Explain with an example. [5]

You can use views to focus, simplify, and customize each user's perception of the database; they also provide an easy-to-use security measure. Views can also be helpful when changes have been made to the structure of a database, but users prefer to work with the structure of the database they are accustomed to.

You can use views to:

➢ Focus on the data that interests them and on the tasks for which they are responsible. Data that is not of interest to a user can be left out of the view.

➢ Define frequently used joins, projections, and selections as views so that users do not have to specify all the conditions and qualifications each time an operation is performed on that data.

➢ Display different data for different users, even when they are using the same data at the same time. This advantage is particularly important when users of many different interests and skill levels share the same database.

Advantages of View with example :

Through a view, users can query and modify only the data they can see. The rest of the database is neither visible nor accessible.

With the **grant** and **revoke** commands, each user's access to the database can be restricted to specified database objects—including views. If a view and all the tables and other views from which it is derived are owned by the same user, that user can grant permission to others to use the view while denying permission to use its underlying tables and views. This is a simple but effective security mechanism.

By defining different views and selectively granting permissions on them, users can be restricted to different subsets of data.

For example:

- Access can be restricted to a subset of the rows of a base table, that is, a value-dependent subset. For example, you might define a view that contains only the rows for business and psychology books, in order to keep information about other types of books hidden from some users.
- Access can be restricted to a subset of the columns of a base table, that is, a value-independent subset. For example, you might define a view that contains all the rows of the *titles* table, except the *royalty* and *advance* columns.
- Access can be restricted to a row-and-column subset of a base table.
- Access can be restricted to the rows that qualify for a join of more than one base table. For example, you might define a view that joins the *titles*, *authors*, and *titleauthor* to display the names of the authors and the books they have written. This view would hide personal data about authors and financial information about the books.

(b) What are the main differences between a file processing system and a database system? [5]

Keeping Organizational information in a typical file-processing system has number of major disadvantages and those are improved in a Database System.

Redundancy and Inconsistency ⇒ In a typical file-processing system has own private files. This can often lead to considerable, redundancy (duplication of same information) in stored data. With resultant waste in storage space and raise many problems for managing a file containing department information for employees.

In a database system, however, redundancy should be controlled-that is, the system should be aware of the redundancy and should assume responsibility for propagating updates. While in a DBMS as it has a centralized system it helps in avoiding unnecessary duplication of record.

Inconsistency ⇒ Data inconsistencies are often encountered in everyday life. For an example consider a situation when an organization changes its address and accordingly informs every one to communicate to the new address, but we find that some of the communications are received at the new address. But we find that some of mailed to the address. Combining all data in a database would involve redundancy as well as inconsistency. So, as DBMS has centralized storage, inconsistency is avoided.

Shared data ⇒ In a typical file-processing system data are scattered in various files and different format, it is difficult to share data with the same format.

While in a Database system, its centralized storage allows the sharing of data to multiple applications and to various users also.

Integrity Problem ⇒ Data Integrity means that data maintained in a database should both accurate and consistent. Inconsistency between two representing the same "fact" is an example of lack of integrity (which of course can occur only if redundancy exists in the stored data). That it should ensure that if there is a reference to certain object, *that object must have existed.*

Even if redundancy is eliminated, however, the database may still contain incorrect data. Therefore, data being inserted for storage must be checked to ensure that they fall within a specified range and are of the correct format. For an example, Amount to be deposited must be greater than 0. This **Integrity is maintained** in a Database System.

Security Problem ⇒ Having complete jurisdiction over the operational data, the DBA (a) can ensure that the only means of access to the database is through the proper channels, and hence (b) can define authorization checks to be carried out whenever access to sensitive data is attempted. Different checks can be established for each type of access (retrieve, modify, delete, etc.) to each piece of information in the database. [Note that without such checks the security of the data may actually be more at the risk in a database system than in a traditional (dispersed) filing system.]

In a typical file-processing system, to provide each such security separate function or program must be written and it is difficult. While in a Database System **Security restrictions can be applied** easily.

Concurrent-access problem ⇒ In a multi-user system multiple users can update the data simultaneously, which can lead to problem of inconsistency. For an example, If two customers withdraw an amount of Rs. 100 from an Account (having balance Rs. 150) at a same time, the result of the concurrent execution may leave the account in an incorrect state. While in a database system solution for the concurrent access is provided.

(c) What is a knowledge based system? Give at least three differences between a knowledge based system and a database system. [5]

One difference between the DBMS and KBMS that has been proposed is that the knowledge base system handles a rather small amount of knowledge, whereas a DBMS efficiently (as measured by response performance) handles large amounts of shared data. However, this distinction is fallacious since the amount of knowledge has no known boundaries and what this says is that existing knowledge base systems handle a very small amount of knowledge. This does not mean that at some future date we could not develop knowledge base systems to efficiently handle much larger amounts of shared knowledge.

In a knowledge base system, the emphasis is placed on a robust knowledge representation scheme and extensive reasoning capability. Robust signifies that the scheme is rich in expressive power and at the same time it is efficient. In a DBMS, emphasis is on efficient access and management of the data that model a portion of the real world. A knowledge base system is concerned with the meaning of information, whereas a DBMS is interested in the information contained in the data. However, these distinctions are not absolute. For our purposes, we can adopt the following informal definition of a KBMS. The important point in this definition is that we are concerned with what the system does rather than how it is done.

A knowledge base management system is a computer system that manages the knowledge in a given domain or field of interest and exhibits reasoning power to the level of a human expert in this domain.

A KBMS, in addition , provides the user with an integrated language, which serves the purpose of the traditional DML of the existing DBMS and has the power of a high-level application language. A database can be viewed as a very basic knowledge base system in so far as it manages facts. It has been recognised that there should be an integration of the DBMS technology with the reasoning aspect in the development of shared knowledge bases. Database technology has already addressed the problems of improving system performance, concurrent access, distribution, and friendly interface; these features are equally pertinent in a KBMS. There will be a continuing need for current DBMSs and their functionalities co-existing with an integrated KBMS. However , the reasoning power of a KBMS can improve the case of retrieval of pertinent information from a DBMS.

OR

Database	Knowledge
1. In DBMS, data models are used to show data and relationship between them.	1. In KBMS, knowledge representation schemes are used to show knowledge.
2. Data independence, is the ability to modify a schema definition in one level affecting in next higher level.	2. A knowledge independence signifies that the knowledge stored in system must be insulated from changes in usage in its physical or logical structure.
3. DBMS, handles large amount of shared data.	3. KBMS, handles small amount of knowledge.
4.In DBMS, emphasis is placed on a efficient access and management of the data that model a portion of real work.	4. In KBMS, emphasis is placed on a robust knowledge representation scheme and extensive reasoning capability. Robust signifies that the scheme is rich in expressive power and at the same time it is efficient.
5.DBMS concerned with information contained in data.	5.KBMS concerned with meaning of information

CS-06 : DATABASE MANAGEMENT SYSTEM
JUNE 2005

Note : *Q.No. 1 is* ***compulsory*** *and carries 30 marks. Answer any* ***three*** *from the rest*

1(a) Suppose you have been designated as a database administrator of an organization. Describe the responsibilities that may be generally assigned to you in order to maintain the centralised database efficiently. Also include at least 2 responsibilities with respect to the Database security. **[7]**

The person who has to administor centralised database of an organisation is called the Database Administrator (DBA). The Responsibilities of the DBA to maintain the centralized database efficiently are the following.

(i) Schema definition :- The DBA creates the original database schema by writing a set of specifications that is translated by the Data Definition language (DDL) compiler at a set of tables that is stored permanently in the data dictionary.

(ii) Schema and Physical–organisation Modification :- Programmers accomplish the relatively rare modifications either to the database schema organization by writing a set of definitions that is used by either the DDL compiler or the data-storage and DDL compiler to generate modifications to the appropriate internal system tables.

(iii) Storage structure and access method :- The Database Administrator creates the appropriate storage structures and access methods by writing a set of definitions, which is translated by the data-storage and data-definition compiler.

The Two responsibilities with respect to the database security are the following :-

(i) Granting of authorization for data access :- The granting of different type of authorization allows the Database Administrator to regulate which parts of the database various users can access. The authorization information is kept in special system structure that is consulted by the database system whenever access to the data is attempted in the system.

(ii) Integrity-Constraint specification :- The data values stored in the database must satisfy certain consistency. The integrity constraints are kept in a special system structure that is consulted by the database system whenever an update takes place in the system.

(b) Create an ER diagram for the loan management system of a finance company. Loans are given on the purchase of various items with different interest rates. The company keeps track of defaulters and takes appropriate steps against them. Make, and state, suitable assumptions (if any). **[8]**

Assumption finance company also sells items

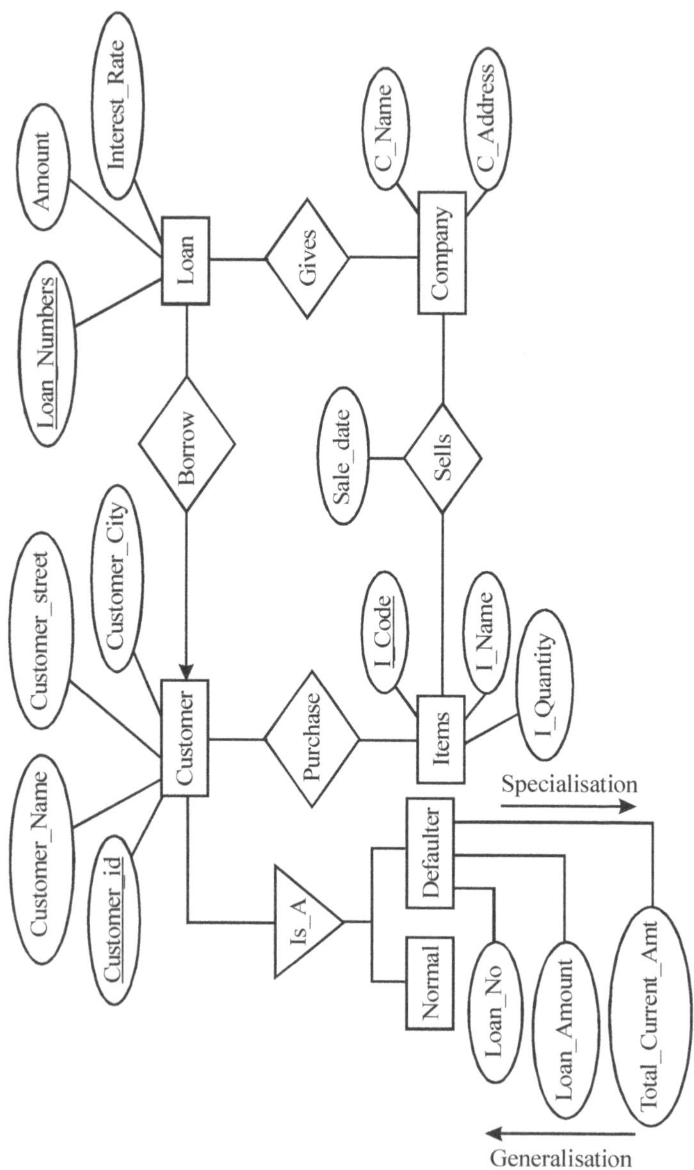

(c). Explain the three-level architecture of DBMS, including the diagram. How is the mapping between these levels achieved? [7]

According the approach of ANSI/SPARC (American National Standard Institute / Standards Planning and Requirements Committee). There are three level of architecture followed in DBMS: external level, conceptual level and internal or physical level.

1. External level : It is the highest level of the abstraction of data. Each external level is defined by means of an External schema. Which consists basically definitions of each of the various types of external record found at that external level.

The external level is that the view that the individual user of the database has. It determines How the data LOOK LIKE, irrespective of how they are stored. It represents a part of the database. The same database may provide different classes of users.

2. Conceptual level : It is the next lower level of abstraction. The conceptual level is defined by means of the conceptual schema. This is also known as user's view that describes WHAT type of data are actually stored. It simply contains the information about structure (or type) of data stored in database. A database administrator, who must decide which information, is to be kept in the database, what are the relations among the tables at conceptual level. The conceptual schema is defined using Data definition Language(DDL).

3. Internal or Physical Level : It is the lowest level of the data abstraction. The Physical level is defined by the means of Internal schema.

It is concerned with the physical storage of the information means what data are stored and How. It also specifies what indexes exist, how stored fields are represented. It gives complete internal structure of storage and their access paths specification of primary, secondary keys, indexes, pointers and sequencing, data compressions and optimization techniques.

Mapping Between the three Levels : Mapping corresponds one record of one level to record of the another level. There are two mappings in three levels architecture .

(1) Mapping between External and Conceptual level.

(2) Mapping between internal and conceptual level.

(3) Internal to physical database. There is not necessary that an internal record at internal level is stored at a physical record, it can be from multiple records on storage device. It provides the relevant mapping.

The figure shows the interrelationship among these three levels of abstraction.

Figure : Illustrating the three-level architecture of DBMS

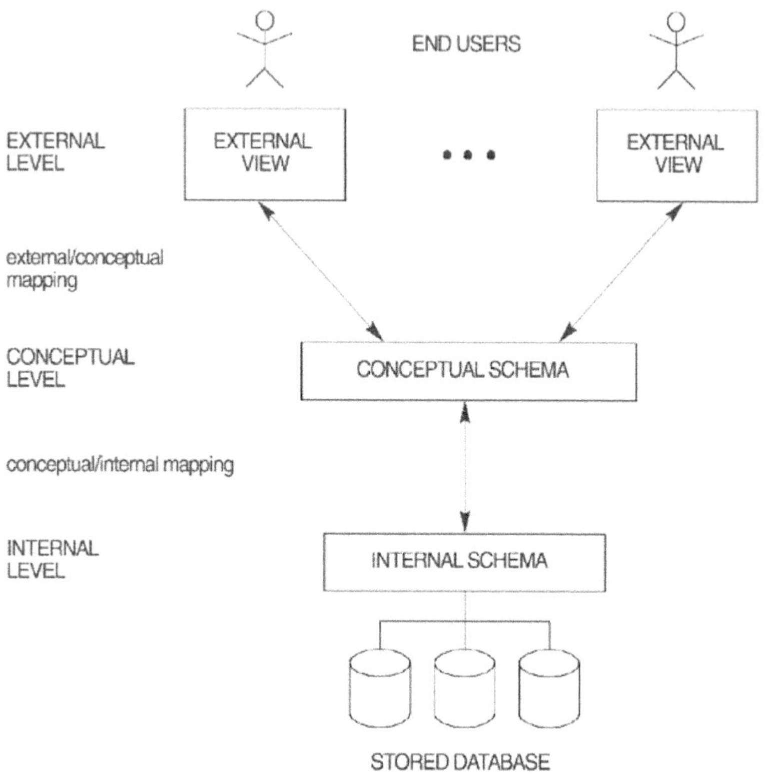

(d) Explain the evolution of Client/Server Architecture. List the components and the usage in Client/Server computing. Mention any two applications of this model. [8]

Evolution of client/serve Architecture:- After twenty years of seventies, the computer based application proliferated the business and scientific application throughput the world. The scenario was dominated by mainframe computers. Till the middle of 70s for over two and half decades proprietary-networking solutions dominated the networking scenario. The solutions used to be very expensive, each company used to set it own networking and connectivity standards. Each company believed in giving the complete network, software and networking solution to the client rendering the solutions extremely high priced and beyond the budget of most Information Technology organizations. Further this did not enable sharing machines from multiple vendors on a network. In 80s networking of PCs in Local Area Network (LAN) in which connectivity between PCs running between DOS and VAX running VMS and PCs, connectivity between almost all standard machines gave rise to a new look in computing scenario.

The R&D labs dealing with software started working on solution, which would distribute the computing load on multiple machines on network, client/serve architecture took birth around these developments. It basically tries to utilized and distribute computing requirements on PCs, UNIX, Servers, VMS Servers, even mainframe depending on the computing requirements.

Components of Client Server Computing are described as follows :

The definition of client/server highlights the four fundamental building components in the client/server architecture. Each component has its own unique characteristics. There are :

(i) Server
(ii) Clients
(iii) Networks
(iv) Applications

APPLICATIONS

(i) Server :- A server performs a set of special tasks for any other device requesting their services. A server is a reactive process activated by requests sent from clients. The server performs requested transactions and does not interact with any other servers. Server can broadly divided into transaction servers and data servers. Here, transaction server provide an interface to which clients can send requests to perform an action, in responds to which they execute the action and send back results to the client while data server allow clients to interact with the server by making requests to read or update, in units such as files or pages.

For example, File servers provide a file systems interact where clients can create update, read and delete files.

The server machine could be running NOVELL LAN or INTEL based server or UNIX from SCO or AT&T or UNIX being run on RISC machines like HP, SUN microsystem, IBM compac etc.

There are server machines should be running on RDBMS engine like Sybase, Oracle, Informix etc. The server machine takes care of data storage, backup, recovery and database services.

(ii) Client :- The client acts as the user entry point into the client/server environment. To be a client a workstation must be intelligent because it must have processing capabilities and make requests to common resources. In the client/server relationship, the client uses the services provided by one or more server processors. It is the proactive member of the relationship, issuing requests to the server and receiving responses. A client is dedicated to an individual user. It comes into existence at the beginning of a user session and ends when the user session ends.

(iii) Network :- The essence of a client/server system network is connectivity in a multi-product, multi-vendor environment. A network connects the workstations with common resources and is a system within which information is transferred. Networks can be classified according to their geographic coverage. LAN serves a single building or a campus of several buildings. MAN serves the entire city or metropolitan area. WAN serves larger geographically spread areas.

(iv) Applications :- Software applications tie the other three components together to form the client/server architecture. The feature that distinguishes client/server from other technology architecture is that it contains cooperative processing capabilities, which physically split the processing performed by the client from that performed by the server while presenting a single logical picture to the user.

2(a) What is a knowledge based system? Mention any two advantages and disadvantages of it. Give any two examples where a knowledge based system is used. Discuss the rule based knowledge representation scheme with the help of an example. [10]

Knowledge base system get their Power from the expert knowledge that has been coded into facts, rules, heuristics and Procedures. The knowledge is stored in a knowledge base separate from the control and inferencing components. This makes it possible to add new knowledge or refine existing knowledge without recompiling the control and inferencing programs. This greatly simplifies the construction and maintenance of knowledge base system.

Advantage :

(i) In a knowledge base system, the emphasis is placed on a robust knowledge representation scheme and extensive reasoning capability. Robust signifies that the scheme is rich in expressive power and at the same time it is efficient.

(ii) Knowledge can be expressed as rules and exception to rules, exception-handling features must be present in the knowledge stored in the system which must be insulated from changes in its physical or logical structure.

Disadvantage :

(i) Knowledge base system, handles small amount of knowledge.

(ii) In knowledge base system, knowledge representation schemes are used to show only knowledge not relationship.

Example of knowledge based System :

(i) MYCIN an knowledge based system developed to diagnose infectious blood diseases.

(ii) RI/XCON

Rule-based Representation ⇒ Production-based system consists of a set of production rules, a data structure that models the system's current state, and a control subsystem or interpreter that interprets the current state and controls its activity by initiating appropriate action. A rule is said to be enabled or triggered when the condition part of the rule is satisfied by the current state of the system. An enabled rule is said to be fired if the action part of a rule is executed. If the system status is such that more than one rule is triggered, the interpreter may be required to fire one or more of these simultaneously enabled rules; this is referred to as a conflict resolution. The conflict resolution can be enacted using its own set of productions. It uses criteria such as priority or ranking, prior selection, arbitrary or random choice, or doing all actions in parallel. The order in which the conditions are examined can be determined and priority could be adjusted dynamically. The action part can be a single action or a set of procedures that will change the status of the system. The latter change can include disabling a subset of the existing productions and enabling other productions.

An example of a rule-based system is given below. This system examines the causes and the corrective actions to be performed after failing to start a car. The execution of each action will modify the state of the starting system under consideration and if there is more than one problem, all the corrective actions will have to be taken.

```
if starter cranks the engine very slowly
   then problem may one or more of: extreme cold
         temperature, battery, cables, connections, voltage
         regulator, alternator; use jumper cable to start
if starter does not crank but solenoid operates
   then check cables and tighten and clean terminals and
         check battery voltage
if problem is low battery voltage
   then problem  may be battery: check specific gravity and
         replace if not acceptable;
```

problem may be loose, worn, or broken alternator belt: do a visual inspection and if belt is okay, tighten belt, otherwise replace it;
problem may be cables: visual inspection, clean and tighten connections, and replace broken connectors or cables;
problem may be voltage regulator: check and replace;
problem may be alternator: check and repair or replace alternator;
problem may be shorts in electrical system: locate and correct

if problem loose or worn alternator belt
then tighten or replace alternator belt

if problem is battery
then check specific gravity and if acceptable charge otherwise replace battery

if problem is voltage regulator
then replace voltage regulator

if problem is alternator
then repair or replace alternator

if battery, cables and connections are good, solenoid operates, but starter does not crank or cranks slowly
then replace the starter

if battery, cables, and connections are good but solenoid does not click
then check ignition switch to solenoid circuit and correct malfunctions

if battery, cables, connections, and ignition switch to solenoid circuit are good but solenoid does not click
then replace solenoid

if starter spins but does not crank the engine
then replace starter

if starter cranks the engine, smell of gas in the exhaust, but the engine does not fire
then check and dry ignition circuit and replace faulty parts

if starter crank the engine but engine does not fire and no smell of gas
then check and correct problems with fuel lines, fuel pump, fuel filter, carburetor, fill tank

Since the action part of a rule can modify the state of the system, additional rules may have to be fired. There are two methods of matching rules to the current state of a system: forward chaining and backward chaining. In **forward chaining**, the initial set of facts are used to determine the rules that apply. If more than one rules applies, one of these is chosen. The search proceeds by firing this rule and arriving at a new set of facts. This procedure is repeated until a solution is reached. In **backward chaining**, all rules that have to be fired are first determined for the desired solution. These rules are then fired sequentially in the forward direction.

In a large system, the production rules limit the interaction between rules and lead to inefficiencies. These inefficiencies become evident when a number of production rules have to be fired, but can only be executed one at a time. Each such firing is proceeded by an interpretation of the current state of the system against the production rules. On average, half of these production rules have to be tested before each firing.

(b) What are the problems caused by data redundancies? Can data redundancies be completely eliminated when a database approach is used? Explain this with the help of an example. [5]

Data Redundancies, is the storage of same set of data two or more times. Storing information several times leads to the waste of storage space and an increase in the total size of the data stored. Updates to the database with such redundancies have the potential of becoming inconsistent. Various anomalies may arise due to redundancy considering the table for example:

Below is the Structure of Sale_Item Table :

Customer_Name Address Sale Item Price/Unit

Update Anomalies ⇒ Multiple copies of the same fact may lead to update inconsistencies when an update is made and only some of the multiple copies are updated. Thus, a change in Price/Unit must be made, for consistency, in all tuples pertaining to the Item.

Insertion Anomalies ⇒ We can not insert new information in the database unless we get other information also to enter. We can not enter Price/Unit for an new Item added in store unless a Customer buys it.

Deletion Anomalies ⇒ If any Customer returns purchased item then information for Price/Unit for that Item is lost.

Data redundancy be completely eliminated when the database approach is used depends on situation sometimes theoretically it is possible but practically not always. As when we develop large application software then we need to divide or normalize the database, but many times after normalization speed becomes an issue. So at that time it may not be possible or practical.

3(a) Write the significance of the evaluation of a database management system. List the technical and administrative issues respectively, required to be taken care of by the evaluation team. [7]

Significance of the evaluation of a DBMS : The evaluation, is not simply a matter of comparison or description of one system against another independent system, and surveying sometimes available through publication do describe and compare the feature of available systems, but a value of an organization depends upon its own problem environment. An organization must therefore look at its own needs of evaluation of the available systems.

In a small organization it is possible that a single individual would have to do the job, but larger organizations need to establish an evaluation team. Even this team's composition would some-what change as the evaluation process moves on. A good role in the initial stage would be played by users and management focusing on the organisational needs. Computers and information technology professionals then evaluate the technical gaps of several candidate system and finally financial and accounting personnel examine the cost estimates, payment alternatives, tax consequences, personnel requirements and contract negotiations. The reasons which inspire the organization to acquire a DBMS should be clearly documented and used to determine the properties and help in making trade offs between conflicting objectives and in the selection of various features that the candidate DBMS may have, depending upon the end-user requirements.

The evaluation team should also be aware of technical and administrative issue.

Technical List:-

(i) Database administration
(ii) Transaction management
(iii) SQL implementation
(iv) Programming interface
(v) DBMS integrity
(vi) Database server environment
(vii) Data storage features
(viii) Connectivity

Administrative List:-

(i) Required hardware platform
(ii) Recurring cost
(iii) Vendor's financial stability

(iv) Documentation
(v) Initial Cost
(vi) Vendor Support

(b) Draw a diagram to illustrate the relationship of different file organizations based on an access key. What is direct file organization? Explain the role of hashing in direct file organization with the help of an example. [8]

Below is the figure illustrating different file organizations based on an access key.

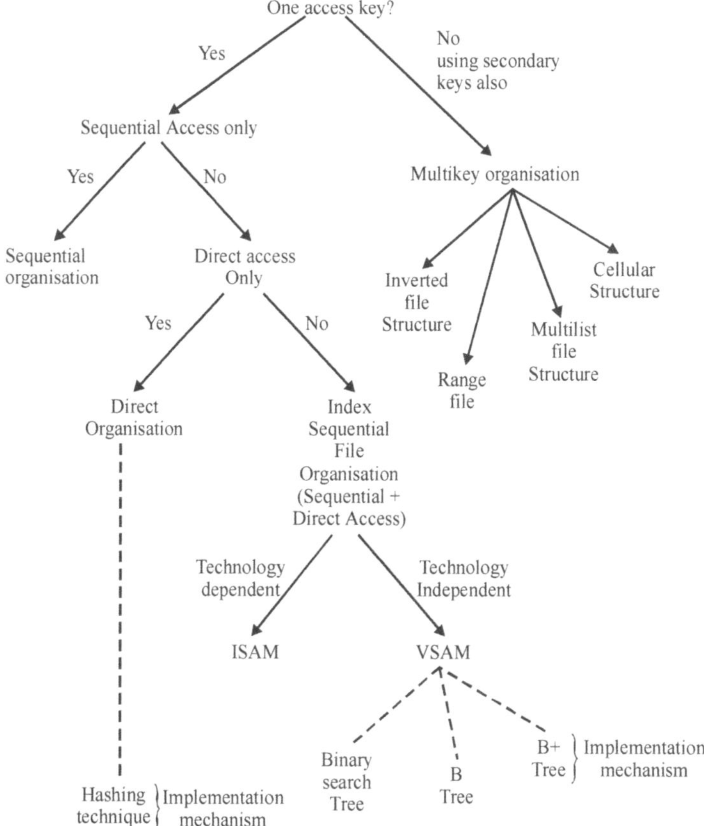

Figure : File organisation techniques

The technique used to represent and store the records on a file is called the File organisation.

Direct File Organisation ⇒ In direct file organisation, the key value is mapped directly to the storage location. The usual method of direct mapping by performing some arithmetic manipulation of the key value.

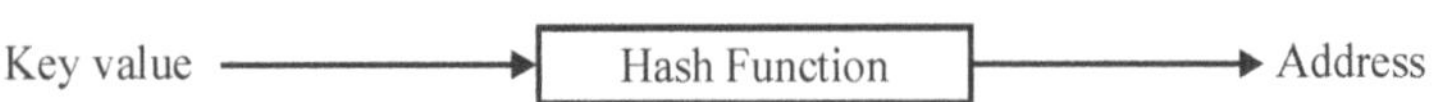

This process is called hashing. Let us consider a hash function h that maps the key value K to the vale h(k). The value h(K) is used as an address and for our application we require that this value be in some range. If our address area for the records lies between S_1 and S_2, that for all values of K it should generate values between S_1 and S_2.

Role of hashing in direct file organisation ⇒ With the help of example, it is obvious that a hash function that maps many different key values to a single address or one that does not map the key values uniformly is a bad hash function. A collision is said to occur when two distinct key values are mapped to the same storage location. Collision is handled in a number of ways. The colliding records may be assigned to the next available space, or they may be assigned to an overflow area. We can immediately see that with hashing schemes there are no indexes to traverse. With well-designed hashing functions where collisions are few, this is a great advantage.

Another problem that we have to resolve is to decide what address is represented by h(k). Let the address generated by the hash function the addresses of buckets in which the y, address pair values of records are stored. Figure shows the buckets containing the y, address pairs that allow a reorganisation of the actual data file and actual record address without affecting the hash functions. A limited number of collisions could be handled automatically by the use of a bucket of sufficiently capacity. Obviously the space required for the buckets will be, in general, much smaller than the actual data file. Consequently, its reorganization will not be that much expensive. Once the bucket address is generated from the key y the hash function, a search in the bucket is also required to locate the address of the required record. However, since the bucket size is small, this overhead is small.

The use of the bucket reduces the problem associated with the collisions. In spite of this, a bucket may be handled by providing overflow buckets and using a pointer from the normal bucket to an entry in the overflow bucket. All such overflow entries are linked. Multiple overflow from the same bucket results in a long list and slows down the retrieval of these records. In an alternate scheme, the address generated by the hash function is a bucket address and the bucket is used to start the records directly instead of using a pointer to the block containing the record.

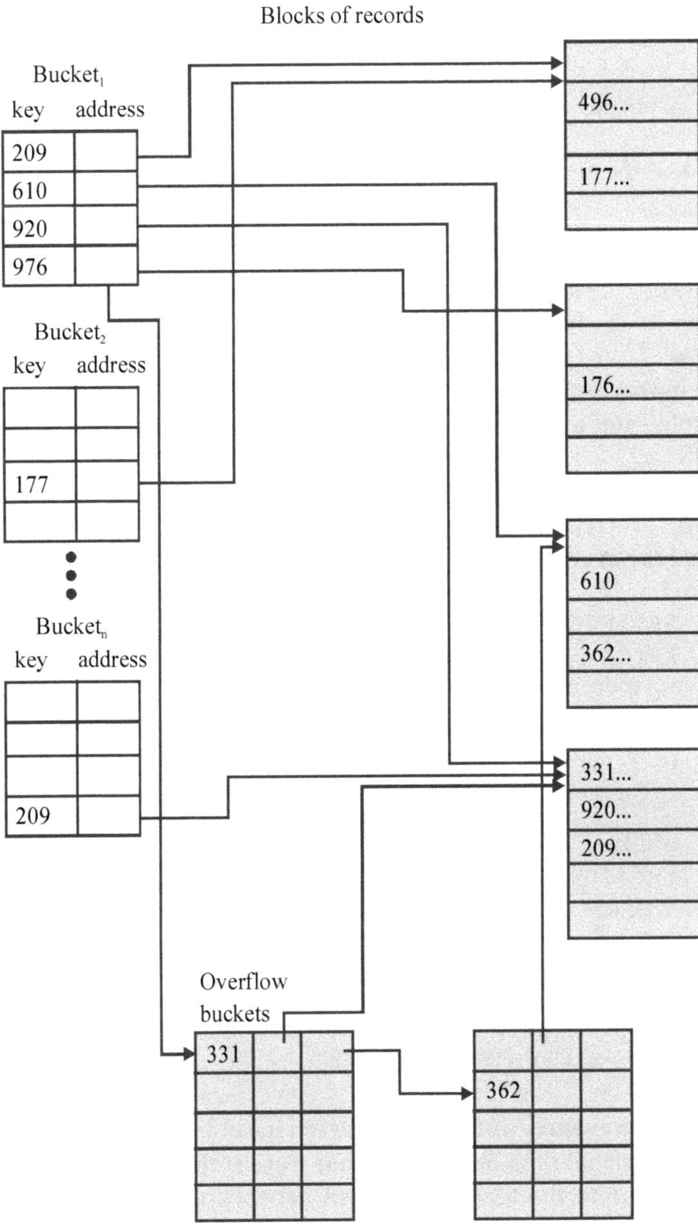

Lets represent the value:

S = upper bucket address value – lower bucket + address value + 1

Here, S gives the number of buckets. Assume that we have some mechanism to convert key values to numeric ones. Then a simple hashing function is

H(K) = Kmod S

Where K is the numeric representation of the key and h(k) produces a bucket address.

4(a) Consider the following schema :

employee (e_no, e_name, address, city, basic_sal, job_status)
projects (p_no, p_name, p_category)
work_in (p_no, e_no, p_duration)

Write appropriate SQL queries for the following : [6]

(i) Display the names of employees who are working in a project on "DBMS".

(ii) Find the employer number of all employees who are working on at least one project.

(iii) Find the average salary of all employees working in a project "based in Delhi".

(i)
```
SELECT E.e _ name
FROM employee E, Projects P, Works_in W
WHERE
(E. e_no = w.e_no) AND
(P. P_no = w.P_no) AND
P_Category = "DBMS" ;
```

(ii)
```
SELECT DISTINCT e_no
FROM Works_in, Projects
WHERE
(Works_in.P_no = Projects. P_no);
```

(iii)
```
SELECT AVG (Basic_sal)
FROM employee
HAVING City = "Based in Delhi";
```

(b) Describe any three differences between the object oriented data model and the relational data model. In what ways is the object oriented data model similar to the hierarchical and network data models? Mention any two examples in which we can use the object oriented databases and relational databases, with the proper justification. [9]

Difference between RDBMS and OODBMS ⇒ RDBMS is Relational Database Management system which is based on establishing relationship among tables is purely based on mathematics. OODBMS is Object Oriented Database Management System which is based on the concept of object. RDBMSs were never designed to allow for the nested structure. These types of applications are extensively found in CAD/CAE, aerospace, etc. OODBMS can easily support these applications. Moreover, it is much easier and natural to navigate through these complex structures in form of objects that model the real world in OODBMS rather than table, tuples and records in RDBMS. It is hard to confuse a relational database with an object-oriented database. The normalized relational model is based on a fairly elegant mathematical theory. Relational databases derive a virtual structure at run time based on values from sets of data stored in tables. Databases construct views of the data by selecting data from multiple tables and loading it into a single table (OODBs traverse the data from object to object).

Relational databases have a limited number of simple, built-in data types, such as integer and string, and a limited number of built-in operations that can handle these data types. You can create complex data types in a relational database, but you must do it on a linear basis, such as combing fields into records. And the operations on these new complex types are restricted, again, to those defined for the basic types (as opposed to arbitrary data types or subclassing with inheritance as found in OODMs).

The object model supports browsing of object class libraries, which allows the reuse, rather than the reinvention, of commonly used data elements. Objects in an OODB survive multiple sessions; they are persistent. If you delete an object stored in a relational database, other objects may be left with references to the deleted one and may now be incorrect. The integrity of the data thus becomes suspect and creates inconsistent versions.

In the relational database, complex objects must be broken up and stored in separate tables. This can only be done in a sequential procedure with the next retrieval replying on the outcome of the previous. The relational database does not understand a global request and thus cannot optimize multiple requests, OODBs can issue a single message that contains multiple transactions.

The relational model, however, suffers at least one major disadvantage, It is difficult to express the semantics of complex objects with only a table model for data storage. Although relational databases are adequate for accounting or other typical transaction-processing applications where the data types are simple and few in number, the relational model offers limited help when data types become numerous and complex.

Object-oriented databases are favoured for applications where the relationships among elements in the database carry the key information. That is, object-oriented models capture the structure of the data; relational models organize the data itself. If a record can be understood in isolation, then the relational database is probably suitable. If a record makes sense only in the context of other records, then an object-oriented database is more appropriate.

5(a) Explain the trade-offs in distributing the database. List the issues involved in storing the relations in the distributed databases. [9]

There are several reasons for distributing database, including sharing of data, reliability and availability, and speedup of query processing. However, along with these advantages come several disadvantages, including software development cost, greater potential for bugs, and increased processing overhead.

Trade-offs in distributing the database :

The major trade-off to support these, and even richer, applications on the Internet is the difficulty of designing, building, testing, and maintaining distributed database using the tools that comprise the state-of-the-art today. And the primary disadvantage/trade-off of distributing database is the added complexity required to ensure proper coordination among the sites where the database is distributed. This increased complexity takes the form of :

Software development cost ⇒ It is more difficult to implement a distributed database system and, thus, more costly.

Greater potential for bugs: Since the sites that comprise the distributed system operate in parallel, it is harder to ensure the correctness of algorithms. The potential exists for extremely subtle bugs. The art of constructing distributed algorithms remains an active and important area or research.

Increased processing overhead ⇒ The exchange of messages and the additional computation required to achieve intersite coordination is a form of overhead that does not arise in centralized systems.

In choosing the design for a database system, the designer must balance the advantages against the disadvantages of distribution of data design ranging from fully distributed designs to designs which included large degree of centralization.

(b) What are the different relational operators used in relational algebra? Consider the following relations A and B, and perform A ∪ B, A ∩ B and A-B. [6]

A →

Flight No.	Airways
IC 2715	Indian Airlines

IC 1007	**Jet Airways**
IC 9119	**Sahara**
IC 3849	**Indian Airlines**

B→

Flight No.	**Airways**
IC 1007	**Jet Airways**
IC 5187	**Cathay Pacific**
IC 1003	**Singapore Airlines**

Relational operators used in relational algebra:-

Union ⇒ The union operation of two relational tables is formed by appending rows from one table with those of a second table to produce a third.

➢ Duplicate rows are eliminated.

The notation for the union of Tables A and B is A UNION B.

The relational tables used in the union operation must be union compatible. Tables that are union compatible must have the same number of columns and corresponding columns must come from the same domain. Next figure shows the union of A and B.

➢ Note that the duplicate rows have been removed. And table A and B are given below.

A UNION B

Flight No	Airways
IC 2715	Indian Airlines
IC 1007	Jet Airways
IC 9119	Sahara
IC 3849	Indian Airlines
IC 5187	Cathay Pacific
IC 1003	Singapore Airlines

Intersection ⇒ The Intersection of two relational tables is a third table that contains common rows. Both tables must be union compatible. The notation for the intersection of A INTERSECT B.

A INTERSECT B

Flight No	Airways
IC 1007	Jet Airways

Difference ⇒ The difference of two relational tables is a third that contains those rows that occur in the first table but not in second. The difference operation requires that the table must be UNION Compatible.

A - B

Flight No	Airways
IC 2715	Indian Airlines
IC 9119	Sahara
IC 3849	Indian Airlines

Product ⇒ The product of two relational tables, also called the Cartesian Product, is the concatenation of every row in one table with every row in second. The product of Table A(having m rows) and table B(having n rows) is the table C(having m × n rows).

A Flight No.	A Airways	B Flight No.	B Airways
IC 2715	Indian Airlines	IC 1007	Jet Airways
IC 2715	Indian Airlines	IC 5187	Cathay Pacific
IC 2715	Indian Airlines	IC 1003	Singapore Airlines
IC 1007	Jet Airways	IC 1007	Jet Airways
IC 1007	Jet Airways	IC 5187	Cathay Pacific
IC 1007	Jet Airways	IC 1003	Singapore Airlines
IC 1007	Singapore Airlines	IC 1007	Jet Airways
IC 1007	Singapore Airlines	IC 5187	Cathay Pacific
IC 1007	Singapore Airlines	IC 1003	Singapore Airlines
IC 3849	Indian Airlines	IC 1007	Jet Airways
IC 3849	Indian Airlines	IC 5187	Cathay Pacific
IC 3849	Indian Airlines	IC 1003	Singapore Airlines

CS-06 : DATABASE MANAGEMENT SYSTEM
DEC - 2005

Note : Question number 1 is compulsory. Attempt any three questions from the rest.

Q1(a). Design an ER diagram for an IT training group database that will meet the information needs for its training program. Clearly indicate the entities, relationships and the key constraints. The description of the environment is as follows :

The company has 12 instructors and can handle upto 100 trainees for each training session. The company offers 5 Advanced technology courses, each of which is taught by a team of 2 or more instructors. Each instructor is assigned to a maximum of two teaching teams or may be assigned to do research. Each trainee undertakes one Advanced technology course per training session.

Ans.
Below are the Entities, attributes, relationship among different entities, E-R diagram and relational database structure :

Entities :
1. Company
2. Instructors
3. Trainees
4. Advance Courses
5. Team

Attributes :

Comp_ID $\rightarrow$ Company ID.
Inst_ID $\rightarrow$ Instructor ID.
Tra_ID $\rightarrow$ Training ID.
Cour_ID $\rightarrow$ Course ID.
Team_ID $\rightarrow$ Team ID.

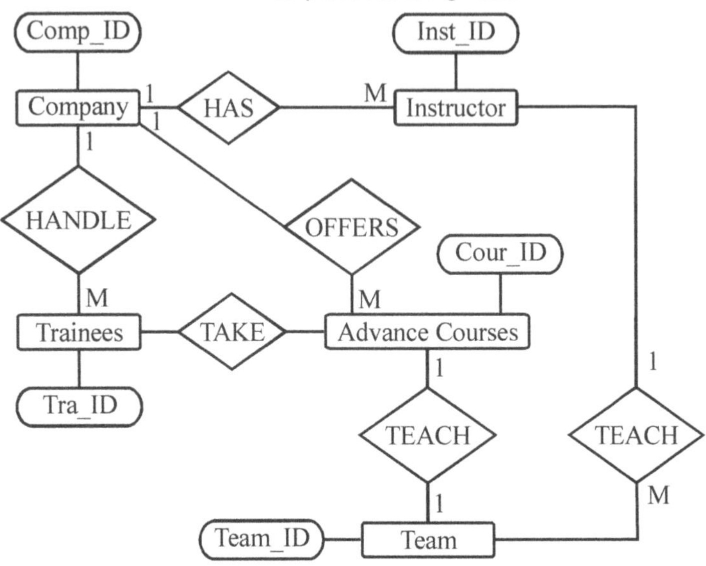

E-R Diagram of IT Trading Company

(b) Examine the table shown below :

Staff No.	Branch No.	Branch Address	Name	Position	Hrs/Week
E101	B02	Sun Plaza, Delhi, 10001	Ram	Assistant	16
E101	B04	2/3 UT, Delhi, 110111	Ram	Assistant	9
E122	B02	Sun Plaza, Delhi, 110001	Mohan	Assistant	14
E122	B04	2/3 UT, Delhi, 110111	Mohan	Assistant	10

(i) Why is the table above not in 2 NF?

Ans. In this table no primary key so the given table is not in 2NF.

(ii) Describe the process of normalizing the data shown in the table above to third normal form (3NF)

Ans. In 3NF decompose the given tables and find out functional dependency.

Key (Staff No., Branch No) → Hrs./Week

(Branch No.) → Branch Address

(Staff No.) → Name

(Name) → Position

Now create the tables.

1. Staff_no and_Branch_No Table :

Staff No.	Branch No	Hrs./Week
E 101	B 02	16
E 101	B 04	9
E 122	B 02	14
E 122	B 04	10

2. Branch_No. Table :

Branch_No.	Branch Address
B 02	Sun Plaza, Delhi-01
B 04	23UP, Delhi -11

3. Staff_No. Table :

Staff_No.	Name
E 101	Ram
E 122	Mohan

Name Table :

Name	Position
Ram	Assistant
Mohan	Assistance

(iii) Identify the primary and foreign keys in your 3NF relations.

Ans. The primary key of after decomposition of the table is Staff No. and foreign key is Branch No.

(c) With the help of an example, explain the Direct file organization method.

Direct File Organisation :

Used for files made up of fixed length records.

Uses a key field to obtain a record's location

Supports random (direct) access to individual records for both reading and writing

Predictable relationship between record key and location on secondary storage F(key value) => record address

Direct files must be stored using direct access storage device (DASD), as it requires the ability to go directly to a particular address.

Two major ways that F(key value) can operate:

1. Direct mapping (Relative), 2. Calculation (hashing)

Direct Mapping

Usually uses *relative addressing* in which key value is address relative to start of file. A file with space for n records will have relative addresses from set {1,2,3,...n-1,n}. Major disadvantage: if density of keys low, lots of waste space.

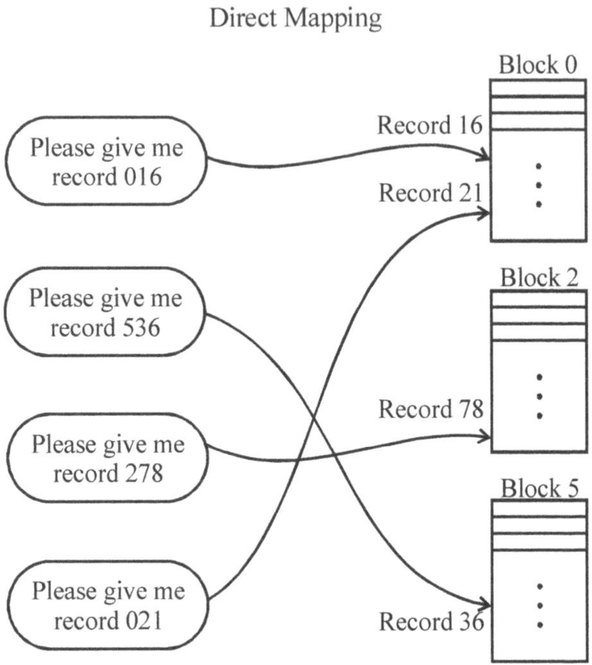

Calculation Or hashing - more common method. Apply a HASH function to key that translates large range of possible addresses to relatively small number of relative addresses.

Problem: a hash function may not produce a unique address every time => collisions may occur where calculation produces non-unique addresses.

f(key 1) = f(key2), but key1 <> key2

Common hash function is division/remainder - where the address is equal to the remainder of a division. Two common methods used to resolve collisions - linear probing and double hashing.

Linear probing involves a sequential search from the home location until an unoccupied position is found. Double hashing is the use of a second hash function to compute a new address

(d) Explain the following integrity rules of a relational model with the help of an example:

(i) Entity Integrity
(ii) Referential Integrity
Refer to Dec.-2001, Q1(b), Page No.-152.

(e) Explain how the "GROUP BY" clause works. What is the difference between the WHERE and HAVING clauses? Explain them with the help of an example for each.

Ans. The GROUP by clause is another section of the select statement. This optional clause is used to group rows based on distinct values that exist for specified columns. The GROUP by clause creates a data set, containing several set of records grouped together based on a condition.

Ex : Retrieve the product number and the total quantity ordered for each product from the sales_order_details table

Table Name : Sales _Order _Details

Det Order No.	Product_ No.	Qty._Ordered	Qty. Disp
019001	P00001	10	10
019001	P00004	3	3
019001	P00006	7	7
019002	P00002	4	4
019002	P00005	10	10
019003	P00003	2	2
019004	P00001	6	6
019005	P00006	4	4
019005	P00004	1	1
019006	P00006	8	8

```
SELECT Product_No, sum (Qty_Ordered) "Total Qty. Ordered"
FROM Sales_Order_Details
                    GROUP by Product_No;
```

Output :

Product_No.	Total_Qty._Ordered
P00001	16
P00002	4
P00003	2
P00004	4
P00005	10
P00006	19

Difference between WHERE & HAVING Clause :

WHERE CLAUSE :

The SELECT statement used until now displayed all rows. This is because there was no condition set to view a specific set of rows from the table. There is the option of using a (WHERE clause) in an SQL query to apply a filter on the rows retrieved when a WHERE clause is added to the SQL query, the SQL engine compares each record in the table with the condition specified in the where clause.

Syntax :

```
SELECT<Column name1>, <Column name2>
        From <table name>
                WHERE<Condition>
```

Example : SELECT >From <sales_Order_Details> WHERE
Det order_No = '019001';

HAVING CLAUSE :

The HAVING clause can be used in conjunction with the GROUP by clause. HAVING imposes a condition on the GROUP by clause, which further filters the groups created by the GROUP by clause.

Example : Retrieve the product_No. and the quantity ordered for products 'P00001' from the sales_Order_Details table.

```
SELECT product_No., sum (Qty_Ordered) "Total Qty Ordered"
    From Sales_Order_Details
        GROUP by Product_No
    HAVING Product_No. = 'P00001' or Product_No. = 'P00004';
```

Where clause is used alone without the need to put group by, while having clause is used with group by clause only.

Q2(a). Consider the following relations:

Employee (empID, FirstName, LastName, address, DOB, sex, position, deptNo)

Department (deptNo, deptName, mgr, emplD)
Project (projNo, projName, deptNo)
Works on (emplD, projNo, hours worked)

Write the SQL statements for the following :

(i) List the name and address of all employees who work for the IT department.

```
SELECT
employee.fname, employee.lname,
employee.add, department.dept name
FROM
department INNER JOIN
employee ON department.deptno = employee.deptno
WHERE ((department.deptname) = "IT");
```

(ii) List the total hours worked by each employee, arranged in order of department number and within department, alphabetically by employee surname.

```
SELECT
employee.fname, employee.lname,
department.deptno, department.deptname,
workson.hoursworked
FROM
(department INNER JOIN employee
ON department.deptno = employee.deptno)
INNER JOIN workson ON
employee.empid = workson.empid
ORDER BY employee.lname;
```

(iii) List the total number of employees in each department for those departments with more than 10 employees.

```
SELECT
count (empid) "Total"
FROM employee
WHERE empid >= 10;
```

(iv) List the project number, project name and the number of employees who work on that project.

```
SELECT
project.projno, project.projname,
```

```
count (employee.empid)
FROM
project INNER JOIN
(employee INNER JOIN workson ON
employee.empid=workson.empid ON
project.projno = workson.projno
GROUP BY
project.projno, project.projname;
```

(b) What is a database model? Explain any two types of data models with an example for each.

Database Model : A database model in a conceptual representation of the data structures that are required by a database. The data structures include the data objects. The associations between data objects and the rules, which govern operation on the objects. As the name implies the data model focuses on what data is required and how it should be organized rather than what operations will be performed on the data. To use a common analogy, the data model is equivalent to an architectures building plans.

A database model is independent of hardware and software constraints. Rather than try representing the data, as a database would see it, the data model focuses on representing the data as the user sees it in the "real world". It serves as a bridge between the concepts that make up real world events and processes and the physical representation of those concepts in a database.

Now Refer to Page No. 154.

Now Refer to Page No. 170.

Q3(a). What is the need for evaluation of a DBMS? List the technical criteria that are to be considered during the evaluation process.

Refer to December-2002, Q. No.3(a), Page No.119.

(b) What are the main features of the Object Oriented Database Management System? How is this advantageous over RDBMS?

Refer to June-2004, Q. No.6(a), Page No.72.

(c) What is a knowledge-base system? With the help of an example for each, explain how it is different from a conventional DBMS.

Refer to December-2002, Q. No.5(a), Page No.123.

Q4(a). Explain the issues that are to be addressed for a distributed database design. Explain how these issues apply to the global system catalogue.

Following are the issues that are to be addressed for a distributed database design :

* **Replication :** The system maintains several identical replicas of the relation. Each replica is stored in a different site, resulting in data replication. The alternative to replication is to store only one copy of relation.

* **Fragmentation :** The relation is partitioned into several fragments. Each fragment is stored in a different site.

* **Replication and Fragmentation :** This is a combination of the above two notions. The relation is partitioned into several fragments. The system maintains several identical replicas of each such fragment.

Now Refer to June-02, Q. No.3(a), Page No.-137.

A distributed database system consists of a collection of sites, each of which maintains a local databases system. When we talk about **Global System Catalogue**, as the name depicts it will be spread out globally and sites will also be available globally. A site may participate in the execution of global transactions those transactions that access data from n several sites across the globe. Here, the concept of distributed database will work better and all the design issues related to distributed databases will apply equally in this case also. Like data replication will be required at all sites, as to access the information anywhere without delay. Fragmentation will also be required. It is essential that the system minimise the degree to which a user needs to be aware of how a relation is stored.

(b) Why is a B+ tree a better structure than a B-tree for implementation of an indexed sequential file? Explain this with an example.

First we will start from the discussion about B-tree and B+ tree. **B Trees** are multi-way trees. That is each node contains a set of keys and pointers. A B Tree with four keys and five pointers represents the minimum size of a B Tree node. A B Tree contains only data pages. B Trees are dynamic. That is, the height of the tree grows and contracts as records are added and deleted.

B+ trees are related to two data structures: ISAM Trees and B-Trees.

ISAM stands for indexed sequential access method. As the name implies, the data is maintained in sorted order. A set of index pages provides fast access to the data pages. ISAM is a relatively static approach. Although it can accommodate additions and deletions, the index pages do not change. Additions are handled through overflow pages. Thus, the efficiency of this access method can degrade if there is a lot of data movement.

A B+ Tree combines features of ISAM and B Trees. It contains index pages and data pages. The data pages always appear as leaf nodes in the tree. The root node and intermediate nodes are always index pages. These features are similar to ISAM. Unlike ISAM, overflow pages are not used in B+ trees.

The index pages in a B+ tree are constructed through the process of inserting and deleting records. Thus, B+ trees grow and contract like their B Tree counterparts. The contents and the number of index pages reflects this growth and shrinkage.

This clearly shows that B+ tree structure is better than B-tree for implementation of an indexed sequential file, as index page facility is there.

(c) With the help of an example, explain the concept of multilist file organization.

Ans. Multi-list file organization is multi-index linked fill organization. In linked organization the sequence of records is governed by the links that determine the next record in sequence. Linking of records can be unordered but such a linking is very expensive for searching of information from a file, through this we can increase primary keys, which facilitates insertion & deletion algorithms.

Example : The records numbers are given as alphabets for better description.

Record No.	Emp. No.	Name	Job	Quali .	Gender	City	Married Single	Salary
A	800	Rama	S/w Eng.	B. Tech	M	ND.	Single	15,000
B	500	Sharma	S/w Eng.	B. Tech	F	ND.	Married	18,000
C	900	Kumar	S/w Eng.	MCA	F	Kochi	Single	16,000
D	700	Rina	S/w Eng.	B. Tech	M	Kochi	Married	12,000
E	400	Muna	S/w Eng.	MCA	F	Kochi	Single	13,000

Upper Value

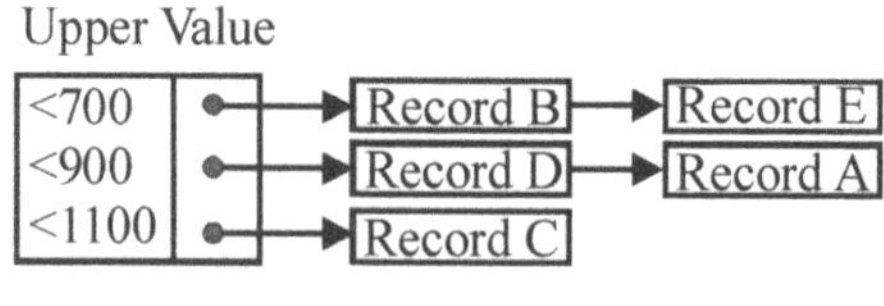

Empid index

Linking together all the records in the same index value

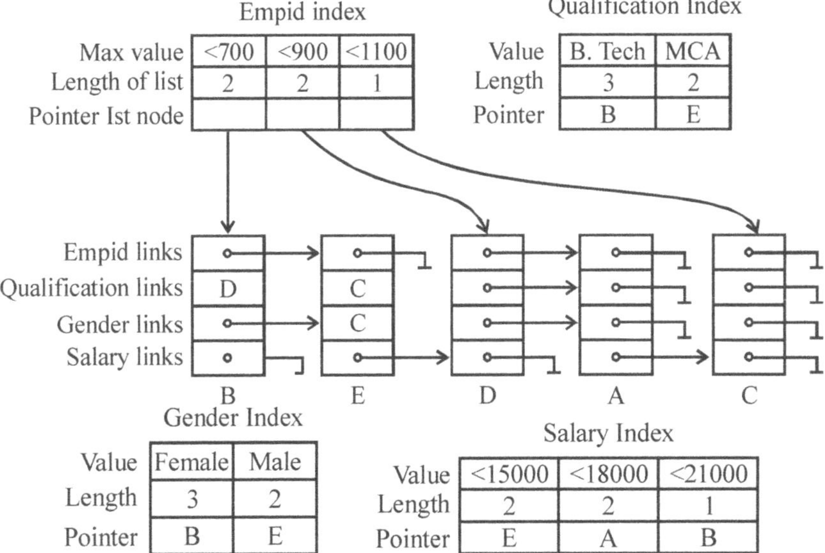

Q5(a). Given the relational schemes :
ENROL (S#, C#, Section) - S# represents student number
TEACH (Porf, C#, Section) - C# represents course number
ADVISE (Porf, S#) - Prof is thesis advisor of S#
PRE_REQ (C#, Pre_C#) - Pre_C# is prerequisite course
GRADES (S#, C#, Grade, Year)
STUDENT (S#, Sname) - Sname is student name
Give queries expressed in relational algebra, tuple calculus and domain calculus for the following

(i) List all students taking courses with Zeba.

Ans $\Pi_{\text{sname, s\# } \sigma \text{ proff= "zeba"}}((\text{Student} \bowtie \text{Teach} \bowtie \text{Enroll}))$

(ii) List all students taking at least one course that their advisor teaches.

Ans. $\Pi_{\text{sname, s\#}}(\text{Student} \bowtie \text{Teach} \bowtie \text{Advice})$

(iii) List those professors who teach more than one section of the same course.

Ans. $\Pi_{\text{proff}}\left[\text{Proff S count section} > 1^{(\text{Teach})}\right]$

(b) What are the design goals of a good relational database design? Is it always possible to achieve these goals? If some of these goals are not achievable, what alternate goals should you aim for and why?

Refer to June-2001, Q. No.5(c), Page No.160.

The differences that arise in the relational approach is in setting up relationships between different tables. This actually makes use of certain mathematical operations on the relation such as projection, union, etc. similarly in order to achieve the organization of the data in terms of tables in a satisfactory manner, a technique called normalization is used.

The second normal forms and the third normal forms. At the moment it is sufficient to say that normalization is a technique which helps in determining the most appropriate grouping of data items into records, segments or tuples. This is necessary because in the relational model the data items are arranged in tables which indicate the structure, relationship and integrity.

Though it is not possible to achieve some of these goals such as redundancy is not removed completely in some situations. This can only be minimized with help of normalization.

If some of the goals are not achievable we can follow the below alternatives :

May want to use non-normalized schema for performance

For example, displaying customer_name along with account_number and balance requires join of account with depositor

Alternative 1: Use denormalized relation containing attributes of account as well as depositor with all above attributes

*faster lookup

*extra space and extra execution time for updates

*extra coding work for programmer and possibility of error in extra code

Alternative 2: use a materialized view defined as account depositor.

Benefits and drawbacks same as above, except no extra coding work for programmer and avoids possible errors

· Some aspects of database design are not caught by normalization

· Examples of bad database design, to be avoided:

Instead of earnings (company_id, year, amount), use; · earnings_2005, earnings_2006, earnings_2007, etc., all on the schema (company_id, earnings).

· Above are in BCNF, but make querying across years difficult and needs new table each year

· company_year(company_id, earnings_2005, earnings_2006, earnings_2007)

· Also in BCNF, but also makes querying across years difficult and requires new attribute each year.

· Is an example of a crosstab, where values for one attribute become column names

· Used in spreadsheets, and in data analysis tools

CS-06 : DATABASE MANAGEMENT SYSTEM
JUNE - 2006

Note : Question number 1 is compulsory. Attempt any three questions from the rest.

Q1(a). With the help of a suitable example, explain a hierarchical database model.

Refer to December-01, Q. No.3(b), Page No.155-157

(b) What are the advantages of index-sequential file organization? With the help of an example explain the structure of index sequential file.

Following are the advantages of index-sequential file organization :

(i) It is fast and efficient when dealing with a large volume of data.

(ii) Index provides the facility for random access to record. Through this access to the sequential records becomes quite easy.

(iii) Facility like overflow area provides additional space for record addition without the need to create.

Structure of Index Sequential Files

An index-sequential file consists of the data plus one or more levels of indexes. When inserting a record, we have to maintain the sequence of records and this may necessitate shifting subsequent records. For a large file this is a costly and inefficient process. Instead, the records that overflow their logical area are shifted into a designated overflow area and a pointer is provided in the logical area or associated index entry points to the overflow location. This is illustrated below. Record 165 is inserted in the original logical block causing a record to be moved to an overflow block.

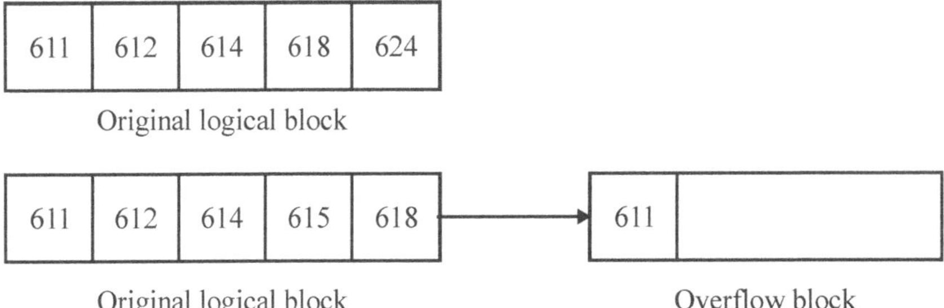

Figure: Overflow of record

Multiple records belonging to the same logical area may be chained to maintained logical sequencing. When records are forced into the overflow area as a result of insertion, the insertion process simplified, but the search time is increased. Deletion of records from index-sequential files creates logical gaps; the records are not physically removed but only flagged as having been deleted. If there were a number of deletions, we may have a great amount of unused space.

An index-sequential file is therefore made up of the following components;

(I) A primary data storage area. In certain systems this area may have used spaces embedded within it to permit addition of records. It may also include records that have been marked as having been deleted.

(II) Overflow area(s). This permits the addition of records to the files. A number of schemes exist for the incorporation of records in these areas into the expected logical sequence.

(III) A hierarchy of indices. In a random enquiry or update, the physical location of the desired record is obtained by accessing these indices.

The primary data area contains the records written by the user's programs. The records are written in data blocks in ascending key sequence. These data blocks are in turn stored in ascending sequence in the primary data area. The data blocks are sequenced by the highest key of the logical records contained in them.

(c) Why are remote procedure calls used? Why is a set of DDE maintained at application level?

With RPC one component communicate with a remote component using simple procedure calls. This involves peer to peer messaging. If an application issues a functional request and this request is embedded in an RPC, the requested function can be located anywhere in the enterprise, the caller is authorized to access. The advantage of this process to process communication is evident when processors are involved in any simultaneous processes. New client applications that use object-level relationships between processes provide need for this type of communication e.g. a client requests information for a server by connecting to the server, making the request by calling low-level procedure native to the database server, and then disconnecting. To respond to a request, the server connects to the application and calls a low-level procedure in the application.

RPC is typically transparent to a user, making it very easy to use. The RPC provides facility for the invocation and execution of requests from processors running different operating systems and using different hardware platforms from the callers.

Through a set of APIs, windows provide calls that support to the DDE protocol for message-based exchange of data among applications. DDE can be used to construct HOT-LINKS between applications where data can be fed from window to window without operation intervention. DDE support WARM-LINKS that we can create so the server application notifies the client that the data have changed and client can issue an explicit request to receive it. We create REQUEST-LINKS to allow direct copy and paste operation between a server and client without the need for an immediate clipboard. No notification of change in data by the server application is provided. EXECUTIVE LINKS cause the execution of one application to be controlled by the another. This provides an easy to use batch processing capability. Using DDE applications can share data, execute commands remotely and check error conditions, therefore DDE is maintained at application level.

(d) Design an ER diagram for any of IGNOU'S study centers. Clearly indicate the entities ,attributes, relationships and the key constraints.
ER-diagram of IGNOU Study Centres.

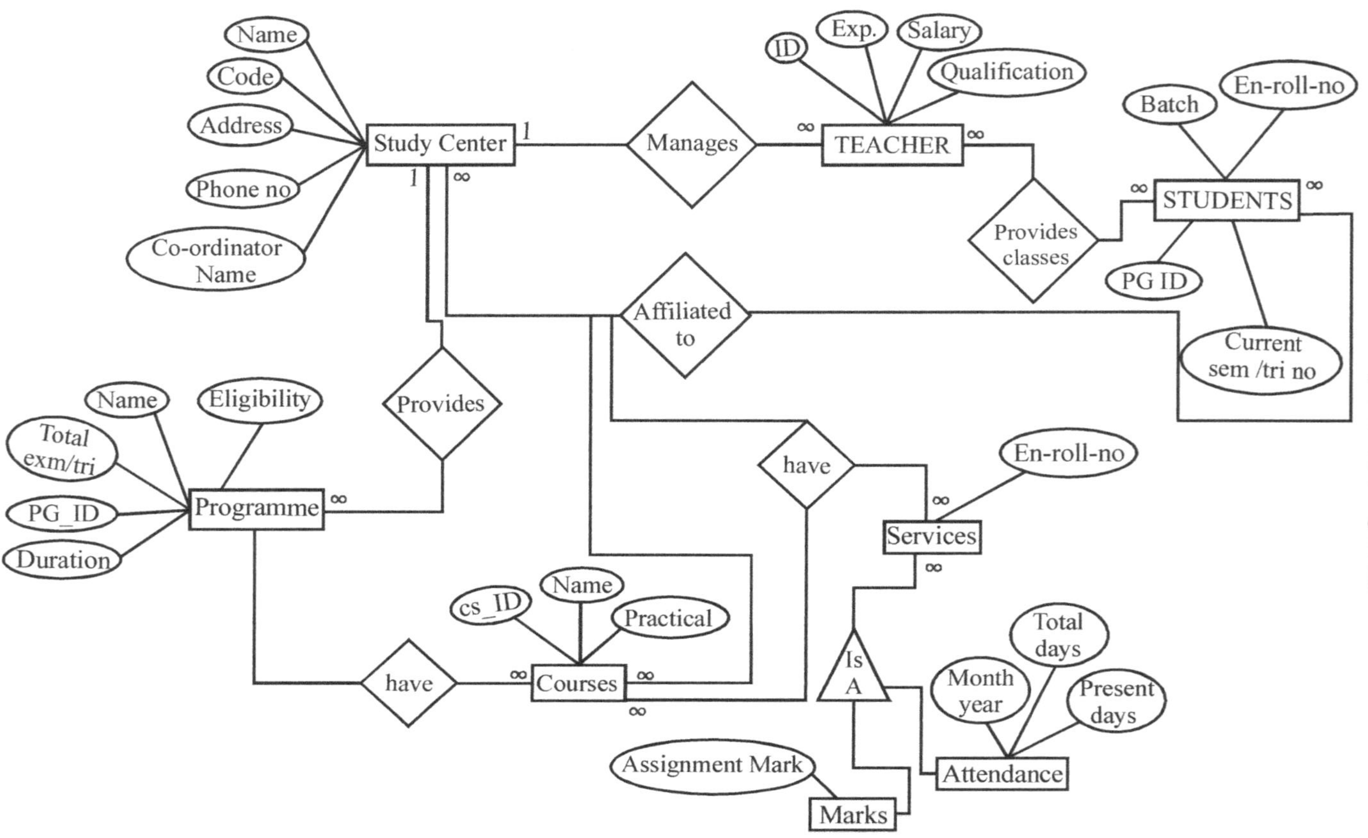
STUDENTS
En-roll-no
Batch
PG ID
Current sem /tri no
Provides classes
TEACHER
Qualification
Salary
Exp.
ID
Manages
Affiliated to
Study Center
Name
Code
Address
Phone no
Co-ordinator Name
Provides
Programme
Eligibility
Name
Total exm/tri
PG_ID
Duration
have
Courses
cs_ID
Name
Practical
have
Services
En-roll-no
Is A
Attendance
Month year
Total days
Present days
Marks
Assignment Mark

(e) With the help of two examples for each, explain the use of multimedia databases and knowledge databases.

Refer to December-03, Q. No.4b(i,ii), Page No.85-86

Q2(a). Consider an employee file with the details given below:

Record	E #	Name	Occup.	Degree	Sex	Location	Salary
A	800	Milind	Prog.	M.E.	M	Delhi	10,000
B	510	Adwet	Analyst	B.E.	M	Mumbai	15,000
C	200	Devendra	Analyst	B.E.	M	Delhi	12,000
D	300	Mukesh	Prog.	M.E.	M	Chennai	9,000

(i) Make a multi list representation of this employee file.

Ans. Multi list Representation :

Let us create a primary index for this file having the E# values in the range:

> = 200 but <500
> = 500 but < 800
> = 800 but < 1100

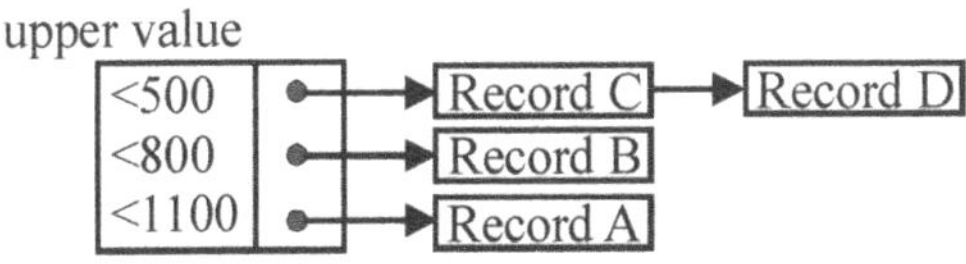

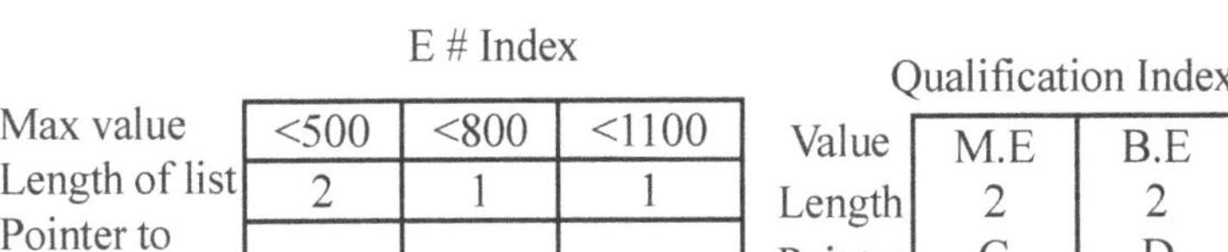

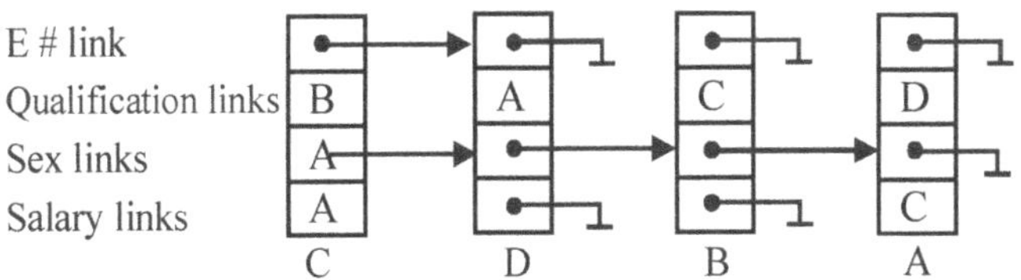

Gender Index

Value	Male
Length	4
Pointer	C

Salary Index

Value	<10,000	<13,000	<15,000
Length	1	2	1
Pointer	C	C	B

(ii) Write a query to retrieve the record of salary > 12,000, Degree = M.E>,
Location = Delhi, Occupation = Analyst, Sex = M

Ans. Select Name, Occup, Degree, salary, sex, location
From Employee
Where salary>12,000 And Degree= "M.E"
And Location = "Delhi" And
Occupation = "Analyst" And Sex = "M";

(b) What are the main features of client-server model ? Explain the stages involved in the development of an application using this model.

Following are the main features of client-server model :

(i) Client / Server model caters to low cost & user friendly environment.

(ii) It can be used to develop highly complex multiuser database application being handled by any mainframe computers until about 8 years back.

(iii) It offers expendability.

(iv) It ensures that the performance degradation is not much with increased load.

(v) It allows connectivity with the heterogenous machines & also with real time date feeders like ATMs, Numerical machines.

(vi) It allows database management including security, performance, backup etc.

Now Refer to Jan-2001, Q. No.6(c), Page No.188

Q3(a). Why is the administration of a database system required ? What are the various functions associated with database administration ?

Most modern applications utilize database management systems (DBMS) to create, store and manage business data. The DBMS software enables end users or application programmers to share data. It provides a systematic method of creating, updating, retrieving and storing information in a database. DBMSs also are generally responsible for data integrity, data access control and automated rollback, restart and recovery. When using a DBMS, **database administration is required** to ensure the efficient and proper care of the data in the database. There comes the role of DBA who has his prime concern dealing with administration of database. Many administrative tools are available in market these days, as DBA alone cannot administer the database without the tools like Administrative Tools, Recovery Tools, Database Security and Integrity tools, Development DBA Tools etc.

Now Refer to June-04, Q. No.5(a), Page No.71.

(b) Define a data manipulation language. Write a syntax for the following and give an example for each.
(i) Select statement
(ii) Update statement
(iii) Delta statement
(iv) Insert statement

Ans. Data manipulation language (DML) which defines the set of commands that modify or process data to create user definable output. The DML precompiler converts DML statements (such as SELECT * From <table name>) in Structured Query Language (SQL) embedded in an application program to normal procedural calls in the host language. The precompiler interacts with the query processor in order to generate the appropriate code:

(i) Select Statement :
It is used for retrieving information from the databases. It can be coupled with many clauses.

Syntax : select <field name> from <table name>;
Ex : select Ename, add1, add2, from employee;

(ii) Update Statement :
It is used to modify database values.

Syntax : UPDATE <table name>
SET <column name> = <value>
Where <condition>;

Ex : Update Employee
SET comm = comm*2
WHERE 2 = (SELECT COUNT (*) from INCR
Where INCR.Empno = employee.empno
Group by empno);

(iii) Delete statement :
It is used to delete any required / particular record from a table

Syntax : DELETE FROM <table name>
WHERE <column name>; (SELECT <column name>
FROM <table name>;

Ex : DELETE FROM EMP
Where EMPNO NOT IN (SELECT EMPNO FROM INCR);

(iv) Insert Development :
It used to insert a new tuple in a relation.
Syntax : INSERT <column name> into
<table name>;
Ex : INSERT <10, 'Gully', 24, 'Vikas'> into PERSONS;

Q4(a). With the help of an example relation and the dependency diagram, explain the concept of functional dependency.

Ans. Let X and Y be two attributes of a relation. Given the value of X, if there is only one value of Y corresponding to it, then Y is said to be functionally dependent on X. This is indicated by the notation:

X → Y

For example, given the value of item code, there is only one value of item name for it. Thus item name is functionally dependent on item code. This is shown as:

Item code → item name

Similarly in table 1, given an order number, the date of the order is known. Thus: order no. Order date

Functional dependency may also be based on a composite attribute. For example, if we write

X, Z → Y

it means that there is only one value of Y corresponding to given values of X, Z. In other words, Y is functionally dependent on the composite X, Z. In table 1 mentioned below, for example, Order no., and Item code together determine Qty. and Price. Thus:

Order no., Item code → Qty., Price

As another example, consider the relation

Student (**Roll no.,** Name, Address, Dept., Year of study)

Order no.	*Order date*	*Item code*	*Quantity*	*Price/unit*
1456	260289	3687	52	50.40
1456	260289	4627	38	60.20
1456	260289	3214	20	17.50
1886	040389	4629	45	20.25
1886	040389	4627	30	60.20
1788	040489	4627	40	60.20

Table 1: Normalized Form of the Relation

In this relation, Name is functionally dependent on Roll no. In fact, given the value of Roll no., the values of all the other attributes can be uniquely determined.

Name and Department are not functionally dependent because given the name of a student, one cannot find his department uniquely. This is due to the fact that there may be more than one student with the same name. Name in this case is not a key. Department and Year of study are not functionally dependent as Year of study pertains to a student whereas Department is an independent attribute. The functional dependency in this relation is shown in the following figure as a dependency diagram. Such dependency diagrams shown in figure 1 are very useful in normalization.

Relation Key: Consider the relation of table 1. Given the Vendor code, the Vendor name and Address are uniquely determined. Thus Vendor code is the relation key. Given a relation, if the value of an attribute X uniquely determines the values of all other attributes in a row, then X is said to be the key of that relation. Sometimes more than one attribute is needed to uniquely determine other attributes in a relation row.

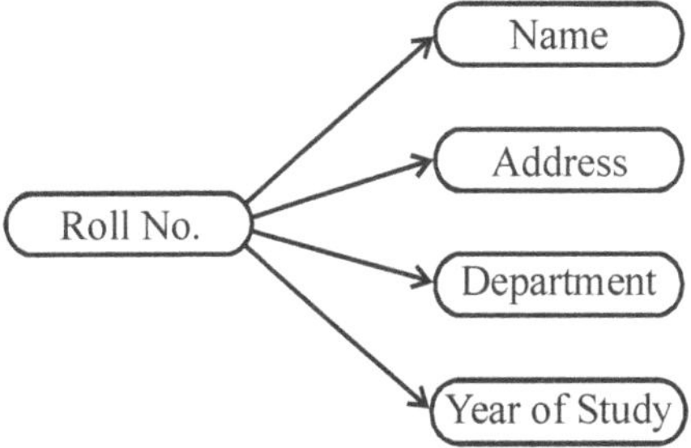

Figure 1: Dependency diagram for the relation "Student"

In that case such a set of attributes is the key. In table 1, Order no. and Item code together form the key. In the relation "Supplies" (Vendor code, Item code, Qty. supplied, Date of supply, Price/unit), Vendor code and Item code together form the key. This dependency is shown in the following diagram (figure 2).

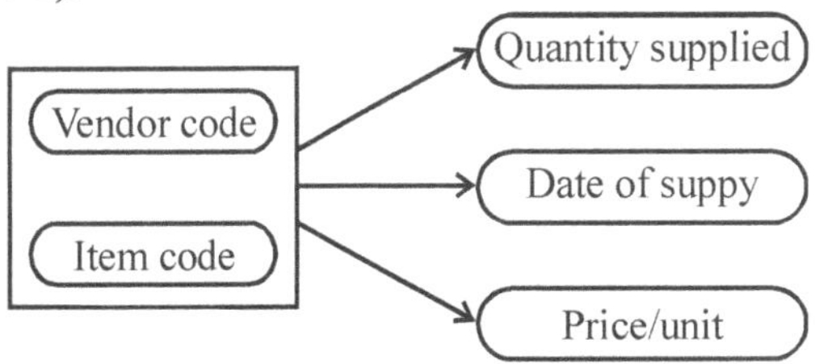

Figure 2: Dependency diagram for the relation "Supplies"

Observe that in the figure the fact that Vendor code and Item code together form a composite key is clearly shown by enclosing them together in a rectangle.

(b) Explain the following tools with respect to client-server environment.
(i) Dynamic data exchange.
(ii) Object linking and embedding
Also mention the usage of these with an example for each.

(i) Ans. Refer to December-01, Q. No.6(c), Page No.162
(ii) Ans. Refer to Jan-01, Q. No.6(b)(ii), Page No.188

Q5(a). Consider the scheme given below :
Branch_scheme (Branch_name, asset, Branch_city)
Customer_scheme (Customer_name, street, customer_city)
Deposit_scheme (Branch_name, account_number, customer_name, balance)
Borrow_scheme (Branch_name, loan_number, customer_name, amount)
Client_scheme (Customer_name, banker_name)

Write the SQL statements for the following:

(i) Find all customers who have a balance of over Rs.1,000/-

```
SELECT          customer_scheme.customer_name,
                      customer _scheme.street,
                      customer_scheme.city
        FROM          customer_scheme        INNER JOIN
                      Deposit_scheme`        ON
                      customer_scheme.customer_name=
        deposit_scheme.customer_name
        WHERE ((deposit_scheme.balance)> = 1000));
```

(ii) Write the query to find the clients of banker Patel, and the city they live in.

```
SELECT     client_scheme.banker_name,
customer_scheme.street,
customer_scheme.city
        FROM          customer_scheme        INNER JOIN
                      client_scheme          ON
                      customer_scheme.customer_name
                      = client_scheme.customer_name
        WHERE ((client_scheme.banker_name) = "Patel");
```

(iii) Write a statement to find all the customers who have a loan amount of more than Rs.1,200/-.

```
SELECT          customer_scheme.customer_name,
                      borrow_scheme.amount
```

```
        FROM          customer_scheme        INNER JOIN
                      Borrow_scheme          ON
                      customer_scheme.customer_name
        = borrow_scheme.customer_name
        WHERE (((borrow_scheme.amount) >= 1200));
```

(iv) Write a statement to find all the customers whose name starts with "R" and who have a balance of more than Rs.10,000/-.

```
SELECT        customer_scheme.customer_name,
                      deposit_scheme.balance
        FROM          customer_scheme        INNER JOIN
                      deposit_scheme         ON
                      customer_scheme.customer_name
        = deposit_scheme.customer_name
        WHERE = (("customer_name"  LIKE 'R %')
              OR      ((deposit_scheme.balance) = 10000));
```

(b) With the help of an example, explain the properties of a Balanced sort tree.

Ans. We will now study the operations possible on a heap and see how these can be combined to generate properties of a balanced sort tree.

The operations on a heap work in 2 steps.

1. The required node is inserted /deleted / or replaced

2. One may cause violation of the heap condition so the heap is traversed and modified to rectify any such violations

Example :

<u>Insertion :</u>

Consider the insertion of a note R in the Heap 1.

1. Initially R is added as the right child of J and given the number 13.

2. But R J, the heap condition is violated

3. Move R up to position 6 and move (J) down to position 13.

4. R P, therefore, the heap condition is still violated.

5. Swap R and P

6. The heap condition is now satisfied by all nodes to get.

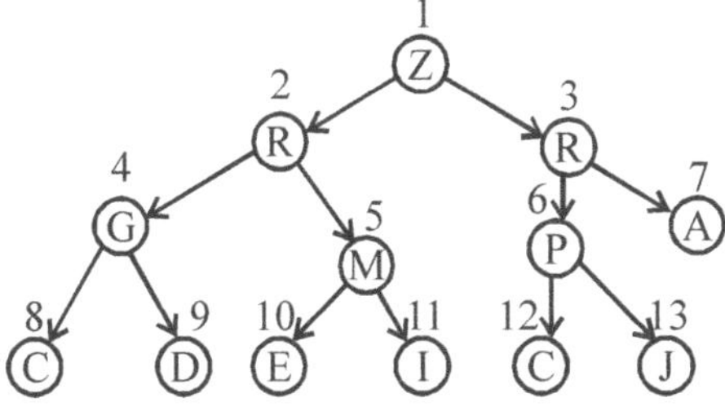

Deletion

Consider the deletion of M from heap 2.

1. The larger of M 's children is promoted to 5.

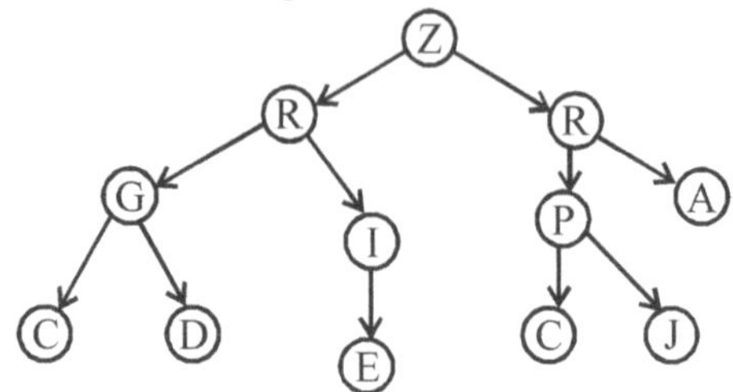

Figure : Heap 3

An efficient sorting method based on the heap construction and node removal from the heap in order. This algorithm is guaranteed to sort n elements in N log N steps.

We will first see 2 methods of heap construction and then removal in order from the heap to sort the list.

1. Top down heap construction

- Insert items into an initially empty heap, keeping the heap condition inviolate at all steps.

2. Bottom up heap construction

- Build a heap with the items in the order presented.
- From the right most node modify to satisfy the heap condition.

We will exemplify this with an example.

Example : Build a heap of the following using both methods of construction.

P R O F E S S I O N A L

Top down construction

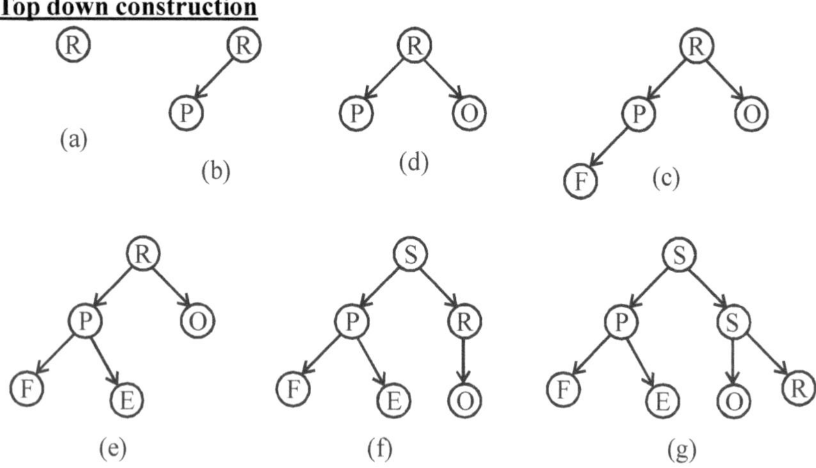

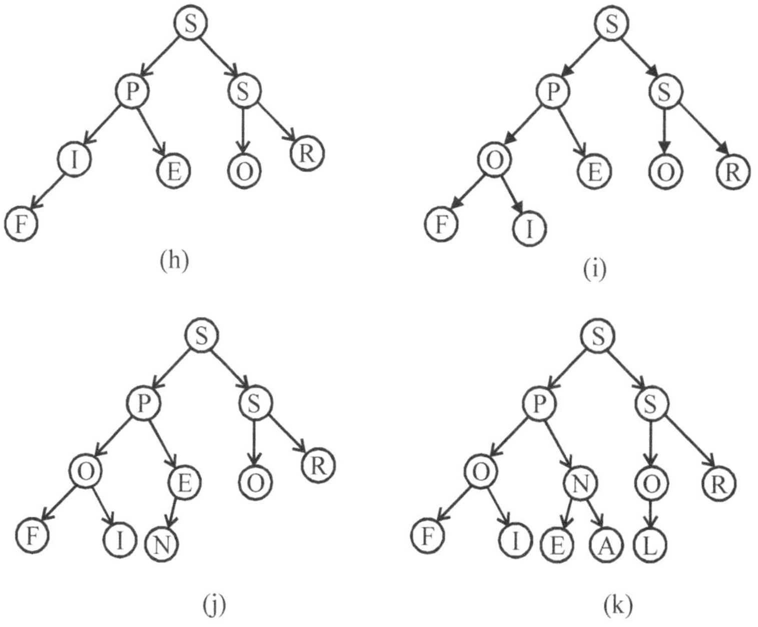

Figure : Heap Sort (Top down Construction)

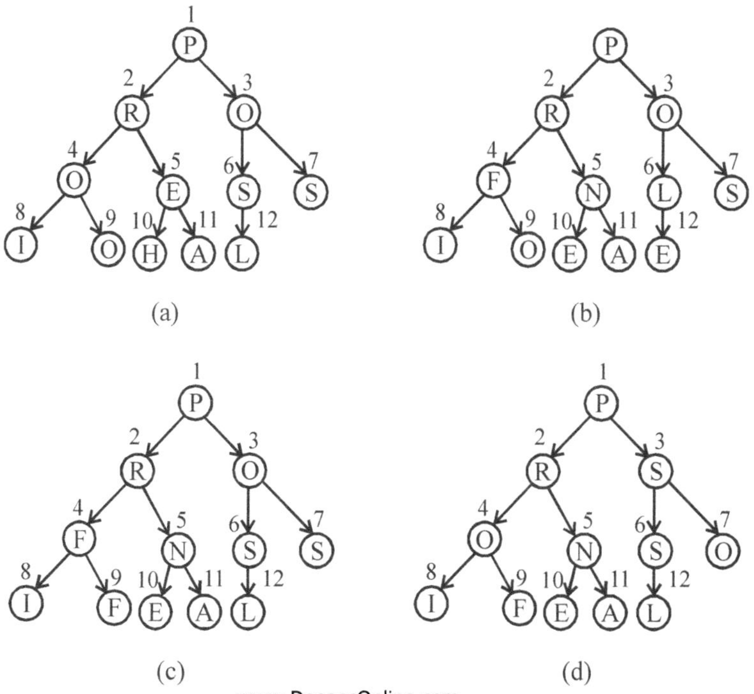

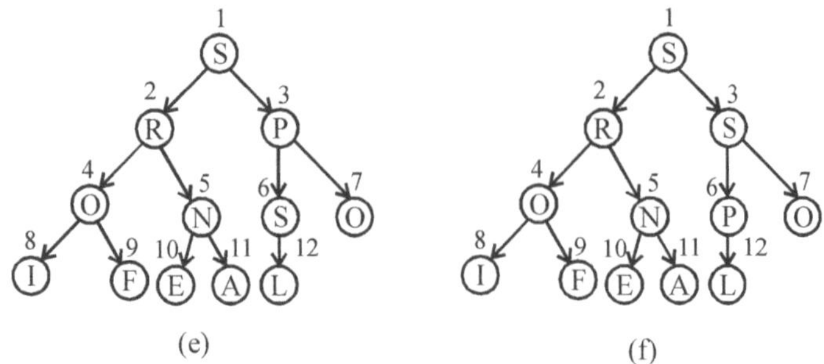

(e) (f)

We will now see how sorting takes place using the heap built by the top down approach. The sorted elements will be placed in X [ ] an array of size 12.

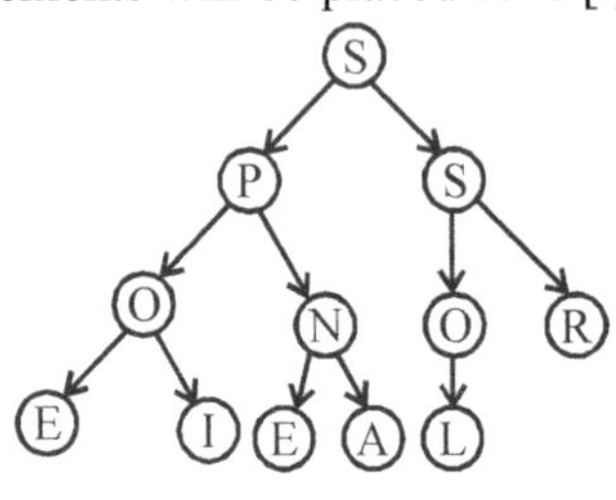

(a)

1. Remove S and store in X [12]

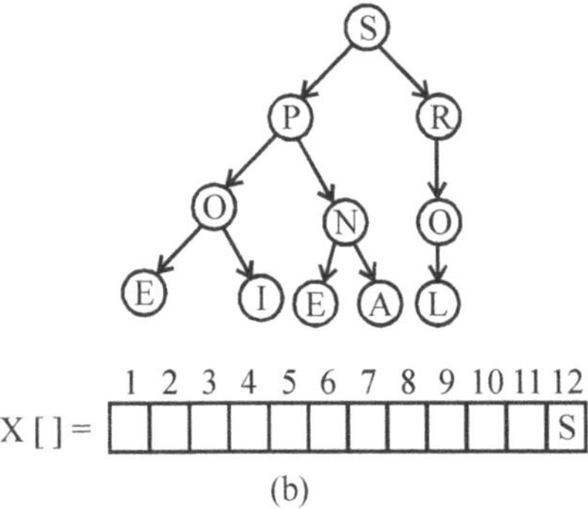

(b)

2. Remove S and store in X [11]

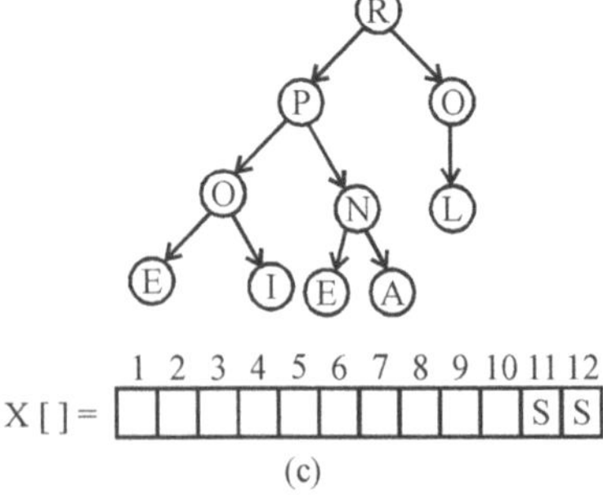

(c)

3. Remove R and store in X [10]

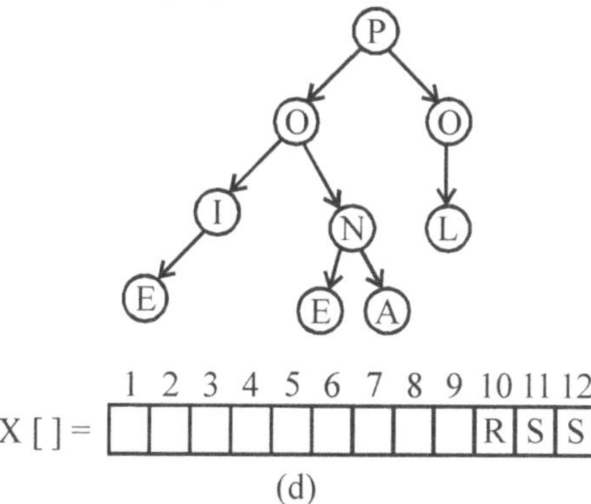

(d)

4. Remove P and store in X[a]

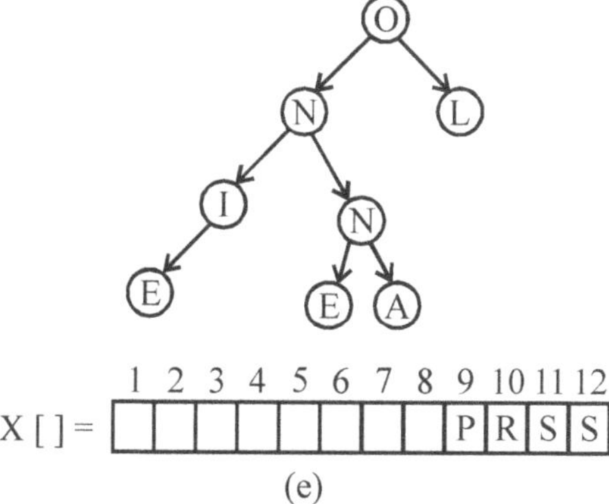

(e)

5. Remove O and store in X[8]

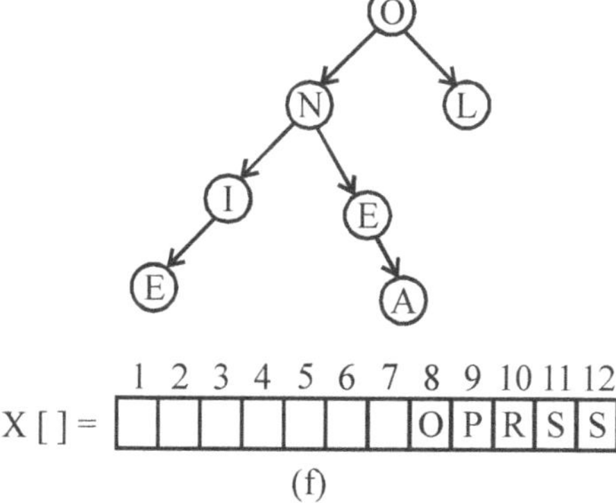

(f)

6. Remove O and store X[7]

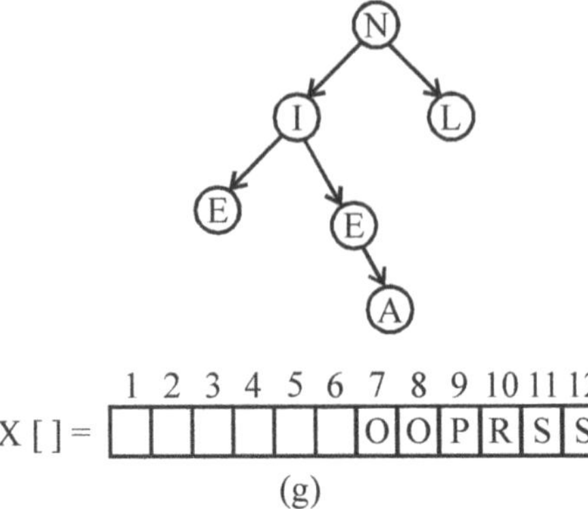

(g)

7. Remove N and store in X[6]

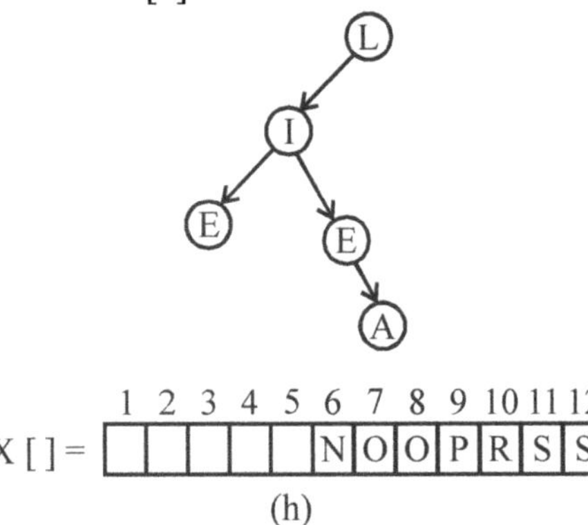

(h)

8. Remove L and store in X[5]

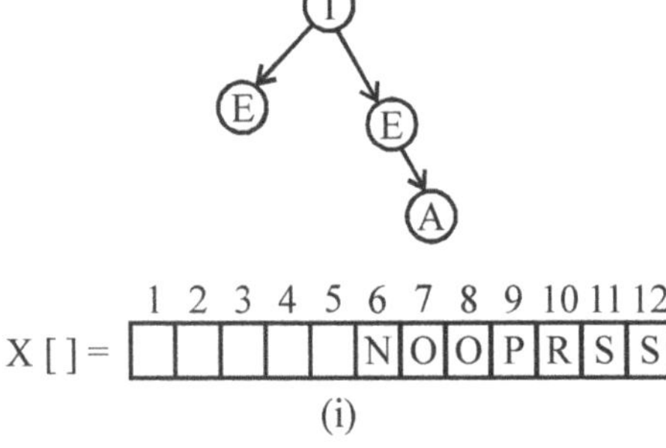

(i)

Similarly the remaining 5 nodes are removed and the heap modified to get the sorted list.

A E E I L N O O P R S S

CS-06 : DATABASE MANAGEMENT SYSTEM
DEC-2006

Note : Question number 1 is compulsory. Attempt any three questions from the rest.

Q1(a). A university registrar's office maintains data about the following entities [10]

(i) *Course*, including number, title, credits, syllabus and prerequisites.

(ii) *Course offering*, including course number, year, semester, section number, instructor (s), timings and classroom.

(iii) *Students*, including student id, name and program.

(iv) *Instructors*, including identification number, name, department and title.

Further, the enrolment of student in courses and grades awarded to students in each course they are enrolled for must be appropriately modelled.

Construct an E-R diagram for the Registrar's office. Document all assumptions that you make about the mapping constraints.

Ans.

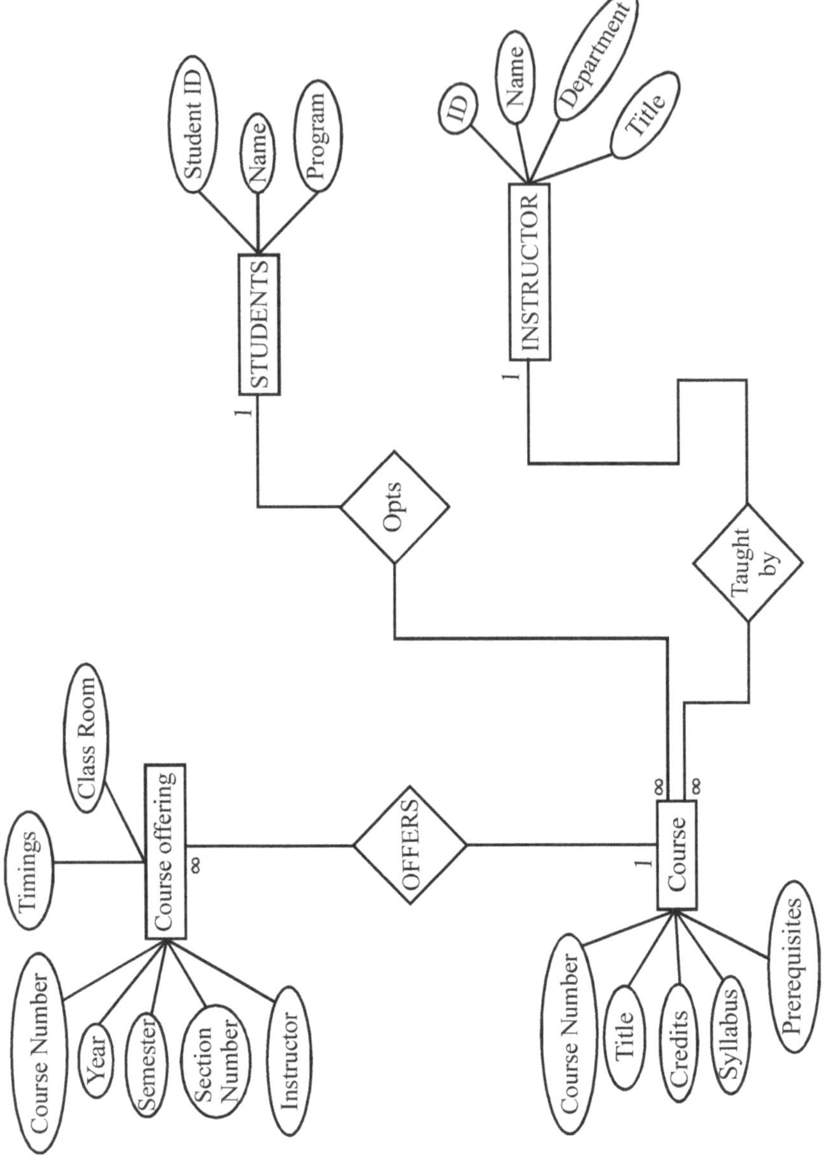

Student ID
Name
Program
STUDENTS
ID
Name
Department
Title
INSTRUCTOR
1
1
Opts
Taught by
Class Room
Timings
Course offering
OFFERS
∞
1
∞
∞
Course
Course Number
Year
Semester
Section Number
Instructor
Course Number
Title
Credits
Syllabus
Prerequisites

(b) Discuss the three level architecture of DBMS. Explain how does it leads to data independence. **[7]**

Refer to Dec.-2003, Q. No.1(b), Page No.79.

As the three levels are assigned different work. Three level architecture allows for changes at one level of the database without affecting other levels. These changes are absorbed by the mappings between the levels. One can change storage mechanisms and formats without having to modify all application programmes. For example:

· method of representation of alphanumeric data (e.g., changing date format to
 avoid Y2000 problem)

· method of representation of numeric data (e.g., integer vs. long integer or floating-point)

· units (e.g., metric vs. furlongs)

· record structure

· file structure (sequential, sorted, indexed, etc.)

Thus, three level architecture of DBMS provides **Data independence**.

(c) With the help of and example, explain the inverted file organization.

Ans. Inverted File Organisation :

Inverted file organization is one file organization where the index structure is most important. The index entries are of variable lengths as the number of records with the same key value is changing, thus, maintenance of index is more complex than that of multi-list file organization. The queries that involve Boolean expressions require accesses only for those records that satisfy the query in addition to the block accesses needed for the indices.

For example :

Qualification Index

B. Tech	B,C,E
MCA	A,D

Salary Index

12000	D
13000	E
15000	A
16000	C
18000	B

(d) What is a view? Explain with the help of an example. Also specify the five conditions that a view must meet in order to allow the updates. **[5]**

Ans. View : View is like a window through which data from tables can be viewed or changed. The table on which a view is based is called base table The format of view statement is as follows:

create view <view name> as <query expression>

Example

(a) For reasons for confidentiality, not all users are permitted to see the Pay_Rate of an employee. For such users the DBA can create a view, for example, EMP_VIEW defined as:

create view EMP_VIEW as
(**select** Empl_No, Name, Skill
from EMPLOYEE)

The five conditions that a view must meet in order to allow the updates are given:

1. No group function,
2. Not any group by clause,
3. Not any distinct keyword,
4. No columns defined by expressions
5. There are not any NOT NULL columns in the base tables that are not selected by view,
6. The select statement used for creating a view should not include sub queries for the creation of views, DISTINCT GROUP BY, HAVING clause.

(e) With the help of an example, explain how knowledge representation can be done through Semantic Network. **[4]**

A lot of knowledge is default knowledge such as birds can fly. You don't want to have to list every attribute of every object, you'd end up with a large amount of data, it would surely be more sensible to create a hierarchy of information. If an entity is a bird you want to make certain assumptions automatically and this results in an inheritance hierarchy.

For example : Tweetie is a canary, canary is a bird, bird is an animal, etc. We would plug in the attributes at the highest possible level e.g..

Animal : Has skin, blood. Can move.
Bird : Is a type of animal. Has feathers. Can fly.
Canary : Is a type of bird. Is Yellow and Small.
Tweetie : Is a canary. Has a toe missing.

Using this technique is obviously efficient as it stores the important attributes only once and only exceptions and extra knowledge are included in each sub-level or sub-class. A structure like this has been shown to be a plausible explanation for the way people remember things.

Semantic nets work along these lines and all semantic nets are constructed from two basic components :

Nodes : These represent the objects, concepts, the things of the domain. Nodes are usually represented by a circle or oval diagrammatically.

Arcs : These represent the relationships between nodes. These can be actions between objects, abstract interactions between concepts, or any number of things in between! Arcs are drawn as arrows connecting the nodes.

(Semantic nets were initially created to demonstrate a theory of long term memory structure in humans by Ross Quillian. His initial aim was to build a program that could understand language but, surprisingly enough, this turned out to be a too ambitious so he dropped his specification down to comparing two word concepts. The results were to be expressed in a pseudo-English language.)

For Example : "Sam is a Vice-President in ABC Corp. He is married to Kay and has a male child named Joe, Joe goes to school. Sam plays golf and owns a silver coloured German made car, Mercedes Benz."

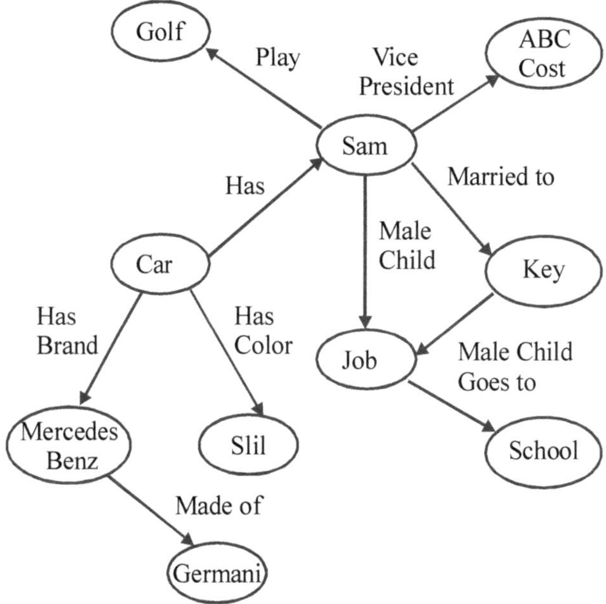

Q2(a). Consider the following 3 tables :

PAINTER

PTR_NUM
PTR_LASTNAME
PTR_FIRSTNAME
PTR_INITIAL
PTR_AREACODE
PTR_PHONE

GALLERY

GAL_NUM
GAL_OWNER
GAL_AREACODE
GAL_PHONE
GAL_RATE

PAINTING

PNTG_NUM
PNTG_TITLE
PNTG_PRICE
PTR_NUM
GAL_NUM

Write the relational algebraic expressions/queries for the following operations : [8]

(i) Find all painters who have painted in GAL_NUM=4.

```
SELECT
Painter.ptr_firstname,
Painter.ptr_lastname, gallery.gal_ num
From gallery INNER JOIN
(Painter INNER JOIN painting ON
        Painter.ptr_num =
Painting.ptr_name) ON gallery.gal_num = pointing.gal_num
WHERE ((gallery.gal_num)=4);
```

(ii) Find all paintings of Gallery whose rate is >1000.

```
SELECT
painting.pntg_num, painting.pntg_title, painting.pntg_price
FROM
        gallery INNER JOIN
painting ON gallery.gal_num
= painting.gal_num
WHERE ((painting.pntg_price)>1000);
```

(iii) Find the Gallery in which painter 'Ramesh' has displayed his paintings.

```
SELECT
gallery.gal_num, gallery.gal_owner,
painter.ptr_firstname
FROM gallery INNER JOIN
(painter INNER JOIN painting ON
painter.ptr_num = painting.ptr_num)
ON gallery.gal_num = painting.gal_num
WHERE ((painter.ptr_firstname) = "Ramesh");
```

(iv) Find the number of paintings displayed in Gallery owned by 'Shyam'.

```
SELECT
painting.pntg_num, gallery.gal_owner
FROM gallery INNER JOIN painting
ON gallery.gal_num = painting.gal_num
WHERE ((gallery.gal_owner) = "Shyam");
```

(b) Explain the concepts of Generalization and Specialization with examples. **[7]**

Generalization is the abstracting process of viewing sets of objects as a single general class by concentrating on the general characteristics of the constituent sets while suppressing or ignoring their differences. It is the union of a number of lower-level entity types for the purpose of producing a higher-level entity type. For instance, student is a generalization of graduate or undergraduate, full-time or part-time students. Similarly, employee is a generalization of the classes of objects cook, waiter, cashier. Generalization is an IS_An relationship; therefore, manager IS_An employee, cook IS_An employee, waiter IS_An employee, and so forth.

Specialization is the abstracting process of introducing new characteristics to an existing class of object to create one or more new classes of objects. This involves taking a higher-level entity and, using additional characteristics, generating lower-level entities. The lower-level entities also inherit the characteristics of the higher-level entities. In applying the characteristic size to car we can create a full-size, mid-size, compact, or subcompact car. Specialization may be seen as the reverse process of generalization: additional specific properties are introduced at a lower level in a hierarchy of objects.

Example :

Below is the Diagrammatic Representation

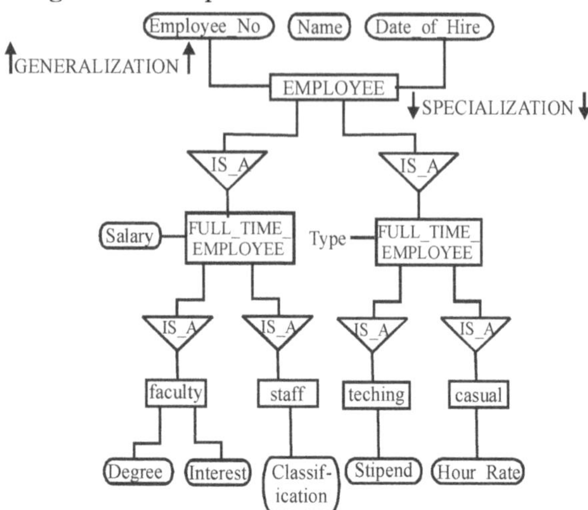

Q3(a). Mention the features of OODBMS and give four advantage of it [8]

Refer to June-2004, Q. No.6(a), Page No.-72.

(b) What are the general resistances faced by an organization while implementing DBMS tool? Explain atleast four of them. [4]

Following are the general resistances faced by an organization while implementing DBMS tool :

(i) The use of the database and its possibility of being shared will, therefore affect many departments within the organization. If the integrity of the data is not maintained, it is possible that one relevant piece of data could have been used by many programs in different applications by different users without they are being aware of it. The impact of this, therefore may be very widespread. Since data can be input from a variety sources, the control over the quality of data become very difficult to implement.

(ii) A part needing a more powerful hardware platform, the software for database management systems are also quite expensive. This means that a significant extra cost has to be incurred by an organization if it wants to adopt this approach.

(iii) The advantages gained by the possibility of sharing of the data with others, also carries with it the risk of data being unauthorisedly accessed. This may range from violation of office procedures to violation of privacy rights of information to down right thefts. The organizations, therefore, have to be ready to cope with additional managerial problems.

(iv) A database management processing system is complex and it could lead to a more inefficient system than the equivalent file-based one.

(v) The staff available for the organization may not be experienced enough to cope with. The training of personnel in the management in use of a database takes times, is expensive and required special attention.

(vi) The work in the organization may not require significant sharing of data or complex access. In other words the data and the way it is used in the functioning of the organization is not appropriate to database processing.

However, for most large organizations, the difficulties in moving over to a database approach are still worth getting over in view of the advantages that are gained, avoidance of data duplication, sharing of data by different programs, greater flexibility and data independence.

(c) What is client/server computing? Discuss the component of client/ server computing.

Refer to June-2003, Q. No.4, Page No.100 to 104.

Q4(a). Given the structure

Proj Num	Project Name	Emp No.	Emp Name	Job Class	Chg/hr	Hrs Billed	Total Charge
13	Banking	103	Ramesh	System Analyst	500	8	4000
		105	Ram	Programme	300	8	2400
26	Telecom	115	Amit	Business Analyst	100	10	1000
		117	Shyam	Engineer	300	7	2100
39	Finance	113	Gopal	Team Leader	1000	4	4000
		120	Suresh	DBA	800	3	2400

(i) Identify the anomalies in the given structure.

Ans.

* **Insertion Anamalies :** Job class of a particular employee can't be recorded

until the employee assigned a project. Project and Employee details are mixed.

* **Deletion Anamalies :** When an employee completes work on a project, the employee's record is deleted. The other information regarding to that employee will also be lost.

* **Updation Anamalies :** For a given employee, the Empno, Project num, Job class, Proj name are repeated several times. Hence if an employee is transferred to another projecct this change will be recorded in every row of the table pertaining to that employee. Any omission will lead to inconsistency.

(ii) Normalise it up to third normal form (3NF).

Ans Development of table;

PROJ NUM	PROJECT NAME	Job class	CHG HR
13.	Banking	Systems Analyse	500
26.	Telecom	Business Analyse	10
39.	Finance	Team	4

ENO	E-Name	HRS BILLED	Total Charge
103	Ramesh	8	4000
115	Amit	10	1000
113	Gopal	4	4000

(b) Explain any three aggregate functions of SQL with an example for each.

Ans. Three aggregate functions are :

Count : It is use in getting consolidated information from a group of tuples.

(a) SELECT COUNT (*)
FROM EMP;

MIN (MINIMUM)

(b) SELECT MIN (SAL)
FROM EMP;

MAX (MAXIMUM)

(c) SELECT MAX (AGE)
FROM EMP;
WHERE DEPTNO ='D1';

Q5(a). Explain the structure of Index sequential file with the help of a diagram. **[5]**

Repeated in June,2006, Q1(b).

(b) Explain briefly **[5]**

(i) Dynamic Data Exchange (DDE)

Refer to Dec.,-2002, Q. No.4(ii), Page No.122

(ii) Object Linking & Embedding (OLE).

Refer to Jan.,-2001, Q. No.6(b)(ii), Page No.188

(c) Illustrate the differences between hierarchical and network data models. Explain why relational data model is a better choice over the two. **[5]**

Ans. Differences between hierarchical and network data models :

(i) In a hierarchical model, data is organized into a tree-like structure, implying a single upward link in each record to describe the nesting, and a sort field to keep the records in a particular order in each same-level list.

In a network model (defined by the CODASYL specification) data is organized using two fundamental constructs, called records and sets. Records contain fields (which may be organized hierarchically, as in the programming language COBOL). Sets (not to be confused with mathematical sets) define one-to-many relationships between records: one owner, many members. A record may be an owner in any number of sets, and a member in any number of sets.

(ii) Hierarchical structures were widely used in the early mainframe database management systems, such as the Information Management System (IMS) by IBM, and now describe the structure of XML documents. This structure allows one 1:N relationship between two types of data. This structure is very efficient to describe many relationships in the real world; recipes, table of contents, ordering of paragraphs/verses, any nested and sorted information. However, the hierarchical structure is inefficient for certain database operations when a full path (as opposed to upward link and sort field) is not also included for each record.

The operations of the **network model** are navigational in style: a program maintains a current position, and navigates from one record to another by following the relationships in which the record participates. Records can also be located by supplying key values.

Relational Model is better than the other two because of the following reasons :

I. High-Level-Programming languages : Programming languages have been developed specially to access databases defined via the relational data model; these languages permit data to be manipulated as groups or files rather than procedurally; one record at a time.

II. Logical Key Pointers : The relational data model uses primary (and secondary) keys in records to represent the association between two records. Because of this model's implementation independence, however, it is conceivable that the physical database (totally masked from the user of a relational database) could use address pointers or one of many other methods.

III. Normalization Theory : Properties of a database that make it free of certain maintenance problems have been developed within the context of the relational model (although these properties can also be designed into a network data model database.

IV. Implementation Independence : The relational model logically represents all relationships implicitly, and hence, one does not know what associations are or are not physically represented by an efficient access path (without looking at the internal data model).

CS-06 : Database Management System
June, 2007

Note : Question number 1 is compulsory. Attempt any **three** questions from the rest.

1. (a) A Bank maintains information about customers and their accounts. Each customer has a name, address (house number, area, city and state code) and telephone number. Account has number, type and balance. We need to record customers who own an account. Account can be operated individually or jointly.
Design and draw an ER diagram, clearly indicating the attributes, keys the cardinality ratio and participation constraints.
Ans.

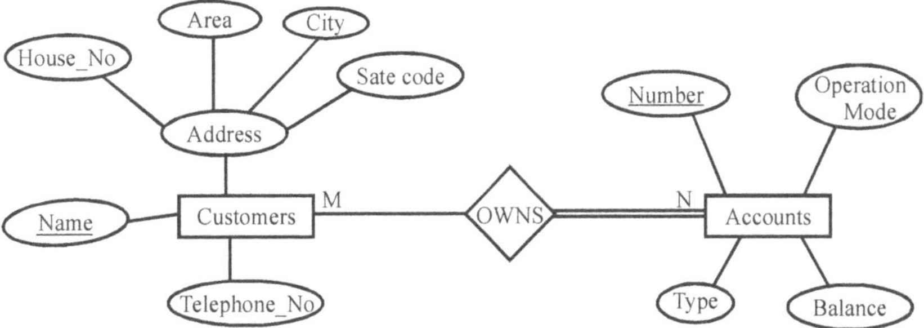

(b) What is meant by data abstraction? Explain the differences between physical level, conceptual level and view level of data abstraction.
Refer to June-2002, Q.No.-2(v), Page No.-136
& Refer to June-2002, Q.No.-2(iii), Page No.-134

(c) Explain at least five important characteristics of OORDBMS.
Ans. ORDBMS combines the advantages of modern object-oriented programming languages with relational database features such as multiple views of data and a high-level non-procedural query language. ORDBMS has following characteristics:
- Provides the capabilities of object-orientation
- Provides multiples views of data
- High-level non-procedural query language
- Provides support for user-defined data types
- Support specialized applications such as image retrieval etc.

(d) For the relation R and S given below. Compute natural join and outer join.

R

A	B	C
1	2	3
4	5	6
7	8	9

S

B	C	D
2	3	10
2	3	11
6	7	11

Ans. R Natural Join S

A	B	C	D
1	2	3	10
1	2	3	11

Full outer Join

A	B	C	D
1	2	3	10
1	2	3	11
7	8	9	
4	5	6	
	6	7	12

(e) Given the following relations:

Vehicle (reg_no, colour, type)
Person (eno, name, address)
Owner (eno, reg_no)

Write expressions in the relational algebra to answer the following queries:

(i) List the reg_no of vehicles owned by "Sandeep".

(ii) List the names of persons who own "Indica" cars.

(iii) List details of all the black coloured vehicles.

Ans. (i) π_{reg_no} ($\sigma_{name = \text{'Sandeep'}}$ (Person® Owner))

(ii) π_{name} ($\sigma_{type = \text{'Indica'}}$ (Person® Owner® Vehicle)

(iii) $\sigma_{colour = \text{'Black'}}$ (Vehicle)

2.(a) Describe DROP TABLE command of SQL with both the options CASCADE AND RESTRICT.

Ans. DROP TABLE command : This command drops the specified table. Dropping a table also drops indexes and grants associated with it. Objects built on dropped tables are marked invalid and cease to work.

CASCADE and RESTRICT options : The DROP TABLE with RESTRICT option destroy the table unless some view or integrity constraint refer to the given table; if so, the command fails. But with the CASCADE option, any referencing views or integrity constraints are (recursively) dropped as well.

(b) Explain the recovery process after system failure, using checkpoint.

Ans. In a large on-line database system there could be hundreds of transactions handled per minute. The log for this type of database contains a very large volume of information. A scheme called checkpoint is used to limit the volume of log information that has to be handled and processed in the event of a system failure involving the loss of volatile information. The checkpoint scheme is an additional component of the logging scheme.

A checkpoint operation, performed periodically, copies log information onto stable storage and put the checkpoint marker at that time in the log. For all transactions active at checkpoint, their identifiers and their database modification actions, which at that time are reflected only in the database buffers, will be propagated to the appropriate storage.

If there is a crash, it scans the log in a backward direction from the time of system crash. Initially, all the transactions are added to the undo list. After that, if it finds that a transaction in the undo list has committed, that transaction is removed from the undo list and placed in the redo list. The redo list contains all the transactions that have to be redone. All transactions that were committed before the checkpoint time need not be considered for the recovery operation. Therefore, the overhead of the recovery from a system crash is reduced. However, in a system that uses the transaction paradigm, checkpoint is a strategy to minimize the search of the log and the amount of undo and redo required to recover from a system failure with loss of volatile storage.

(c) How is the knowledge representation done through semantic network? Give an example of semantic network.

Ans. Semantic network (or also called as associative network) is used for graphical representation of knowledge. It is one of effective and popular method used in knowledge databases. The objects are represented by modes (ovals) and the relation (predicates or properties) are represented by directed edges. Example: Ram is a programmer. He works for ABC company.

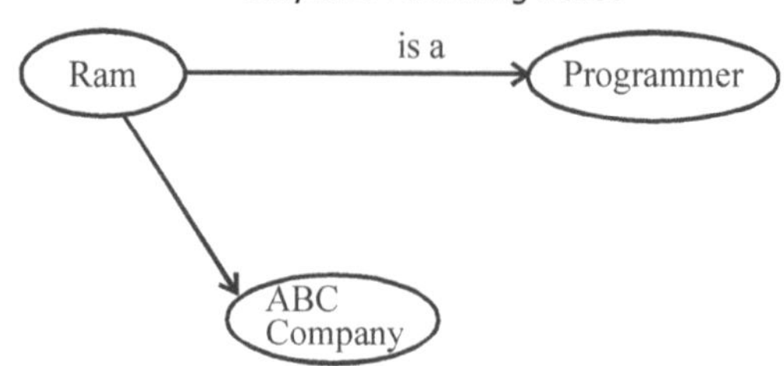

3.(a) How does data fragmentation support the distributed databases? Explain horizontal and vertical fragmentation using an example of given relation.

Project (Project_name, Emp_no, Emp_name, Job_class, Emp_location, Salary) Note: Assume the suitable data.

Ans. First Refer : June-2004, Q.No.-2(c), Page No.-67

Horizontal Fragmentation

Assumption : Data is fragmented based on Emp_location value.

The relations will be

Project1(Project_name, Emp_no, Emp_name, Job_class, Emp_location, Salary)
Project2(-----------------)
:
:
Projectn(-----------------)

Vertical Fragmentation

Assumption : Project and Employee details are fragmented.

Project(Project_name, Job_class, Emp_no)
Employee(Emp_no, Emp_name, Emp_location, Salary)

(b) What is NULL? Give an example to illustrate testing for NULL in SQL.

Ans. NULL is a special value represent nothing in the data item. The NULL value is tested by using IS NULL or IS NOT NULL condition.

Example :

Select * From Emp Where City IS NULL;

(c) Define and differentiate between ordered indexing and hashing.

Ans. Ordered Indexing or Index-Sequential : Provides random access to records and the sequential nature of the file provides easy access to next record. Updation do not require generation of a new file. It uses magnetic disks for direct access. In indexed sequential file overflow is a real problem in volatile tables. ISAM is good for static tables because there are usually fewer index levels.

Hashing : In direct file organization the key value is mapped directly to storage location. The usual method of direct mapping is by performing arithmetic manipulation of the key value. This procedure is called hashing.

4. (a) Construct a B+ tree for the following set of key values where the number of key values that fit in a node is 3.
Key values : (12, 2, 15, 4, 123, 45, 6, 7, 9, 1, 3)
Show the steps involved in the deletion of key values 7 and then 6.

Ans. Insertion

Keys: 12, 2, 15

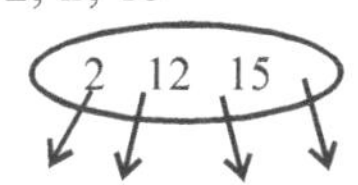

Keys: 4

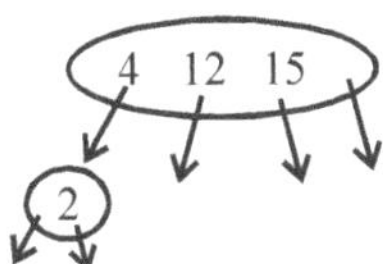

Keys: 123, 45

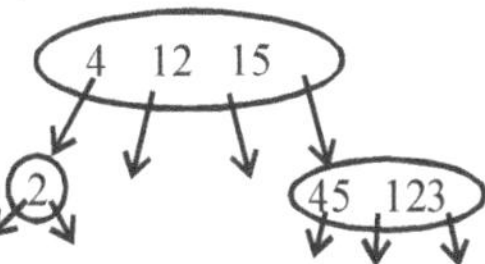

Keys: 6, 7, 9

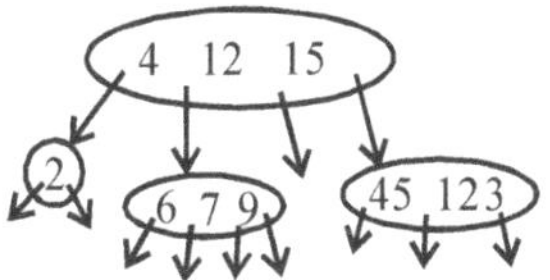

Keys: 1, 3

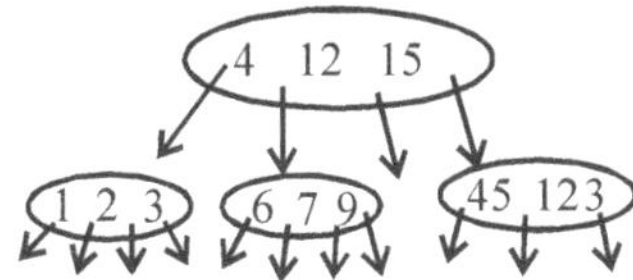

Deletion

Keys: 7, 6

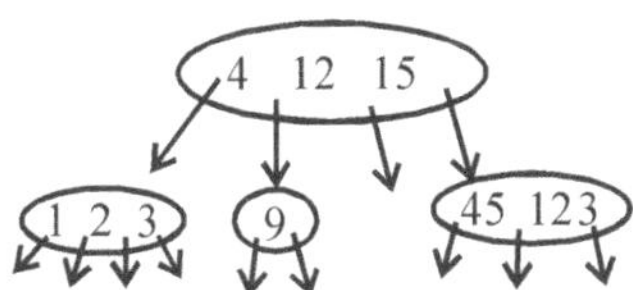

(b) Why is BCNF a more desirable normal from than any of the lower

order normal forms? Give an example of a relational schema that a in 3NF but no in BCNF.

Ans. A relation is in Boyce/Codd normal form (BCNF) if and only if every determinant is a candidate key. [A determinant is any attribute on which some other attribute is (fully) functionally dependent.]

Boyce-Codd normal form is stricter than **3NF**, meaning that every relation in BCNF is also in 3NF; however, a relation in 3NF is *not necessarily* in BCNF. A relation schema is an **BCNF** if whenever a functional dependency X->A holds in the relation, then X is a superkey of the relation. The only difference between BCNF and 3NF is that condition of **3NF** (i.e 3NF also require prime attribute), which allows A to be prime if X is not a superkey, is absent from BCNF.

Consider, as an example, the relation **Professor:**
Professor (**Professor code,** Dept., Head of Dept., Parent time)
Assuming that

1. The percentage of the time spent in each department is given.
2. A professor can work in more than one department
3. Each department has only one Head of Department

The relationship diagram for the above relation is given below. The two possible composite keys are professor code and Dept. or Professor code and Head of Department. Observe that department as well as Head of Department are not non-key attributes. They are a part of composite key.

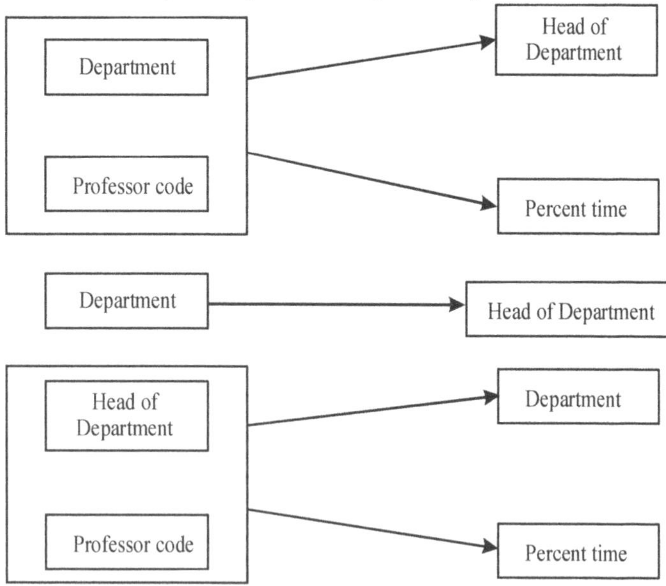

Dependency Diagram of Professor Relation

Professor Code	Department	Head of Dept.	Parent
P1	Physics	Ghosh	50
P1	Mathematics	Krishnan	50
P2	Chemistry	Rao	25
P2	Physics	Ghosh	75
P3	Mathematics	Krishnan	100

The relation given in above table is in 3NF. Thus, from the above case it is clear that BCNF is more desirable normal form than any of the lower order. As the given case is better than 3NF and 3NF is better than 2 NF and so on.

5. (a) Define the following with respect to SQL. Also give an example of each.
(i) UNIQUE function
(ii) ORDER-BY clause
(iii) LINK predicate

Ans. (i) UNIQUE: It is used to specify UNIQUE constraint.
Example:
Alter table student
Add constraint UNIQUE(ENRL No);

(ii) ORDER BY: It is used with select statement to arrange the output of select statement.

Example : Select * From Emp Order By Emp_name;

(iii) LIKE: LIKE predicate is used for pattern matching using wild card characters '%' and '_'.

Example : Select * From Emp Where Emp_name LIKE 'A%';

(b) Explain different methods of implementing the following data models:
(i) Hierarchical Data Model
(ii) Network Data Model

Ans. (i) Hierarchical Data Model can be implemented using tree data structure.
(ii) Network Data Model can be implemented using Linked Lists or graphs.

(c) What is the difference between a database schema and a database state?

Ans. Database Scheme: The *description* of a database. Includes descriptions of the database structure and the constraints that should hold on the database.
Database State: Refers to the content of a database at a moment in time.
Distinction: The database schema changes very *infrequently*. The database state changes *every time the database is updated*. Schema is also called intension, whereas state is called extension.

CS-06 : Database Management System
December, 2007

Note : There are five questions in this paper. Question number 1 is **compulsory.** Attempt any **three** questions from the rest.

1. (a) Explain the characteristics of Relational Model. Write its two advantages and disadvantages. How is relational model different from other models? Explain with a suitable example.

Ans. Refer to Dec-2004, Q.No.-3(b), Page No.-233

(b) A marketing based organization has many branches in different states. The organization sells items in bulk to the dealers who sell them to retailers. The retailers ultimately sell it to the customers. Draw an E-R diagram for this distribution channel, clearly indicating the entities, attributes, relationships, keys and the cardinality ratio.

Ans.

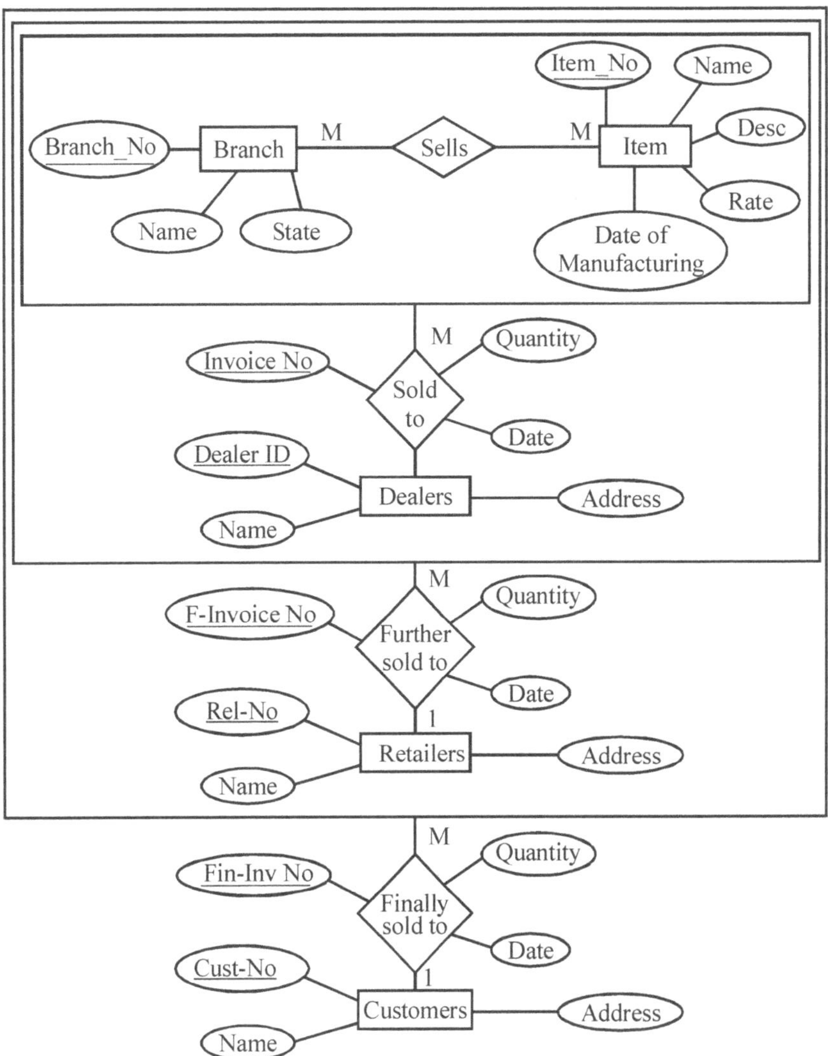

(c) What is data integrity? Explain the significance of data integrity in database management system, with the help of a suitable example.

Ans. Data integrity means that the data contained in the database is both accurate and consistent. Therefore, data values being entered for storage could be checked to ensure that they fall within a specified range and are of the correct format. For example, the value for the age of an employee may be in the range of 16 and 75. Another integrity check that should be incorporated in the database is to ensure that if there is a reference to certain object, that object must exist. In the case of an automatic teller machine, for example, a user is not allowed to transfer funds from a nonexistent saving account to a checking account.

(d) Construct a B-tree of order 5 by inserting the following data: { D, H, K, Z, B, P, Q, E, A, S, W, T, C, L, }

Ans. (i) After Inserting: D, H, K, Z

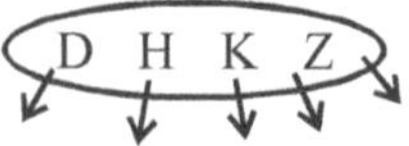

(ii) After Inserting: B

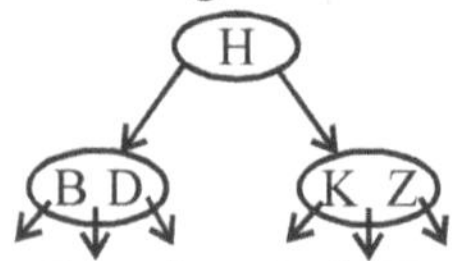

(iii) After Inserting: P, Q, E, A

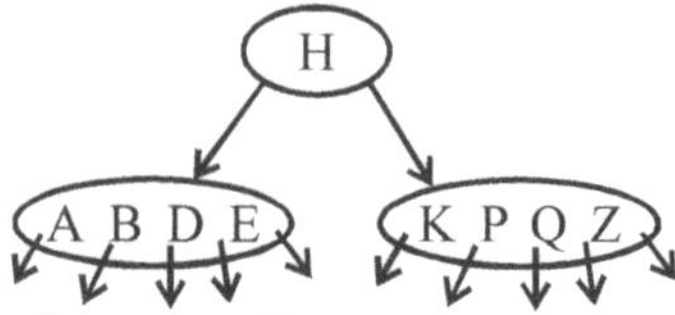

(iv) After Inserting: S

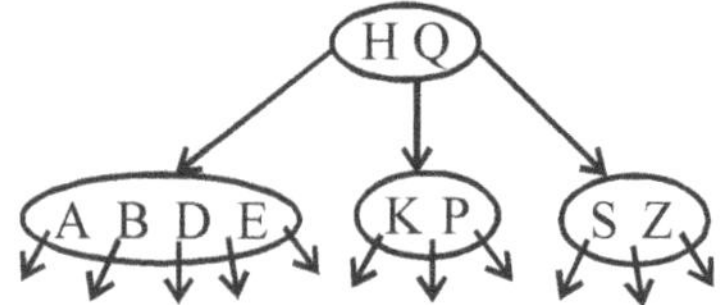

(v) After Inserting: W, T

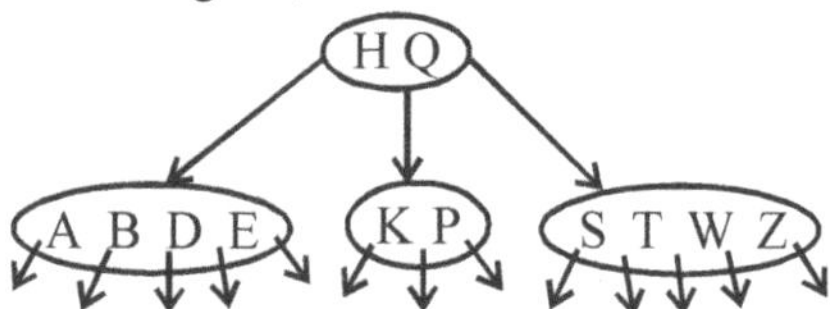

(vi) After Inserting: C

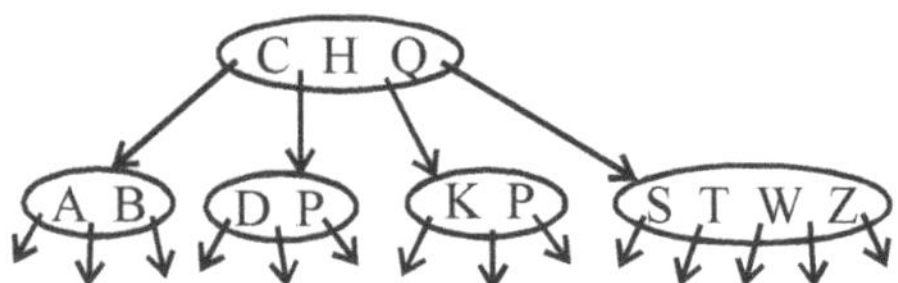

(vii) After Inserting: L

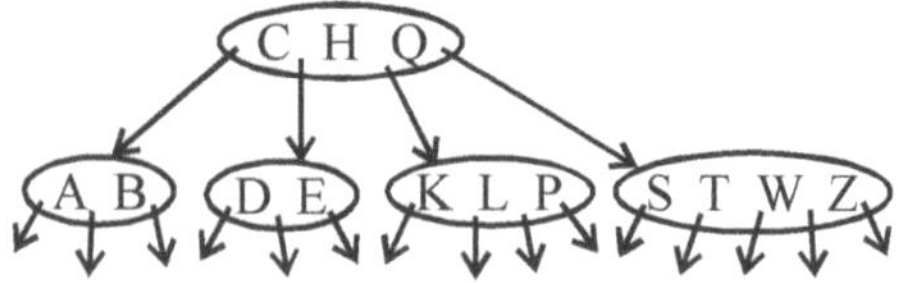

2. (a) Consider the following relations:
Item (I_code, I_name, I_price, I_qty)
Customer (c_code, c_name, c_address, c_phone)

Issue (Is_code, Is_date, I_code, c_code, is_qty)
Write the appropriate SQL queries for the following:
(i) Find the name of the customers who have taken any item with price above Rs. 1000/-
(ii) Find the details of the costliest item.
(iii) Find the issue code and quantity of all the items issued today.
(iv) Find the details of those customers who bought a particular item, given the I_code.

Ans. (i) Select Distinct C_name From Item, Customer, Issue Where item.i_code = issue.i_code AND customer.c_code = issue.c_code AND i_price > 1000;
(ii) Select * From item Where i_price = (Select max(i_price) From item);
(iii) Select is_code, is_qty From issue Where is_date = Sysdate;
(iv) Select * From customer Where c_code in (Select c_code From issue Where I_code = 'ABC')

(b) What are major anomalies in a database? Explain the method to deal with these anomalies, with a suitable example.

Ans. First Refer : June-2003, Q.No.-2(i), Page No.-95

Normalization is used to reduce the anomalies from the database.These anomalies are created due to the data redundancy in the database and with the help of normalization we can reduce the data redundancy and its implication.

3. (a) What is a view? Discuss the difference between a view and a base relation. Explain what happens when a user accesses a database through a view. Give an example of a base relation and a view.

Ans. Refer to June-2003, Q.No.-2(ii) Page No.-96

Now Refer to Dec-2006, Q.No.-1(d), Page No.-278

Basis	Base Relation	View
Storage	Physically Stored	Virtually Stored
Default Order of Records	Based on creation of the records	Specified by the Order By clause
Records belongs to	Only one relation	May belongs to multiple relations
Updatation	Not restricted	Some Update restrictions are there on views

For example : Base Relation: EMP(EMPNO, ENAME, ADDRESS, DEPTNO)
View: Create View EMP_V1 as Select * From EMP Where DEPTNO=20 Order By EMPNO;
In this case if we want to execute a query e.g., Select EMPNO, ENAME From EMP_V1 Where ENAME like 'A%'
then first this query will refer the view EMP_V1 which in turn refer the base relation EMP to return the result.

(b) Explain the process of data fragmentation with suitable example. Discuss different types of data fragmentation. Compare it with data triplication.

Ans. First Refer : June-2002, Q.No.-3(a), Page No.-137

The act of tripling, or making threefold, or adding three together. *Data Triplication* is the term for this phenomenon of copying the data three times(at three different storage media). Its main advantage when implemented is : **Data** unavailability reduced and Data Availability improved.

4. (a) Write five major steps in the process of conversion from old system to a new system. Mention two technical and administrative criteria for evaluation of a database.

Ans. The following five steps required in the process of conversion from old system to a new system::

(1) Determining conversion priority in strategic information system plans, building block systems and critical needs to replace system.

(2) Redesign and implement new data structures.

(3) Write software utility tools to convert the files or database in the old system to the new database.

(4) Modify all application programs to make use of the new data structures.

(5) Implement all software.

Now Refer : June-2005, Q.No.3(a), Page No.-216

(b) Compare the working mechanism of virtual records with replication. Explain the method of accessing the data records in hierarchical data structure, with suitable example.

Ans. In the case of many-to-many relationships, record **replication** is necessary to preserve the tree-structure organization of the database. Record replication has two major drawbacks:

1. Data inconsistency may result when updating takes place.
2. Waste of space is unavoidable.

There are several ways to eliminate these drawbacks. To eliminate record replication, we need to relax our requirement that the logical organization of data be constrained to a tree structure. Do it carefully otherwise we will end up with the network model. The solution is to introduce the concept of a **virtual record**. Such a record contains no data value; it does contain a logical pointer to a particular physical record. Instead of replication, we keep a single copy of the physical record, and everywhere else we keep virtual records containing a pointer to that physical record. More specifically, we let R be a record type that is replicated in several tree-structure diagrams—say, T1, T2, ··· ,Tn. To eliminate replication, we create a new virtual recordtype virtual-R, and replace R in each of the n - 1 trees with a record of type virtual-R.

Now Refer : Dec-2001, Q.No.-3(b), Page No.-155

5. (a) With the help of an example explain the Multilist file organization method. How is it different from inverted file organisation?

Ans. Refer to Dec-2004, Q.No.-5(b), Page No.-237

(b) Differentiate between a knowledge base system and a database system. List any three major knowledge representation schemes. Explain the working mechanism of Frame Base Representation Scheme.

Ans. Refer to June-2004, Page No.-64

Three major knowledge representation schemes:

1. Frame Structure

2. Semantic Network

3. Conceptual Graph

Now : Refer to June-2003, Q.No.6(ii), Page No.-108

CS – 06 : Database Management System
June, 2008

Note: Question number 1 is **compulsory**. Attempt any **three** questions from the rest.

Q1. (a) A construction company XYZ maintains information about customers and their bookings. Each customer has a name, address, mobile number, telephone number and e-mail address. Each booking has a booking amount, type of flat booked (i.e. 2BR/3BR), name of the block in which flat is located and number of the flat. You need to design a database which can absorb changes in bookings by customers, such as deposit of booking amount, change of flat etc.
Design and draw an ER diagram, clearly indicating the attributes, keys, the cardinality and participation constraints.
Ans.

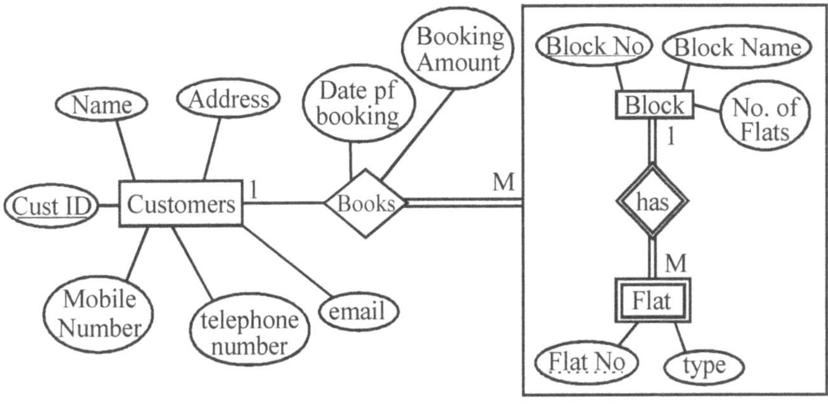

(b) Explain the advantages of a Relational DBMS over the Hierarchical DBMS model.

Refer to Q.No.-5(c) Page No.-285, 286
Also Refer Q.No.-(1) Page No.-5

(c) Explain the distributed computing environment. Explain the following terms w.r.t. it:
(i) Two Phase Commit (2PC)
(ii) Replicated Server/Table

Refer to Q.No.-1(g) Page No.-167

(d) Explain any ten Codd's rules.

Ans. Dr. E.D. Codd, an IBM researcher, first developed the relational data model in 1970. In 1985, Dr. Codd published a list of 12 rules that concisely define an ideal relational database, which have provided a guideline for the design of all relational database systems ever since. The term "guideline" is used because, to date, no commercial relational database system fully conform to all 12 rules. They do represent the relational ideal, though. Following is a list of Codd's 12 rules, including his original name for each rule and a simplified description.

Rule 1: The Information Rule: All data should be presented to the user in table form.

Rule 2: Guaranteed Access Rule: All data should be accessible without ambiguity. This can be accomplished through a combination of the table name, primary key and column name.

Rule 3: Systematic Treatment of Null Values: A field should be allowed to remain empty. This involves the support of a null value, which is distinct from an empty string or a number with a value of zero. Of course, this can't apply to primary keys. In addition, most database implementations support the concept of a non-null field constraint that prevents null values in a specific table column.

Rule 4: Dynamic On-Line Catalog Based on the Relational Model: A relational database must provide access to its structure through the same tools that are used to access the data. This is usually accomplished by storing the structure definition within special system tables.

Rule 5: Comprehensive Data Sublanguage Rule: The database must support at least one clearly defined language that includes functionality for data definition, data manipulation, data integrity and database transaction control. All commercial relational database use forms of the standard SQL (Structured Query Language) as their supported comprehensive language.

Rule 6: View Updating Rule: Data can be presented to the user in different logical combinations, called views. Each view should support the same full range of data manipulation that direct-access to a table has a available. In practice, providing update and delete access to logical views is difficult and is not fully supported by any current database.

Rule 7: High-level Insert, Update and Delete: Data can be retrieved from a relational database in sets constructed of data from multiple rows and/or multiple tables. This rule states that insert, update and delete operations should be supported for any retrievable set rather than just for a single row in a single table.

Rule 8: Physical Data Independence: The user is isolated from the physical method of storing and retrieving information from the database. Changes can be made to the underlying architecture (hardware, disk storage methods) without affecting how the user accesses it.

Rule 9: Logical Data Independence: How a user views data should not change when the logical structure (tables structure) of the database changes. This rule is particularly difficult to satisfy. Most databases rely on strong ties between the user view of the data and the actual structure of the underlying tables.

Rule 10: Integrity Independence: The database language (like SQL) should support constraints on user input that maintain database integrity. This rule is not fully implemented by most major vendors. At a minimum, all databases do preserve two constraints through SQL.

- No component of a primary key can have a null value.
- If a foreign key is defined in one table, any value in it must exist as a primary key in another table.

Rule 11: Distribution Independence: A user should be totally unaware of whether or not the database is distributed (whether parts of the database exist in multiple locations). A variety of reasons make this rule difficult to implement.

Rule 12: Nonsubversion Rule: There should be no way to modify the database structure other than through the multiple row database language (like SQL). Most databases today support administrative tools that allow some direct manipulation of the data structure.

Q2. (a) Write and explain CREATE and INSERT statements in SQL. Also, give an example for each.

Ans. CREATE statement : To make a new database, table, index or stored query. Perhaps the most common CREATE command is the CREATE TABLE command. The typical usage is:

CREATE [TEMPORARY] TABLE *[table name]* (*[column definitions]*) *[table parameters]*.

Column Definitions: A comma-separated list consisting of any of the following

- Column definition: *[column name] [date type] {NULL|NOT NULL} {column options}*
- Primary key definitions: *PRIMARY KEY* (*[comma separated column list]*)
- CONSTRAINTS: *{CONSTRAINT} [constraint definition]*
- RDBMS specific functionality

For example, the command to create a table named **employees** with a few sample columns would be:

```
CREATE TABLE    employee    (
    id              INTEGER      PRIMARY KEY,
    first_name      CHAR (50)    NULL,
    last_name       CHAR (75)    NOT NULL,
    dateofbirth     DATE         NULL
);
```

INSERT statement : This statement is used to insert a row of data in a table. All inserted non numeric values are enclosed using single quote strings. The syntax of this command is :

```
insert into tablename
[(column1name, column2name...columnxname)]
values (value1, value2...valuex);
```

Example :

```
insert into citylist
(name, state, population, zipcode)
values ('Gullybaba', 'India', 100, '110035');
```

(b) Describe the following relational operators with an example for each: (i) UNION (ii) INTERSECTION (iii) CARTESIAN PRODUCT

Refer to Q.No.-6(a) Page No.-203-204

Q3. (a) Describe the methodologies used in the evaluation of a DBMS. What are the merits and demerits of each of these?

Refer to Q.No.-3(a) Page No.-119-120

(b) Give the structure of a distributed database system with the help of a diagram. Also, give its trade-offs. List two distinct applications where we can use the distributed databases.

Refer to Q.No.-2(b) Page No.-230-231

Q4. (a) What is meant by Client/Server computing? Explain the significance of it. Describe its components.

Refer to Q.No.-4 Page No.-100-104

(b) Explain why Project-Join Normal Form is more desirable than 4NF.

Refer to Q.No.-6(a) Page No.-124-126

Q5. (a) Explain the trade-off that should be considered in the design of an inversion index for multikey file.

Refer to Q.No.-5(b) Page No.-241-242

(b) What is a Knowledge based system? Compare and contrast Knowledge based system with a Database system. Explain the context of use of the Knowledge based systems with examples.

Refer to Q.No.-6(c) Page No.-244-246

CS – 06 : Database Management System
December, 2008

Note: Question number 1 is **compulsory**. Attempt any **three** questions from the rest.

Q1. (a) A chemical testing laboratory has several chemists who work on one or more projects. Chemists may have a variety of equipment on each project. The laboratory management wants to record the equipment issued data when given equipment item is assigned to a particular chemist working on a specified project. A chemist must be assigned to atleast one project and one equipment item. A given equipment item need not be assigned and a given project need not be assigned either a chemist or an equipment item. Design and draw an ER diagram, clearly indicating the entities, attributes, keys, the cardinality and participation constraints.

Note : Make necessary assumptions.

(b) What is CODD's Rules? Explain the Integrity Rule and the View Updating Rule.

Refer to Q.No.-1(d), June 2008

Also Refer to Q.No.-4(a), Page No.-127

(c) Describe the Client/ Server Architecture and its main components. Explain its need and advantages.

Refer to Q.No.-4(a), Page No.-100, and Refer to Q.No.-4(b), Page No.-103

(d) Write syntax of the following SQL commands. Provide an example of each :

(i) CREATE (ii) ALTER

(iii) REPLACE (iv) DELETE

(v) INSERT

Refer to Page No.-38,39. Also Refer Q.No.-2(a), June 2008

Q2. (a) Draw and explain the three-level architecture of a Database Management System.

Refer to Q.No.-(b), Page No.-79.

(b) Describe the JOIN operations and its various types with the help of examples.

Refer to Page No.-32,33,34 and 42.

(c) Compare Relational Database Management System with Object Oriented Database Management System.

Refer to Q.No.-4(a), Page No.-140,
Also Refer to Q.No.-(f), Page No.-166, and Refer to Q.No.-6(a), Page No.-187.

Q3. (a) What is meant by Distributed Computing Environment? What are the three possible methods by which we can integrate the distributed RDBMS applications.

Refer to Q.No.-(g), Page No.-167

(b) Explain the problems of database inconsistency and redundancy of data. How can this problem be solved in the relational model. Support your answer with an example.

Refer to Q.No.-(b), Page No.-243
Now Refer to Q.No.-(b), Page No.-233 and Similar Question.

Q4 (a) Explain the Hierarchical Model. How are following functions performed in this model.

(i) Representation of many-to-many relationship

(ii) Accessing of data records.

(iii) Implementing of the Hierarchical Data Model.

Ans. A DBMS belonging to the hierarchical data model uses tree structures to represent relationship among records. Tree structures occur naturally in many data organizations because some entities have an intrinsic hierarchical order. For example, an institute has a number of programmes to offer. Each program has a number of courses. Each course has a number of students registered in it. The following figure depicts, the four entity types Institute, Program, Course and Student make up the four different levels of hierarchical structure. The figure below shows an example of database occurrence for an institute. A database is a collection of database occurrence.

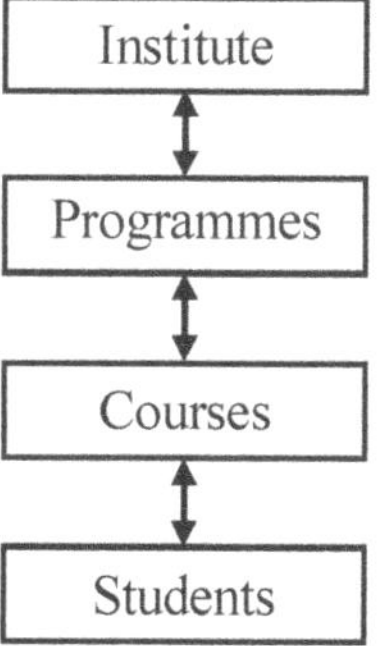

Fig : A simple Hierarchy

A hierarchical database therefore consists of a collection of records which are connected with each other through links. Each record is a collection of fields (attributes), each of which contains one data value. A link is an association between precisely two records.

(i) Representation of many-to-many relationship : The hierarchical model cannot support a many-to-many relationship directly. In the hierarchical model, the many-to-many relationship can be expressed using one of the following methods: **replication** or virtual record. When more than one employee works in a given department, then for the hierarchical tree with **EMPLOYEE** as the root node we have to replicate the record for the department and have this replicated record attached as a child to the corresponding occurrence of the **EMPLOYEE** record type.

Replication of data would mean a waste of storage space and could lead to data inconsistencies when some copies of replicated data are not updated. The other method of representing the many-to-many relationship in the hierarchical data model is to use an indirect scheme. In the hierarchical model the solution is to use the so-called **virtual record**. A virtual record is essentially a record containing a pointer to an occurrence of an actual physical record type. This physical record type is called the **logical parent** and the virtual record is the **logical child**. When a record is to be replicated in several database trees, we keep a single copy of that record in one of the trees and replace, each other record with a virtual containing a pointer to that physical record. To be more specific, let R be a record type that is replicated in several hierarchical diagrams say H_1, H_2, … H_n. To eliminate replication we create a new virtual record type virtual – R and replace R in each of the n-1 trees with a record of type virtual – R. Virtual – R will contain no data.

(ii) The Accessing of Data Records in Hierarchical Data Structure: The tree type data structure is used to represent hierarchical data model shows the relationships among the parents, children, cousins, uncles, aunts and siblings. A tree is thus a collection of nodes. One node is designated as the root node; the remaining nodes form trees or subtrees.

An **ordered tree** is a tree in which the relative order of the subtrees is significant. This relative order not only signifies the vertical placement or level of the subtrees but also the left to right ordering. Figures below give two examples of ordered trees with A as the root node and **B, C** and **D** as its children nodes. Each of the nodes **B, C** and **D**, in turn, are root nodes or subtrees with children nodes **(E, F), (G)** and **(H, I, J)**, respectively. The significance in the ordering of the subtrees in following diagrams is discussed below.

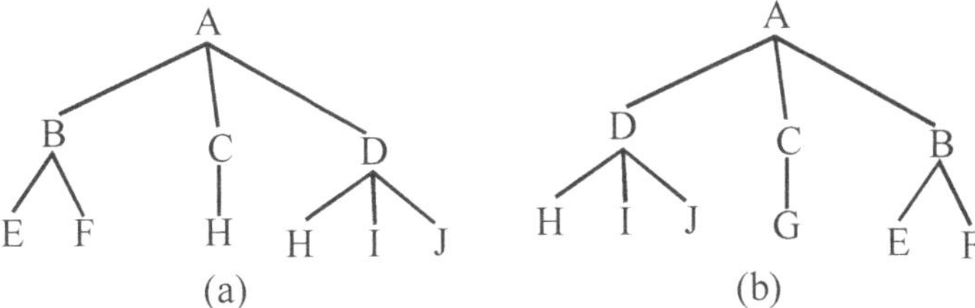

Fig : Example of two trees

Traversing an ordered tree can be done in a number of ways. The order of processing the nodes of the tree depends on whether or not one processes the node before the node's subtree and the order of processing the subtrees (left to right or right to left). The usual practice is the so-called **preorder traversal** in which the node is processed first, followed by the leftmost subtree not yet processed.

The preorder processing of the ordered trees of figure below will process the nodes in the sequence **A, B, E, F, C, G, D, H, I. J.**

The significance of the ordered tree becomes evident when we consider the sequence in which the nodes could be reached when using a given tree traversing strategy. For instance, the order in which the nodes of the hierarchical tree of figure are processed using the preorder processing strategy is not the same as the order for figure above, even though the tree of part b contain the same nodes as the tree of part a.

Two distinct methods can be used to implement the preorder sequence in the ordered tree. The first method, shown in figure below uses hierarchical pointers to implement the ordered tree. Here the pointer in each record points to the

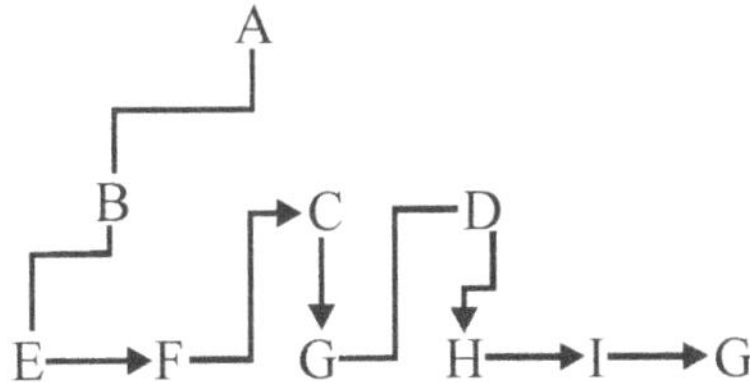

Fig : Preorder Traversal of figure above

next record in the preorder sequence. The second method, shown in figure below uses two types of pointers, the **child** and the **sibling pointers**. The child pointer is used to point to the

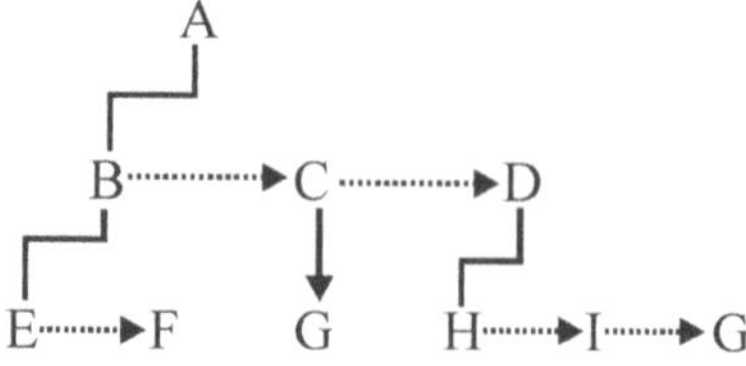

Fig : Child/Sibiling Pointers

leftmost child and the sibling pointer is used to point to the right sibling. The siblings are notes that have the same parent. Thus, the binary tree corresponding to tree in the figure is obtained by connecting together all siblings of a node and deleting all links from a node to its children except for the link to its leftmost child. Using this transformation, we obtain the tree representation as shown in figure above.

(iii) Implementation of the Hierarchical Data Model: Each occurrence of a hierarchical tree can be stored as a variable length physical record, the nodes of the hierarchy being stored in preorder. In addition the stored record contains a prefix field. This field contains control information including pointers, flags, locks and counters, which are used by DBMS to allow concurrent usage and enforce data integrity.

A number of methods could be used to store the hierarchical trees in the physical medium affects not only the performance of the system but also the operations that can be performed on the database. For example, if each occurrence of the hierarchical tree is stored as a variable length record on a magnetic tape like device, the DBMS will allow only sequential retrieval and insertion or modification may be disallowed or performed only by recreating the entire database with the insertion and modification storage of the hierarchical database on a direct access device allows an index structure to be supported for the root nodes and allows direct access to an occurrence of a hierarchical tree. The storage of one occurrence of the hierarchical definition tree of figure above using the variable length record approach is given in the following figure.

$$\left\{ a_1\ b_1\ e_{11}\ I_{12}\ f_1\ b_2\ e_{21}\ e_{22}\ f_2\ c_1\ g_1\ d_1\ h_1\ I_1\ J_1\ d_2\ h_{21}\ h_{22}\ I_2\ I_2 \right\}$$

Fig : Sequential storage of hierarchical database

The hierarchy can also be represented using pointer of either preorder hierarchical type or child/sibling type. In the hierarchical type of pointer, each record occurrence has a pointer that points to the next record in the preorder sequence. In the child/sibling scheme, each record has two types of pointers. The **child** pointer points to its leftmost child record occurrence. The **sibling** pointer points to its right sibling (or twin). A record has one sibling pointer and as many child pointers as the number of child types associated with the node corresponding to the record. The following two figures illustrates preorder hierarchical pointer and child sibling pointers respectively of hierarchical tree shown in figure below.

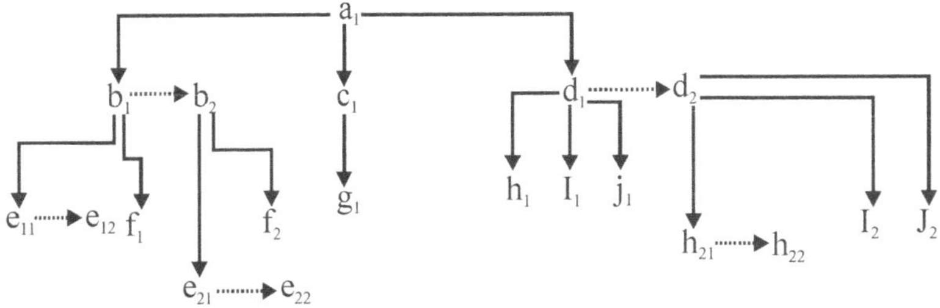

Fig : Preorder Hierarchical Pointer

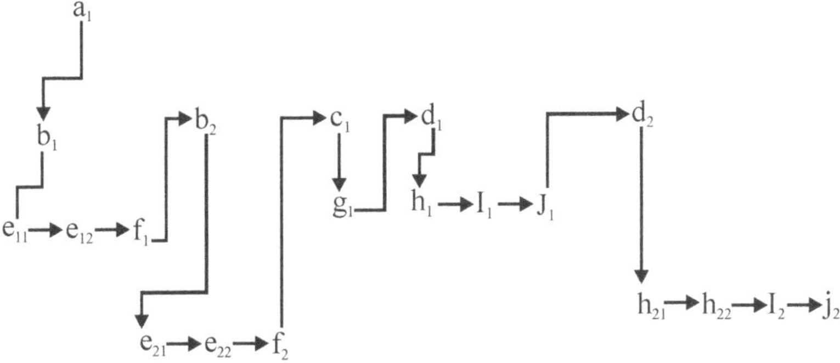

Fig : Child Sibling Pointers

(b) What are Database anomalies? Explain the three types of anomalies that may exist in a database.

Database anomalies are the problems in relations that occur due to redundancy in the relations. These anomalies affect the process of inserting, deleting and modifying data in the relations. Some important data may be lost if a elations is updated that contains database anomalies. It is important to remove these anomalies in order to perform different processing on the relations without any problem.

Now Refer to Page No.-95

5 (a) What is Normalization? Explain the conditions under which a relation

need to be normalized to 3 NF to BCNF, with the help of suitable example.

Refer to Q. No.-5(b), Page No.-143, and Q.No.-(b), Page No.-291

(b) Explain any six reasons as to why organisations resist from using DBMS tools.

Refer to Q. No.-3(b), Page No.-282

CS-06 : Database Management System
June, 2009

Note : Question number **1** is **compulsory**. Attempt **any three** questions from the rest.

Q1. (a) A publishing company produces academic books on various subjects. Books are written by authors who specialise in one or more particular subjects. The company employs a number of editors who do not have particular specialisations but who take sole responsibility for editing one or more publications. A publication (i.e. Book) covers a single subject area, but may be written by one or more authors - the contribution each author is recorded as a percentage for the purposes of calculating royalties.

On the basis of this case attempt the following questions :

(i) Design an ERD for the above case.

Ans.

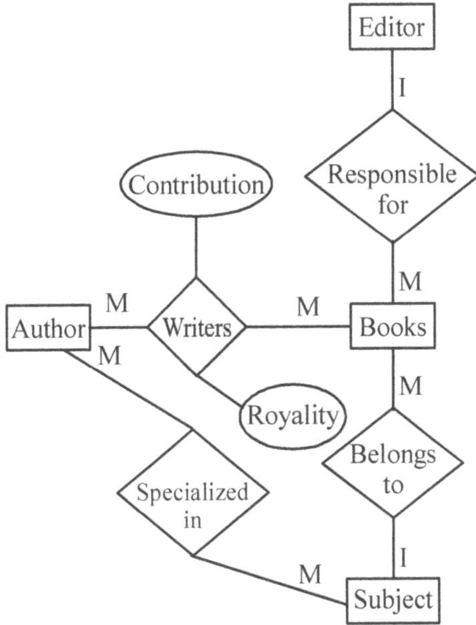

(ii) Assume the following changes to the specification :

An author can develop a publication covering more than one subject area and that the schema must be able to store the percentage of the pages concerned with each of the subjects. Modify your ERD to reflect the above changes.

Ans.

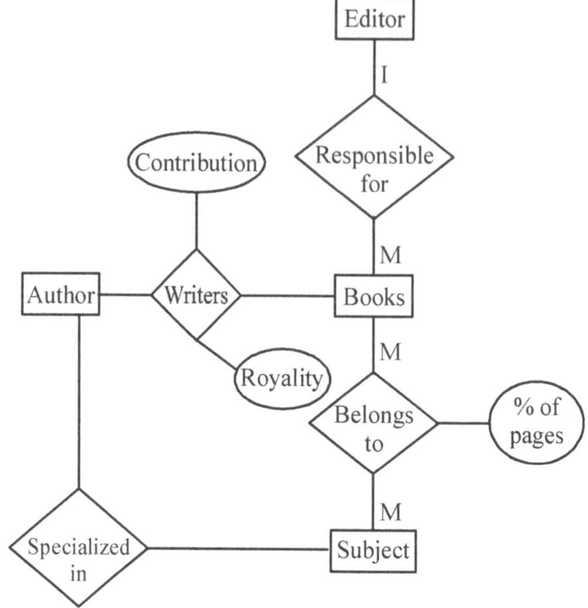

(b) What is a Knowledge Base System? Explain its various components. How does a KBS differ from a Database System? Give at least five differences.

Refer to Dec-2002, Q.No.-5(a), Page-123

Components of KBS-

(c) Explain the process of normalization. What is the difference between Third Normal Form and BCNF. Consider the following database relation: ***ClientRental (clientNo, propertyNo, CName, pAddress, rentstart, rentFinish, rent, ownerNo, Oname)*** **with following functional dependencies**

$clientNo, propertyNo \rightarrow rentstart, rentFinish$

$clientNo \rightarrow Cname$

$propertyNo \rightarrow pAddress, rent, ownerNo, OName$

with the Primary Key (*clientNo, PropertyNo*)

Find the normal form in which the relation clientRental is.

Refer to Chapter-2, Page No.-7-11

Refer to Q.No.-5(b), Page No-143 and Q.No.-4(b) Page No.-291and now....

The relation client rental is in 1NF only because all the attributes except rent start & rent finish are partly functionally dependent on the primary Key of the relation.

Q2. (a) Explain "program-data-independence" in a DBMS.
Refer to June-2002, Q.No.-2(iv), Page No.-136

(b) What are CODD's Rules? Explain "The View Updating Rule" and "The Physical Independence Rule".
Refer to June-2008, Q.No.-1(d), Page No.-300-301

(c) Explain the advantages and disadvantages of data distribution in Distributed Databases.
Refer to June-2004, Q.No.-2(b), Page No.-65

Q3. (a) What is Index Sequential File Organisation? Explain the Primary, Clustering, Secondary and Multilevel Indexing Schemes.
Refer to June-2006, Q.No.-1(b), Page No.-259

(b) What are Views? What is the syntax for creating views? Explain the advantages and disadvantages of views.
Refer to June-2003, Q.No.-2(ii), Page No.-96, 97

Q4. (a) Consider the functioning of an institute where Director is the Head of Institute and Two Deans, one Administrative Dean, another Academic Dean. The institute is organised into Departments, where each Department has an H.O.D. who supervises the faculty members. Create a Hierarchical Database model for above specifications and show how data will be stored in it.

Ans. Hierarchical Models- A hierarchical model uses tree like structure to represent relationship among records.

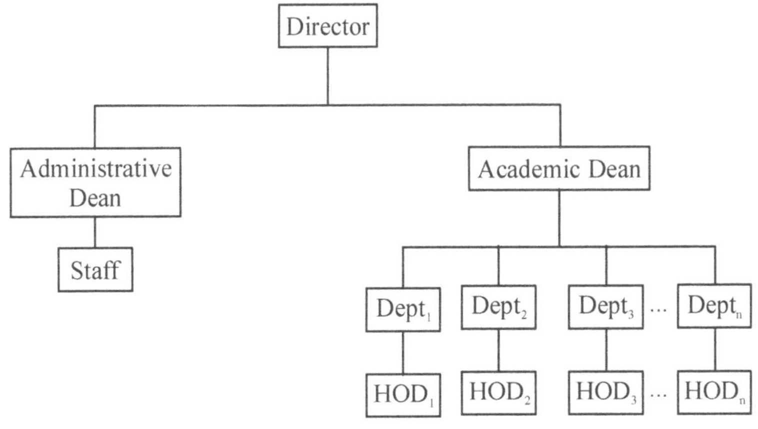

(b) Compare Network Model with Hierarchical Model. Mention atleast three differences.

Refer to December-2006, Q.No-5(c), Page-285

(c) What is the difference between data and knowledge? How DBMS are different from knowledge based systems.

Refer to June-2004, Q.No.-1(d), Page No.-63

Q5. Consider the following three relations :
EMPLOYEE (Emp_name, Dept_no, Salary, Emp_id, Emp_supervise)
DEPARTMENT (Dept_no, Dept_name, Manager_id)
DEPENDENT (Dependent_name, Dependent_id, Emp_id)
Write Relational Algebra statements for the following :

(a) Select tuples for all employees who either work in *Dept_no* 10 and get annual salary of more than 80,000/- or work in *Dept_no* 12 and get annual salary more than 90,000/-.

Ans. Select * from Employee
where (Dept_no =10 and salary > 80000) or (Dept_no=12 and Salary > 9000);

(b) Retrieve the name and salary of all employees who work in *Dept_no* 10.

Ans. Select Emp_name, salary from Employee Where Dept_no =10;

(c) Retrieve the id of all employees who work in *Dept_no* 10 and whose supervisor is name is "John".

Ans. Select emp_id from Employee
Where dept_no =10 and Emp-Superwise='John';

(d) Retrieve the name of the manager of each department.

Ans. Select Emp_name from Employee e,
department d where emp_id=d, Manager_id

(e) Retrieve the names of employees who have no dependents.

Ans. Select Emp_name from Employee
where emp-id not in (select emp_id form department)

CS-06: Database Management System
December, 2009

Note : Question number **1** is **compulsory**. Attempt **any three** questions from the rest.

Q1. (a) A bookshop has millions of books available and therefore requires a database to track its sales. For each book that is available online, they store a Title, an author, count of the no. of pages a regular price, a sale price, information about its availability (in stock, from publisher etc.) and an ISBN number. To help customers find the book they require that each book is assigned to one or more categories such as Literature and Fiction or computing. The bookshop also operates a best seller list, which changes each month, although customers may wish to look at the best seller for a previous month. Each customer who purchases books through the system must open an account. However customers are free to browse without an account. A customer's name, mailing address, credit card details and previous purchases are all stored in the system. The bookshop wishes to be able to provide each customer with a history of the books they have purchased.

Identify the entities and the relationships among them. Construct an ERD for the above specifications.

Ans. Entities with their attributes are given bellow:-

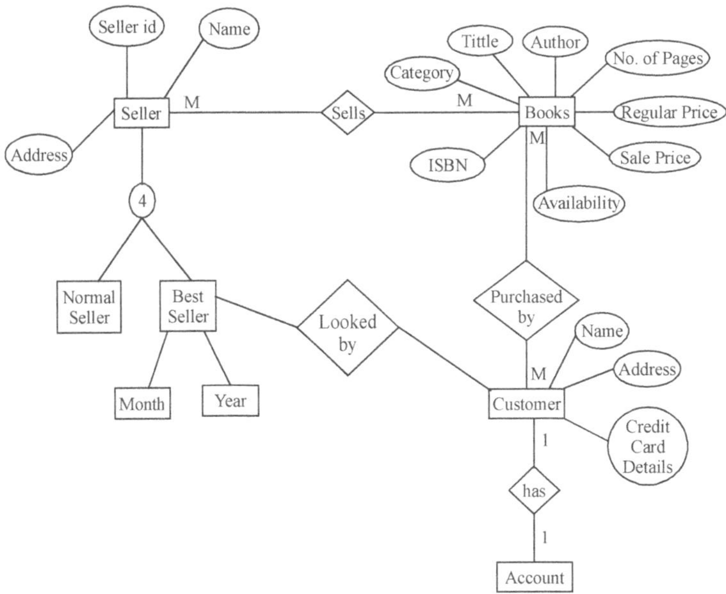

(b) What are different types of keys in a RDBMS. Also explain their significance. Using a single example explain the difference between following keys:
Primary key, candidate key, superkey, Foreign key.
Ans. Refer to Dec-2003, Q.No.-2(b), Page-82-83, Page-7-8

(c) What is a RDBMS? Write the advantages and disadvantages of a DBMS. When you should not use a DBMS?
Refer to Page No.-140

Q2. (a) Explain the following terms w.r.t. the Network Model.
(i) DBTG Set
Ans. Database Task Group (DBTG) set was a group of people who had introduced the concept of network data model of DBMS in late 1960's in the Conference on Data Access System Language (CODASYL).

(ii) Implementation of the Network Data Model.
Ans. Network data Models: Network model was given in late 1960 by DBTG. It contains details of the network data model. It consists of two different data structures.
(1) Record Type: It is used to represent an entity type. E.g. Department and employee are two record types.
(2) Set types: It is used to show relationship b/w two record type. One is called the owner of record type and second is called the member of the record type.
E.g.

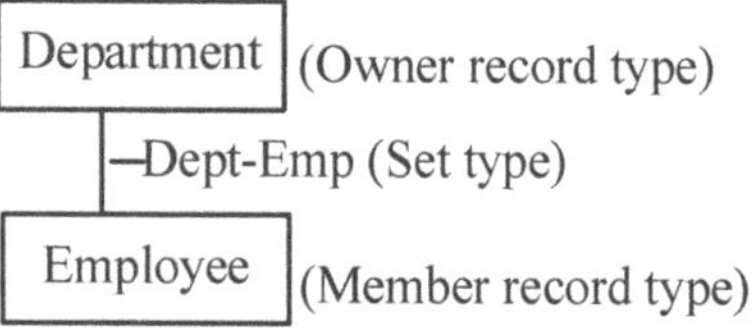

Normally there is one to one relationship b/w owner and member record type. and now refer to June-2001, Q.No.-3(a) Page No-170

(b) Consider the following relations from a property database:
Property (Property No., pAddress)
Property Inspection (Property No., iDate, iTime, comments, staff No, S.Name, CarReg)
With the following functional dependencies
Property No $\rightarrow$ pAddress
Property No, iDate $\rightarrow$ iTime, comments, Staff No., SName, CarReg)
Staff No $\rightarrow$ S.Name
Staff No, iDate $\rightarrow$ carReg
CarReg, iDate, iTime $\rightarrow$ Property No, comments, Staff No, S.Name
Staff No., iDate, iTime $\rightarrow$ Property No, Comments
Identify in which Normal Form, the above database is convert the database in 3NF.

Ans. Property

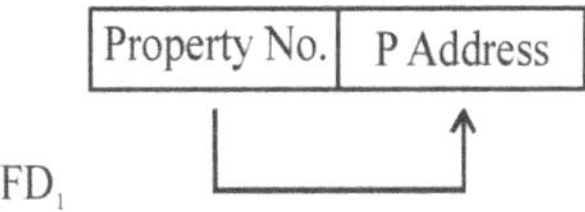

Property Inspection

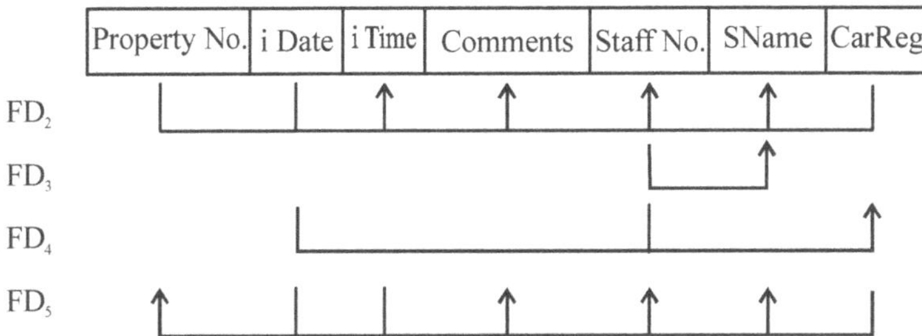

The above database is in 2NF because FD_3 Shows the Transitive FD.
The 3NF decomposition of the above database is :
Property (Property No, pAddress)
Property, Inspection (Property No, iDate, iTime, Comments, Staff No, CarReg)
Staff (Staff No, SName)

Q3. (a) What is ISAM? How are overflow records managed in ISAM?
Refer to June-2004, Q.No.-1(b), Page No.-59

(b) What are Integrity rules? Explain the two Integrity rules with the help of examples.
Refer to June-2004, Q.No.-3(b), Page No.-69

(c) Explain the advantages and disadvantages of distributing the database.
Refer to December-2003, Q.No.-6(b), Page No.-88

Q4. (a) How OODBMS are better than RDBMS. Mention atleast five reasons.
Refer to Q.No.-4(a), Page No.-140, Q.No.-1(f), Page No.-166 and Q.No 4(a), Page No.-187

(b) What is the client/server Architecture? Explain its advantages. List and discuss the role of its various components.
Refer to Q.No.-4(a) and 4(b) Page-100-103

(c) Explain the JOIN operator, its relevance and its various types.
Refer Page No.-32-34, 42

Q5. (a) Consider the following relations:
EMP (E-no, E-name, Job, Hiredate, Basic-sal, commission, Dept-no)
DEPT (Dept-no, Dept-name, Location)
CLIENT-MASTER (Client-no, Client-name, Address, Balance-due)
PRODUCT-MASTER (Prod-no, Description, Profit-perc, Units, Qty-available, sell-price, cost-price)
Write SQL queries for the following:
(i) List names, job and department no. of all employees whose names start with "K".
Ans. Select E-name, job, dept. dept_no from Emp Where ename like 'K%';

(ii) Select the average salaries of each department where dept-no is DOO1 or DOO2.
Ans. Select dept_no avg(basic-sal) from emp group dept_no having dept_no in ('D001', 'D002');

(iii) Display names of all salesmen who have been hired after 30th August, 2008.
Ans. Select e-name from emp where job='Salesman' and hiredate > '30 Aug 2008';

(iv) Increase the basic salary of all employees by Rs. 2000/-
Ans. Update emp set-basic-sal = basic-sal + 2000;

(v) Display a list of all products whose quantity is less than 5 and therefore need to be ordered.
Ans. Select * from product_master
where Qty-available<5;

(b) What is Multivalued Dependency? Explain the Fourth and Fifth Normal Form with the help of an example.
Refer to Dec-2002, Q.No.-6(a), Page No.-124

CS-06: DATABASE MANAGEMENT SYSTEM
June, 2010

Note: *Question number **1** is **compulsory**. Attempt **any three** from the rest.*

Q1. (a) A marketing company maintains information about salespersons, Areas and Products. Salespersons have a unique identification number, name, designation and area allocated to each one. Areas are divided with a number and names. Products have their number, name, cost, discount, and the areas where these product need to be marketized. Sales persons can sale any product in their areas, and maintains a monthly statement which shows the number of products sold, along with their cost, discount and date of delivery.

On the basis of the above specification answer the following questions:

(i) Design an ΣR diagram indicating attributes, keys and cardinality ratios.

Ans.

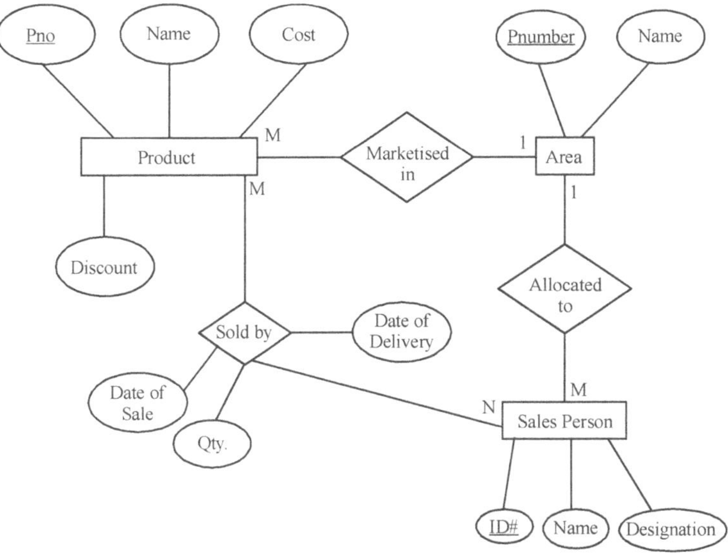

(ii) Derive the number of tables from the ΣR diagram.

Ans. Product (<u>Pno</u>, name, cost, discount, number)

Area (<u>Anumber</u>, name)

Sales Person (<u>ID#</u>, name, designation, Anumber)

Sold by (<u>Pno, ID#, date of sale</u>, Qty, date of delivery)

(iii) Create the BCNF normalized table and describe the integrity constraints (including referential integrity constraints) on these tables. Note : Make and state necessary assumptions, if any.

Ans. The above four relations Product, Area, Sales Person and sold_by are already in BCNF becomes there is no partial and transitive functional dependencies exist in the relations as well as all the determinants are super key of the relation.

```
Create table Area
(Anumber number primary key
name varchar2 (20));
Create table product
(Pno number primary key,
name varchar2 (20),
cost number,
discount number,
Anumber number, references area);
Create table sales person
(ID# number primary key,
name varchar2 (20),
pnumber number references area);
Create table sold_by
(Pno number references product,
ID# number references sales person,
date of sale date,
Qty number,
date-of-delivery date,
Primary key (pno, id#, date-of-sale));
```

(b) What are the different problems in relational databases from the view of organization of data (Discuss any three). How these problems can be overcome by using Object Oriented RDBMS.

Ans. Refer to Page-187, Q.No.-6 (a)

(c) "Data Independence means programs are not dependent on the physical attributes of data". Is it True or False? Justify your answer.

Ans. Yes, data independence means programs are not dependent on the physical attributes of data.

Now refer to Page-136, Q.No.-2(iv)

Q2. What are the main features of client server model? Explain the stages involved in the development of an application using this model.

Ans. Refer to P-264, Q.No.-2(b)

(b) Why a B + tree is a better structure than B - tree for implementation of an indexed sequential file. Explain how using a B + tree increases the efficiency of processing in DBMS.

Ans. Refer to Page No.-255, Q.No.-4(b)

Now Refer www.gullybaba.com download section.

Q3. (a) What are the different technical and administrative criteria for evaluation of a DBMS? Explain.

Ans. Refer to Page No.-216, Q.No.-3(a)

(b) Explain the significance of multimedia and knowledge databases. Also, give two example for each.

Ans. Refer to Page No.-85-86, Q.No.-4(b)(i)(ii)

(c) Explain the role and functions associated with database administration.

Ans. Refer to Page No.-264, Q.No.-3(a)

Q4. (a) Explain the concept of functional dependency using a suitable example with the help of a dependency diagram. Why is it difficult to identify functional dependencies by just looking at a table? Explain with an example.

Ans. Refer to Page No.-266, Q.No.-4(a)

It is difficult to identify functional dependencies by just looking at the table, because:

(i) Sometimes the attributes are not common.

(ii) The relationship among the attributes may varies in different context.

(iii) The cardinality of the relation between attributes may vary in different contest.

(b) What are the problems of file management system? Explain, how does the database approach overcome these problems.

Ans. Refer to Page-243, Q.No.-6(b)

Q5. Consider the following relations:

(a) Where primary keys are underlined:

AIRBUS (Name, Start_Station, Dest_Station, ANumber)

TICKET (PNRNO, Start_Station, Dest_Station, Fare)

PASSENGER (Name, Address, PNRNO, ANumber)

Write SQL Queries for the following:

(i) Retrieve the name of passengers who are travelling from the Start_Station to the Dest_Station of the Airbus.

Ans. Select P.name from Airbus A, Ticket T, Passenger P
Where P.PNRNo=T.PNRNo and A.Anumber=P.Anumber
and T.Start-station = A.start_station and T.Dest-station=A.Dest-station;

(ii) Retrieve the names of all the passengers who have paid more than Rs. 50,000/- as fare.

Ans. Select name from Passenger where PNRNo=(select PNRNo from Ticket where fare>5000);

(iii) Retrieve the name of the Airbuses travel between Delhi and Chennai as start station and dest_station.

Ans. Select name from Airbus where start-station='Delhi' and dest-station= 'Chennai';

(iv) Insert a new Airbus named GOLIGHT, number G_1372 from Delhi to Bangalore.

Ans. Insert into Airbus values ('GOLIGHT', 'Delhi', Benglore', 'G-1372');

(v) Cancel a ticket with PNRNO 7321523108, and passenger name Rajiv.

Ans. Delete from Passenger where PNRNo-7321523108 and name= 'Rajiv';

(b) Discuss the advantages and disadvantages of data replication in distributed databases. Is there any use of data replication in relational databases?

Ans. Refer to Page No.-98, Q.No.-3(a)

CS-06: DATABASE MANAGEMENT SYSTEM
December, 2010

Note: *Question number 1 is* ***compulsory****. Attempt* ***any three*** *from the rest.*

Q1. (a) Assume a Film or movie production house which maintains information about films, actors and studios. Films have a name, year of production duration and the category of the film. Actors have a name, address and contact number. Studios have an owner and a banner. Films are shot in only one studio. Actors are connected to one or more studios but can act in any films which may or may not be owned by the studio. On the basis of the above specifications Design an ERD indicating attributes, keys and the cardinality ratios.

Ans.

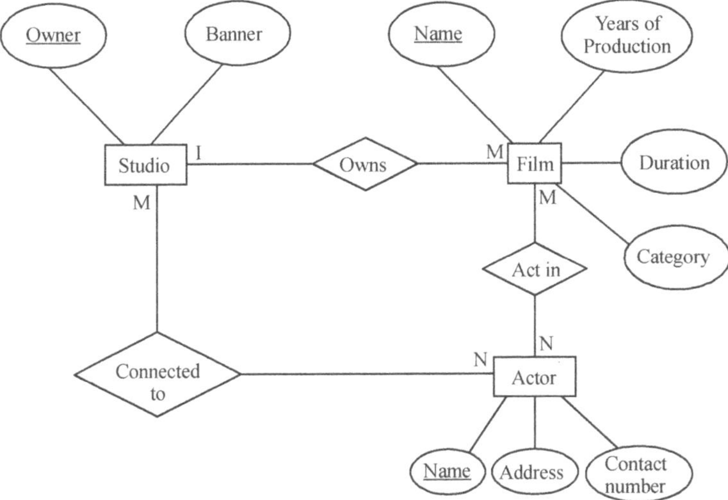

(b) What is data independence? Explain, how is data independence achieved, using an example.

Ans. Refer to Page No.-136, Q.No.-2(iv) **and now**

Data independence is achieved by three levels of data abstraction in DBMS which is provided by three-schema architecture of DBMS. In three-schema architecture, data is described at three levels and the schema of upper level needs not to change if any change takes place in lower level schema. Sometimes, it is required to change the mappings between two schemas only.

(c) What is a multivalued dependency (MVD)? How is it related to functional dependency? What do you understand by a Trivial MVD? Explain using an example explain the normal form based on MVD using example.

Ans. Multivalued dependencies are a consequence of first normal form (1NF), which disallowed an attribute in a tuple to have a set of *values.* If we have two or more multivalued *independent* attributes in the same relation schema, we get into a problem of having to repeat every value of one of the attributes with every value of the other attribute to keep the relation state consistent and to maintain the independence among the attributes involved. This constraint is specified by a multivalued dependency.

Formal Definition of Multivalued Dependency

A **multivalued dependency (MVD)** $\chi \twoheadrightarrow Y$ specified on relation schema R, where χ and Y are both subsets of R, specifies the following constraint on any relation state r of R: If two tuples t_1 and t_2 exist in r such that $t_1[\chi] = t_2[\chi]$, then two tuples t_3 and t_4 should also exist in r with the following properties, where we use Z to denote $(R - (\chi \cup Y))$:

$t_3[\chi]=t_4[\chi] = t_1[\chi]=t_2[\chi]$.
$t_3[Y]=t_1[Y]$ and $t_4[Y]=t_2[Y]$.
$t_3[Z]=t_2[Z]$ and $t_4[Z]=t_1[Z]$,

where the t_1, t_2, t_3, and t_4 are not necessarily distinct.

Now refer to Page No.-13, for 4NF

(d) What do you understand by a knowledge base? Explain any two representational schemes in knowledge bases using examples for each.

Ans. Refer to Page No.-298, Q.No.-5(b)

Q2. (a) How does indexed sequential file organization maintain and retrieve the data? What are its advantages over sequential organization?

Ans. Refer to P-47 (Index files) and then Page No.-92, Q.No.-1(b)

(b) Explain the concepts of Generalization and Specialization with an example for each. How is a specialized entity different from a weak entity?

Ans. Refer to Page No.-281, Q.No.-2(b)

A Weak Entity is an entity that cannot be uniquely identified by its attributes alone; therefore, it must use a foreign key in conjunction with its attributes to create a primary key. The foreign key is typically a primary key of an entity it is related to.

An entity can be a more specialized version of a general entity. This means that the specialized entity has all the attributes, associations, events etcetera of the more general entity.

Q3. (a) Explain the "Rule of entity integrity" and "comprehensive sublanguage rule", CODD's Rule, with an example for each.
Ans. Refer to Page No.-152, Q.No.-1(b)(i), Page No.-129, (Rule-5) & Page No.-300, Q.No.-1(d)

(b) What are the limitations of relational DBMS? Explain the advantages of distributed and object oriented DBMS over relational DBMS.
Ans. Refer to Page No.-187, Page No.-6(a)
Refer to Page No.-65, Page No.-6(b)

(c) Explain how is superkey different from a candidate key using an example.
Ans. Super key is a key which uniquely identifies each row of the relation. The key may consists of one or more attributes.
Candidate key: A minimal super key is called as candidate key. Every candidate key is super key but reverse is not true. A super key can have extraneous attribute but candidate key does not.
Example:
Student (Roll No, Name, City, Marks)
F={Roll No $\rightarrow$ Name, Roll No $\rightarrow$ City, Marks, Roll No. Name $\rightarrow$ City}
Super key = {Roll No, Name}
Candidate key= {Roll No}

Q4. (a) Why is BCNF a more desirable normal form than lower forms? Give an example of a relational scheme that is in third normal form but not in BCNF. Also explain using an example why it is not practically feasible always.
Ans. Refer to Page No.-291, June-07, Page No.-4(b)

(b) What are the advantages & disadvantages for distribution of data. Discuss any two issues in design of distributed databases.
Ans. Refer to Page No.-88, Q.No.-6(b)
Q5. Consider the following relations, where primary keys are underlined.

SHOP(SHOP_NO,SH_NAME,SH_ADDRESS)

SHOP_OWNER(OWNER_NAME,OWNER_ADDRESS)

WAS_STOCK(SHOP_NO,ITEM)

SUPPLIES(SHOP_NO,C_NAME,ITEM,PRICE)

Write SQL for the following.

(a) Retrieve the names of shop owners who supply some item to the address C_133, Karol Bagh, New Delhi.

Ans. Select SH.SH_Name From Shop Sh, Supplies S, Customers C
Where Sh.Shop_No=S.Shop_No and C. C_Name= S. C_Name and C_address= 'C_133, Karol Bagh, New Delhi';

(b) Retrieve the name & address of customer who has been supplied items of maximum total value.

Ans. Select C.* from customer C, Supplies S
Where c.c_name=S.C_Name and price =(select max (price) from Supplies);

(c) Retrieve the names of customers who requires the items which have not been supplied. List both the customers and the items.

Ans. Select R.* From Requires R, Supplies S
Where R. C_Name=S.C_Name and R.Item ⇒ S.Item;

(d) List the names of shops who has at least 50 items on their stock.

Ans. Select shop_no from was_stock
Group by Shop_no
having count (*)>=50;

(e) List the shops which stock required items of some customers but supply none.

Ans. Select S.Shop_No From Requires R, Was.stock W, Supplies S
Where Not (R. C_Name= S. C_Name and R. Item = S. Item) and w.Shop_No=S.Shop_No and W.Item= S.Item;

CS-06: DATABASE MANAGEMENT SYSTEM
June, 2011

Note: *Question number 1 is **compulsory**. Attempt **any three** from the rest.*

Q1. (a) Consider a database that contains information about person and skills. At a particular time, the following persons are represented in the database, and their skills are as indicated.

Person	Skill
Vivek	Programming
Aditi	DEO and Programming
Vinay	DEO, Programming, H/W Maintenance
Akash	DEO, and H/W Maintenance

For each person the database contains various personal details such as Date of birth, father's name, address, email address, telephone no. and educational qualifications. For each skill it contains an identification of the appropriate basic training course, an associated job grade code and other information. Also the database contains the date each person attended each course.

(i) Identify the entities and the relationships among them. Draw an ERD for the above specifications.

Ans.

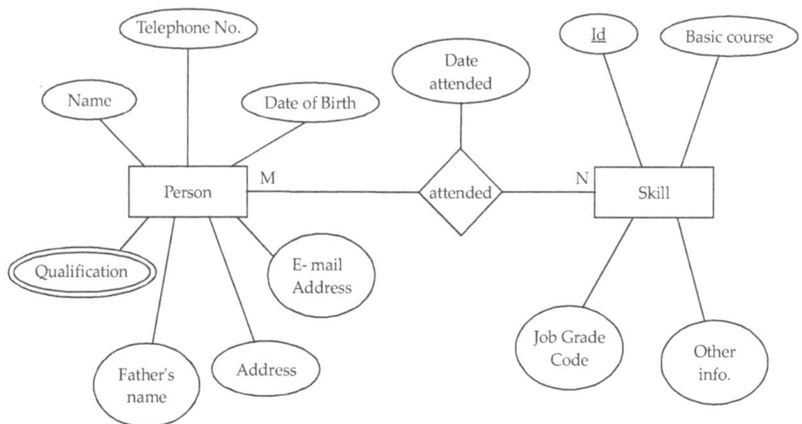

(ii) Design a Relational structure for this data.

Ans. Relational Structure

- Person (Name, Father's name, Date of Birth, Address, Email address, Telephone no.)
- Qualification Detail (Name, Qualification)
- Skill (Id, Basic course, Job grade code, other info.)
- Attended (Name, Id, Date attended)

(iii) Design a Network structure for this data.

Ans.

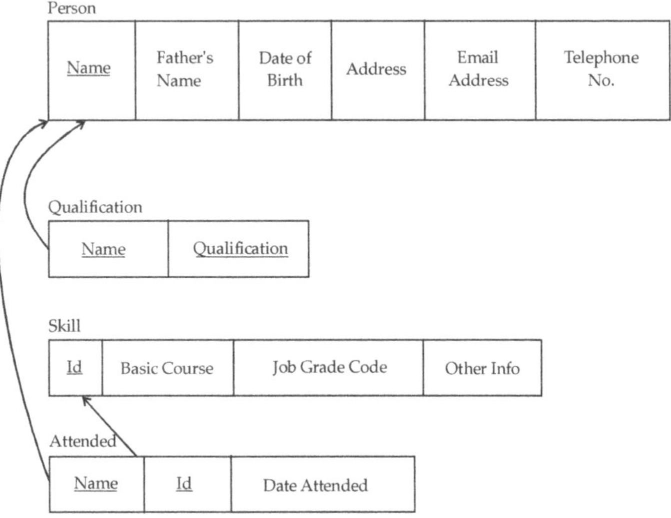

(b) Explain the concept of clustering and secondary indexes with the help of an example.

Ans. Clustering

There are several types of ordered indexes. A primary index is specified on the orderin key field of an ordered file of records. An ordering key field is used to physical order the file records on disk, and every records has unique value for that filed. If the ordering field is not a key field – that is, if numerous records in the file can have the same value for the ordering field.

Clustering Index

If records of a file are physically ordered on a non key field which does not have a distinct value for each record- that field is called the clustering field.

Clustering Index can use to speed up retrieval of records that have the same value for the clustering field. This differs from a primary key index, which requires that the ordering filed of the data file have a distinct value for each record.
A Secondary Index is also an ordered file with two field. The first field is of the same data type as some nonordering field of the data file that is an indexing filed. The second field is either a block pointer or record pointer. There can be many secondary indexes (and hence, indexing field) for the same file.

(c) Explain the concept of frame-based Representation with the help of an example showing the frames and facets/slots.
Ans. Refer to Page No.-229, Dec-04, Q.No.-1(e)

Q2. (a) Consider the following Relations:
EMPLOYEE (EMPLOYEE - NAME, STREET, CITY)
WORKS (EMPLOYEE - NAME, COMPANY - NAME, SALARY)
Write the SQL statements for the following:
(i) Find the street and city of all the employees who works in "CICIP Bank".
Ans. Select street, city from employee, works where employee.employee_ name and works. Employee_ Name and company_name = 'CICIP Bank';

(ii) Find the Company Name of all the employees who have salary greater than Rs. 10,000.
Ans. Select company_name, employee_ name from works where salary>10000.

(iii) Find the names of all the Employees who do not work for "ABC Enterprises".
Ans. Select employee_name from works where company_name <> 'ABC Enterprises'

(iv) Find all the employees-names who works in the PATEL-MARG street of MUMBAI.
Ans. Select employee_name from employee where city = 'Mumbai' and street='Patel-Marg'

(b) Explain the difference between Cartesian Product and Natural Join Operations with illustrations for each.
Ans. Refer to Page No.-237, Dec-04, Q.No.-5(a)

Q3. (a) How do you implement a hierarchical data model ? Explain through an illustration.
Ans. Refer to Page No.-308 [Implementation of a hierarchical data model]

(b) Explain the concept of Semantic Net with the help of an example which should contain both the one-way link representation as well as the representation of a reverse-link.
Ans. Refer to Page No.-278, Dec-06, Q.No.-1(e)

Q4. (a) Explain the role of API, RPC and dynamic data exchange (DDE) in the communication process between the heterogeneous databases.
Ans. Refer to Page No.-162, Dec-01, Q.No.-6(c), & Page No.-122, Dec-02, Q.No.-4(i)(ii)

(b) Discuss a "B-Tree" with the help of an example. Also, mention its properties.
Ans. Refer to Page No.-104, June-03, Q.No.-5(a) & Page No.-174, June-01, Q.No.-6

Q5. Write short notes on the following:
(a) OODBMS and multimedia databases.
Ans. Refer to Page No.-114, Dec-02, Q.No.-1(c)(ii), & Page No.-142, June-02, Q.No.-4(b)(ii)

(b) Distributed database design.
Ans. Refer to Page No.-114, Dec-02, Q.No.-1(c)(i)

(c) Multilist file organization.
Ans. Refer to Page No.-237, Dec-04, Q.No.-5(b)

CS-06: DATABASE MANAGEMENT SYSTEM
December, 2011

Note: *Question number 1 is* **compulsory.** *Attempt* **any three** *from the rest.*

Q1. (a) Consider the following Relations:

BRANCH	**(Branch_name, Street, Branch_city)**
CUSTOMER	**(Customer_name, Street, Customer_city)**
DEPOSIT	**(Branch_name, Act_no, Customer_name, Balance)**
BORROW	**(Branch_name, Loan_number, Customer_name, Amount)**
CLIENT	**(Customer_name, Banker_name)**

Write the SQL statements for the following:

(i) Find all the customers who have a balance of over Rs. 1,00,000 in any of the Bank's.

Ans. Select customer-name from deposit where balance>100000.

(ii) Find all the customers whose loan amount is exceeding 20 lakhs in any of the Branch.

Ans. Select customer-name from borrow where amount>2000000.

(iii) Find all the customers details whose name starts with "A".

Ans. Select * from customer where customer_name like 'A %'.

(iv) Find the address of the Branch whose Branch city is given.

Ans. Select * from Branch where Branch city = '& city'.

(b) A publishing company produces scientific books on various subjects. The books are written by Authors who specialize in one particular subject. The company employs Editors who, not necessarily being specialists in a particular area, each take sole responsibility for editing one or more publications. A publication covers essentially one of the specialist subjects and is normally written by a singly Author. When writing a particular book, each author works with one Editor, but may submit another work for publication to be supervised by other editors. To improve their competitiveness, the company tries to employ a variety of authors, more than one author being a specialist in a particular subject.

Draw an ER diagram, identifying all the entities, attributes, relationships, cardinality etc.

Ans.

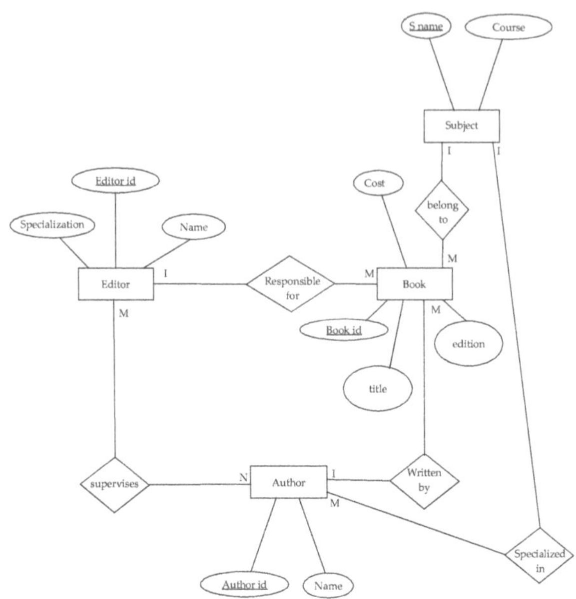

(c) With the help of an example, explain the structure of Index Sequential File Organization.

Ans. Refer to Page No.-259, June-06, Q.No.-1(b)

(d) Consider a Relation:

A	B	C
a_1	b_1	c_1
a_1	b_1	c_2
a_2	b_1	c_1
a_2	b_1	c_3

List all the functional dependencies satisfied by this relation.

Ans.

$A \rightarrow B$

$C \rightarrow B$

Q2. (a) Discuss a "Balanced Sort Tree" with the help of a suitable example. Also, mention its properties.

Ans. Refer to Page No.-269, June-06, Q.No.-4(b)

(b) Explain Aggregation and specialization, with the help of a suitable example for each.

Ans. Refer to Page No.-182, June-01, Q.No.-2(c)(i), & Page No.-154, Dec-01, Q.No.-2(d)(ii)

Q3. (a) Write the important issues in Knowledge Representation and with the help of a suitable example explain the Rule Based Representation.

Ans. Knowledge Representation is a non-trivial problem, which continues to engage some of the, best minds in this field even after the successful development of many a Knowledge Base System. Some of the important issues in Knowledge Representation arc the following:

(i) Expressive Adequacy: What knowledge can be and cannot be represented in a particular Knowledge Representation scheme?

(ii) Reasoning Efficiency: How much effort is required to perform inferencing over the KB? There is generally a tradeoff between expressive adequacy and reasoning efficiency,

(iii) Incompleteness: What can be left unsaid about 'a domain and how does one perform inferencing over incomplete knowledge?

(iv) Real World Knowledge: How can we deal with attitudes such as beliefs, desires and intentions?

Now Refer to Page No.-148, June-02, Q.No.-6(a)

(b) Explain the process of hashing. Draw the bucket and block organization for hashing. Also write the advantages and disadvantages of hashing.

Ans. Refer to Page No.-73, June-04, Q.No.-6(b), & Page No.-217, June-05, Q.No.-3(b)

Q4. (a) Define 2NF and 3NF. Normalize the following table to 3NF.

Id-No	Name	Dept	Course	Hostel
111	Ajay	Chemistry	BSc	Blk - I
112	Deepak	Physics	BSc	Blk - I
113	Simran	Maths	MSc	Blk - III
114	Kranth	English	MA	Blk – III
115	Phani	Social-Work	BA	Blk – I
116	Digvijay	Computers	MCA	Blk – IV

Ans. Refer to Page No.-226, Dec-2004, Q.No.-1(b)

The FDs of the given relation are:

Id-No. → Name, Dept., Course, hostel

Dept → Course, hostel
Course → Hostel
The key of the relation is Id-No.
Hence, the key of the relation is simple them there is no chance of partial functional dependency in the relation and therefore it is in 2NF.
But, there are transitive functional dependencies exist in the relation:
Dept → Course
Course → Hostel
Therefore, it is not in 3NF. The 3NF decompositions of this relation are:
R_1 (Id No., Name, Dept)
R_2 (Dept, Course)
R_3 (Course, Hostel)

(b) Explain the features of OORDBMS. What are its Applications? Also, list the alternative OODB strategies.

Ans. Refer to Page No.-287, June-07, Q.No.-1(c), & Page No.-231, Dec-04, Q.No.-3(a)

Q5. Write short notes on:

(a) Inverted file organization

Ans. Page No.-240 [Inverted file organization]

(b) Distributed computing environment.

Ans. Refer to Page No.-167, June-01, Q.No.-1(g)

(c) Semantic nets.

Ans. Refer to Page No.-109 [Semantic Nets]

www.ingramcontent.com/pod-product-compliance
Ingram Content Group UK Ltd.
Pitfield, Milton Keynes, MK11 3LW, UK
UKHW021708190726
13853UKWH00001B/457